ESSENTIALS OF STRATEGIC MANAGEMENT

Fifth Edition

ESSENTIALS OF STRATEGIC MANAGEMENT

J. David Hunger
Saint John's University
Iowa State University

Thomas L. Wheelen
Formerly with University of Virginia
Trinity College, Dublin, Ireland

Prentice Hall
Boston   Columbus   Indianapolis   New York   San Francisco
Upper Saddle River   Amsterdam   Cape Town   Dubai   London   Madrid
Milan   Munich   Paris   Montreal   Toronto   Delhi   Mexico City   Sao Paulo
Sydney   Hong Kong   Seoul   Singapore   Taipei   Tokyo

Editorial Director: Sally Yagan
Editor in Chief: Eric Svendsen
Acquisitions Editor: Kim Norbuta
Director of Editorial Services: Ashley Santora
Editorial Project Manager: Claudia Fernandes
Editorial Assistant: Meg O'Rourke
Director of Marketing: Patrice Lumumba Jones
Marketing Manager: Nikki Ayana Jones
Marketing Assistant: Ian Gold
Senior Managing Editor: Judy Leale
Production Project Manager: Debbie Ryan
Operations Specialist: Clara Bartunek
Creative Art Director: Jayne Conte

Cover Designer: Bruce Kenselaar
Manager, Visual Research: Beth Brenzel
Manager, Rights and Permissions: Shannon Barbe
Image Permission Coordinator: Christie Barros
Manager, Cover Visual Research & Permissions: Karen Sanatar
Cover Art: Fotolia
Full-Service Project Management: Sadagoban Balaji/ Integra Software Services, Ltd.
Composition: Integra Software Services, Ltd.
Printer/Binder: R R Donnelley/Harrisonburg
Cover Printer: R R Donnelley/Harrisonburg
Text Font: 10/12 Palatino

Credits and acknowledgments borrowed from other sources and reproduced, with permission, in this textbook appear on appropriate page within text.

Many of the designations by manufacturers and seller to distinguish their products are claimed as trademarks. Where those designations appear in this book, and the publisher was aware of a trademark claim, the designations have been printed in initial caps or all caps.

Library of Congress Cataloging-in-Publication Data
Hunger, J. David
    Essentials of strategic management / J. David Hunger, Thomas L. Wheelen.—5th ed.
        p. cm.
    Includes bibliographical references and index.
    ISBN-13: 978-0-13-600669-5 (alk. paper)
    ISBN-10: 0-13-600669-8 (alk. paper)
    1. Strategic planning.   2. CASE method.   I. Wheelen, Thomas L.   II. Title.
HD30.28.H867 2010
658.4'012—dc22
                                                                2010007380

10 9 8 7 6 5 4 3 2

Prentice Hall
is an imprint of

PEARSON

www.pearsonhighered.com

ISBN 10:   0-13-600669-8
ISBN 13: 978-0-13-600669-5

Dedicated To

Kathy, Richard, & Tom

*Betty, Kari & Jeff, Suzi & Nick, Lori &
Dave, Merry & Dylan; Maddie & Meggie,
Summer & Kacey; and Wolfie the dog*

BRIEF CONTENTS

CONTENTS

PREFACE

We wrote this book to provide you with a short, concise explanation of the most important concepts and techniques in strategic management. There is no fluff in this book. *Essentials of Strategic Management* is significantly shorter than our other books, but we have not "dumbed it down" or made it "cutesy." It is a rigorous explanation of many topics and concerns in strategic management. We condensed the content of the field into eleven carefully crafted chapters. The key concepts and techniques are here. We cite only enough examples to help you understand the material. Although the content is based on rigorous research studies, we don't report every study and we don't provide endless footnotes. Our goal was to keep the length of this book under 200 pages so that it could be easily affordable by all. For those who want more research detail and illustrative examples, please see our other textbook, *Strategic Management and Business Policy*.

WHAT'S NEW IN THIS EDITION

The fifth edition of *Essentials of Strategic Management* contains many new content topics plus updated data and illustrations. Older examples have been replaced with newer ones, information has been updated where appropriate, and a few errors have been corrected. In addition, the following content topics have been added to the book:

- Added the natural physical environment to the discussion of the societal and task environments in Chapters 1 and 3.
- Contrasted agency theory with stewardship theory in the section on corporate governance in Chapter 2.
- Added paragraphs on sustainability and moral relativism plus information on enterprise strategy and social capital to the section on social responsibilities and ethics in Chapter 2.
- Added PESTEL analysis to environmental scanning in Chapter 3.
- Added a discussion of brands to marketing resources in Chapter 4.
- Replaced the section on advantages and limitations of portfolio analysis with a section on strategic alliance portfolio analysis in Chapter 6.
- Added open innovation to the discussion of R&D strategy.
- Added purchasing and logistics strategies to functional strategies in Chapter 7.
- Included offshoring in the discussion of outsourcing in Chapter 7.
- Added real options to the discussion of risk in Chapter 7.
- Included the concept of core rigidities in the discussion of the organizational life cycle in Chapter 8.
- Added an explanation of integration managers to managing mergers and acquisitions in Chapter 9.

TIME-TESTED FEATURES

The fifth edition of *Essentials of Strategic Management* contains many of the same features that made previous editions successful. Some of these features are the following:

- A strategic decision-making model based on the underlying processes of environmental scanning, strategy formulation, strategy implementation, and evaluation and control is presented in Chapter 1 and provides an integrating framework for the book.
- Michael Porter's approach to industry analysis and competitive strategy (plus competitive tactics!) is highlighted in Chapters 3 and 5. Hypercompetition and cooperative strategies, such as strategic alliances, are also discussed.
- The resource-based view of the firm (including Barney's VRIO framework), in Chapter 4, serves as a foundation for organizational analysis. Sections on business models and value-chain analysis are also used to assess a company's strengths and weaknesses and to identify core and distinctive competencies.
- Functional analysis and functional strategies receive major attention in Chapters 4 and 7. Sections on R&D and R&D strategies emphasize the importance of technology to strategy and product-market decisions.
- Strategy implementation deals not only with organization design and structure, but also with executive leadership and succession, reengineering, Six Sigma, TQM, MBO, and action planning in Chapters 8 and 9.
- Chapter 10, on evaluation and control. explains the importance of measurement and incentives to organizational performance. Benchmarking and economic value-added measures are highlighted.
- International considerations are included in all chapters and are highlighted in special sections in Chapters 3, 6, 8, 9, and 10.
- Environmental scanning and forecasting is given an emphasis equal to that given to industry analysis in Chapter 3.
- Suggested EFAS and IFAS Tables and a SFAS Matrix in Chapters 3, 4, and 5 enable the reader to better identify and evaluate strategic factors.
- Top management and the board of directors are examined in detail as strategic managers in Chapter 2.
- Social responsibility and ethics are discussed in Chapter 2 in terms of their importance to strategic decision making.
- To aid in in-depth case analysis, a complete listing of financial ratios, recommendations for oral and written analysis, and ideas for further research are presented in Chapter 11. The strategic audit is proposed as an aid to case analysis. This chapter is most useful for those who wish to supplement this book with cases.
- Each chapter begins with a brief situation vignette of an actual company that helps illustrate the chapter content.
- Each chapter ends with a list of key terms (which are also boldfaced within the text) and a set of discussion questions.

SUPPLEMENTS

Supplements are available for adopting instructors to download at www.pearsonhighered. com/irc. Registration is simple and gives the instructor immediate access to new titles and new editions. Pearson's dedicated technical support team is ready to help instructors with the media supplements that accompany this text. The instructor should visit http://247.pearsoned.com/ for answers to frequently asked questions and for toll-free user support phone numbers. Supplements include the following:

- Instructor's Manual with Test Bank—An instructor's manual has been carefully constructed to accompany this book. It includes a summary of the most important concepts of each chapter, answers to discussion questions, a series of multiple-choice questions, and a set of additional discussion/essay questions for use in exams.
- PowerPoint Slides—The PowerPoint slides highlight text learning objectives and key topics and serve as an excellent aid for classroom presentations and lectures.

COURSESMART

CourseSmart textbooks online is an exciting new choice for students trying to economize. As an alternative to purchasing the print textbook, students can subscribe to the same content online and save up to 50 percent off the suggested list price of the print version. With a CourseSmart e-textbook, students can search the text, make notes online, print out reading assignments that incorporate lecture notes, and bookmark important passages for later review. For additional information on this option, visit www.coursesmart.com.

ACKNOWLEDGMENTS

We thank Kim Norbuta, Editor, and Claudia Fernandes, Project Manager, at Prentice Hall, who supervised this edition. Without their support and encouragement, this edition would never have been written. We are very grateful to Clara Bartunek and Sadagoban Balaji (Integra Software Services) for their patience, expertise, and even disposition during the copyediting and production process. We also thank Betty Hunger for her work in preparing the index.

In addition, we express our appreciation to Wendy Klepetar, Management Department Chair of Saint John's University/College of Saint Benedict, for her support of this endeavor. Both of us thank Mary Clare McEwing and Michael Payne of Addison Wesley Publishing Company for their help in developing the first edition of this book. We remember how hard it was to get an essentials book approved since there was no such book in print in the strategy area at that time!

Finally, to the many strategy instructors and students who have moaned to us about the increasing size and cost of textbooks: We have tried to respond to your concerns as best we could by providing a comprehensive yet usable text that is half the size and cost of other books on the market. Instead of the usual five-course meal (complete with heartburn), we are offering you "lean cuisine." This book should taste good with fewer empty calories. Enjoy!

J. David Hunger

Thomas L. Wheelen

1

BASIC **CONCEPTS** OF **STRATEGIC** MANAGEMENT

How does a company become successful and stay successful? Certainly not by playing it safe and following the traditional ways of doing business! Taking a strategic risk is what Ford Motor Company did when top management, led by its new CEO Alan Mulally, decided to change the way it made automobiles. Already a successful CEO at Boeing, Mulally had been handpicked in 2006 by William (Bill) Clay Ford, Jr., to replace him as CEO of the company. This was a highly unusual selection, given that Mulally had no previous experience in the auto industry. Led by Bill Ford as Chairman, the board had wanted a CEO who would take a new approach and break Ford Motor out of its bureaucratic lethargy. Even though the company in 2006 was still profitable—thanks to its Financial Services segment, it had not made a profit in autos since 2000. Top management had already instituted a turnaround plan to lay off employees, close factories, and modernize plants, but this was not enough to move the company forward. The company needed a new direction.

As Ford's new CEO, Mulally wanted to concentrate on making smaller, more fuel-efficient cars and on matching production with consumer demand. He supported a plan to redesign factories to make multiple models instead of just one. He also endorsed the global strategy of building one auto for multiple markets worldwide instead of multiple models tailored to national or regional tastes. The company had tried building a "world car" before but had failed due to conflict among its regional divisions. To fund these strategic changes, Mulally raised $23.5 million from 40 banks, using all of the firm's buildings, stock, intellectual property, stakes in foreign automakers, and even its trademark blue logo as collateral. As CEO, he overcame internal opposition to divest the money-losing, but prestigious, Jaguar, Land Rover, and Aston Martin brands.

At that time, marketing, manufacturing, and product development were competent, but needed "makeovers" to be competitive. For example, the Mercury and Lincoln brands had lost their distinctive identities and needed to be repositioned. Based on dealer suggestions, Lincoln would emphasize premium sedans and SUVs, while Mercury would offer premium small cars and crossover vehicles. Unhappy with the "deflated football" design of the Taurus sedan, Mulally challenged Ford's design team to deliver a new Taurus in 24 months using the existing platform, but with a new look. Selected by CEO Mulally to be the head of global car development, Derrick Kuzak worked with the company's far-flung fiefdoms to collaborate on vehicle development by improving interiors; building small, fuel-efficient engines; and creating cost savings by ensuring that SUVs and trucks shared more parts. He aimed to reduce by 40 percent the number of chassis on which vehicles were built.

By 2009, some of the changes had begun to pay off. At a time when General Motors and Chrysler were asking for government assistance and declaring bankruptcy, Ford had enough cash to continue operations without government help. Although the company was still losing money, all three Ford domestic brands were rated "above average" in J. D. Power and Associates' 2009 Vehicle Dependability Study. Thanks to its successful Ford Fusion mid-size hybrid sedan, Ford had become the largest domestic maker of hybrid cars. The "world car" strategy would be tested in 2010 when the company began selling the same cars in North America as it did in Europe. The first of these autos were the carlike Transit Connect utility vehicle, a Fiesta subcompact, and a new Focus subcompact codesigned for both continents. Would this be enough to make the company profitable once again? Would Ford Motor Company soon be competitive with industry leaders Toyota and Honda? According to Jim Farley, Group VP of Marketing and Communications, a Toyota veteran who had been hired by Mulally, "Ford reminds me of what Toyota was like 20 years ago." At Ford, "there is a single-mindedness to the business plan and the product execution."[1]

Ford's actions suggest why the managers of today's business corporations must manage firms strategically. They cannot make decisions based on long-standing rules, historical policies, or simple extrapolations of current trends. Instead, they must look to the future as they plan organization-wide objectives, initiate strategy, and set policies. They must rise above their training and experience in such functional and operational areas as accounting, marketing, production, or finance, and grasp the overall picture. They must be willing to ask three **key strategic questions**:

1. Where is the organization now? (Not where does management hope it is!)
2. If no changes are made, where will the organization be in one year? two years? five years? ten years? Are the answers acceptable?
3. If the answers are not acceptable, what specific actions should management undertake? What risks and payoffs are involved?

1.1 THE STUDY OF STRATEGIC MANAGEMENT

Strategic management is that set of managerial decisions and actions that determines the long-run performance of a corporation. It includes environmental scanning (both external and internal), strategy formulation (strategic planning), strategy implementation, and evaluation and control. The study of strategic management therefore emphasizes the monitoring and evaluating of external opportunities and threats in light of a corporation's strengths and weaknesses in order to generate and implement a new strategic direction for an organization.

How has Strategic Management Evolved?

Many of the concepts and techniques dealing with strategic planning and strategic management have been developed and used successfully by business corporations such as General Electric and the Boston Consulting Group. Nevertheless, not all organizations use these tools or even attempt to manage strategically. Many are able to succeed for a while with unstated objectives and intuitive strategies.

From his extensive work in this field, Bruce Henderson of the Boston Consulting Group concluded that intuitive strategies cannot be continued successfully if (1) the corporation becomes large, (2) the layers of management increase, or (3) the environment changes substantially. The increasing risks of error, costly mistakes, and even economic ruin are causing today's professional managers to take strategic management seriously in order to keep their companies competitive in an increasingly volatile environment. As top managers attempt to better deal with their changing world, strategic management within a firm generally evolves through four sequential **phases of development**:

Phase 1. *Basic financial planning:* Seeking better operational control by trying to meet annual budgets.

Phase 2. *Forecast-based planning:* Seeking more effective planning for growth by trying to predict the future beyond the next year.

Phase 3. *Externally oriented strategic planning:* Seeking increased responsiveness to markets and competition by trying to think strategically.

Phase 4. *Strategic management:* Seeking a competitive advantage by considering implementation and evaluation and control when formulating a strategy.[2]

General Electric, one of the pioneers of strategic planning, led the transition from strategic planning to strategic management during the 1980s. By the 1990s, most corporations around the world had also begun the conversion to strategic management.

Has Learning Become a Part of Strategic Management?

Strategic management has now evolved to the point where its primary value is to help the organization operate successfully in a dynamic, complex environment. Strategic planning is a tool to drive organizational change. Managers at all levels are expected to continually analyze the changing environment in order to create or modify strategic plans throughout the year. To be competitive in dynamic environments, corporations must become less bureaucratic and more flexible. In stable environments such as those that have existed in the past, a competitive strategy simply involved defining a competitive position and then defending it.

As it takes less and less time for one product or technology to replace another, companies are finding that there is no such thing as a permanent competitive advantage. Many agree with Richard D'Aveni, who says, in his book *HyperCompetition*, that any sustainable competitive advantage lies not in doggedly following a centrally managed five-year plan, but in stringing together a series of strategic short-term thrusts (as Intel does by cutting into the sales of its own offerings with periodic introductions of new products).[3]

This means that corporations must develop *strategic flexibility*—the ability to shift from one dominant strategy to another. Strategic flexibility demands a long-term commitment to the development and nurturing of critical resources. It also demands that the company becomes a **learning organization**: an organization skilled at creating, acquiring, and transferring knowledge and at modifying its behavior to reflect new knowledge and insights. Learning organizations avoid stagnation through continuous self-examination and experimentation. People at all levels, not just top management, need to be involved in strategic management: scanning the environment for critical information, suggesting changes to strategies and programs to take advantage of environmental shifts, and working with others to continuously improve work methods, procedures, and evaluation techniques. For example, Hewlett-Packard uses an extensive network of informal committees to transfer knowledge among its cross-functional teams and to help spread new sources of knowledge quickly.

What is the Impact of Strategic Management on Performance?

Research has revealed that organizations that engage in strategic management generally outperform those that do not. The attainment of an appropriate match or "fit" between an organization's environment and its strategy, structure, and processes has positive effects on the organization's performance. Strategic planning becomes increasingly important as the environment becomes unstable. For example, studies of the impact of deregulation on the U.S. railroad and trucking industries found that companies that changed their strategies and structures as their environment changed outperformed companies that did not change.[4]

Nevertheless, to be effective, strategic management need not always be a formal process. Studies of the planning practices of organizations suggest that the real value of strategic planning may be more in the strategic thinking and organizational learning that is part of a future-oriented planning process than in any resulting written strategic plan. Small companies, in particular, may plan informally and irregularly. The president and a handful of top managers might get together casually to resolve strategic issues and plan their next steps.

In large, multidivisional corporations, however, strategic planning can become complex and time consuming. It often takes slightly more than a year for a large company to move from situation assessment to a final decision agreement. Because a strategic decision affects a relatively large number of people, a large firm needs a formalized, more sophisticated system to ensure that strategic planning leads to successful performance. Otherwise, top management becomes isolated from developments in the divisions and lower-level managers lose sight of the corporate mission.

1.2   INITIATION OF STRATEGY: TRIGGERING EVENTS

After much research, Henry Mintzberg discovered that strategy formulation is typically not a regular, continuous process: "It is most often an irregular, discontinuous process, proceeding in fits and starts. There are periods of stability in strategy development, but also there are periods of flux, of groping, of piecemeal change, and of global change."[5] This view of strategy formulation as an irregular process reflects the human tendency to continue on a particular course of action until something goes wrong or a person is forced to question his or her actions. This period of so-called strategic drift may simply be a result of the organization's inertia, or it may reflect the management's belief that the current strategy is still appropriate and needs only some fine-tuning. Most large organizations tend to follow a particular strategic orientation for about 15 to 20 years before they make a significant change in direction. This phenomenon, called *punctuated equilibrium*, describes corporations as evolving through relatively long periods of stability (equilibrium periods) punctuated by relatively short bursts of fundamental change (revolutionary periods). After this rather long period of fine-tuning an existing strategy, some sort of shock to the system is needed to motivate management to seriously reassess the corporation's situation.

A **triggering event** is something that stimulates a change in strategy. Some of the possible triggering events include:

- **New CEO.** By asking a series of embarrassing questions, the new CEO cuts through the veil of complacency and forces people to question the very reason for the corporation's existence.
- **External intervention.** The firm's bank suddenly refuses to agree to a new loan or suddenly calls for payment in full on an old one. A key customer complains about a serious product defect.
- **Threat of a change in ownership.** Another firm may initiate a takeover by buying the company's common stock.
- **Performance gap.** A performance gap exists when performance does not meet expectations. Sales and profits either are no longer increasing or may even be falling.
- **Strategic inflection point.** This is a major environmental change, such as the introduction of new technologies, a different regulatory environment, a change in customers' values, or a change in what customers prefer.

1.3   BASIC MODEL OF STRATEGIC MANAGEMENT

Strategic management consists of four basic elements: (1) environmental scanning, (2) strategy formulation, (3) strategy implementation, and (4) evaluation and control. **Figure 1.1** shows how these four elements interact. Management scans both the external environment for opportunities and threats and the internal environment for strengths and weaknesses.

What is Environmental Scanning?

Environmental scanning is the monitoring, evaluating, and disseminating of information from the external and internal environments to key people within the corporation. The **external environment** consists of variables (opportunities and threats) that are outside the organization and not typically within the short-run control of top management. These variables form the context within which the corporation exists. They may be general forces and trends within the natural or societal environments or specific factors that operate within an organization's specific task environment—often called its industry. (These external variables are defined and discussed in more detail in Chapter 3.)

The **internal environment** of a corporation consists of variables (strengths and weaknesses) that are within the organization itself and are not usually within the short-run control of top management. These variables form the context in which work is done. They include the corporation's structure, culture, and resources. (These internal variables are defined and discussed in more detail in Chapter 4.)

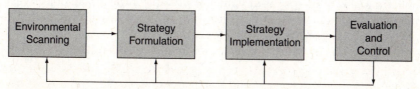

FIGURE 1.1   Basic Elements of the Strategic Management Process

What is Strategy Formulation?

Strategy formulation is the development of long-range plans for the effective management of environmental opportunities and threats, in light of corporate strengths and weaknesses. It includes defining the corporate mission, specifying achievable objectives, developing strategies, and setting policy guidelines.

WHAT IS A MISSION?

An organization's **mission** is its purpose, or the reason for its existence. It tells what the company is providing to society, such as housecleaning or manufacturing automobiles. A well-conceived **mission statement** defines the fundamental, unique purpose that sets a company apart from other firms of its type and identifies the scope of the company's operations in terms of products (including services) offered and markets served. It puts into words not only what the company is now, but also a vision of what it wants to become. It promotes a sense of shared expectations in employees and communicates a public image to important stakeholder groups in the company's task environment. A mission statement reveals who the company is and what it does.

One example of a mission statement is that of Google:

> *To organize the world's information and make it universally accessible and useful.*

A mission may be defined narrowly or broadly. A *broad* mission statement is a vague and general statement of what the company is in business to do. One popular example is, "Serve the best interests of shareowners, customers, and employees." A broadly defined mission statement such as this keeps the company from restricting itself to one field or product line, but it fails to clearly identify either what it makes or which product or market it plans to emphasize. In contrast, a *narrow* mission statement clearly states the organization's primary products and markets, but it may limit the scope of the firm's activities in terms of product or service offered, the technology used, and the market served.

WHAT ARE OBJECTIVES?

Objectives are the end results of planned activity. They state *what* is to be accomplished by *when* and should be *quantified* if possible. The achievement of corporate objectives should result in the fulfillment of the corporation's mission. For example, by providing society with gums, candy, iced tea, and carbonated drinks, Cadbury Schweppes has become the world's largest confectioner by sales. One of its prime objectives is to increase sales 4–6 percent each year. Even though its profit margins were lower than those of Nestle, Kraft, and Wrigley, its rivals in confectionary, or those of Coca-Cola and Pepsi, its rivals in soft drinks, Cadbury Schweppes' management established the objective of increasing profit margins from around 10 percent in 2007 to the mid-teens by 2011.[6]

The term *goal* is often confused with *objective*. In contrast to an objective, a **goal** is an open-ended statement of what one wishes to accomplish with no quantification of what is to be achieved and no timeframe for completion.

Some of the areas in which a corporation might establish its goals and objectives include:

- Profitability (net profits)
- Efficiency (low costs, etc.)

- Growth (increase in total assets, sales, etc.)
- Shareholder wealth (dividends plus stock price appreciation)
- Utilization of resources (ROE or ROI)
- Reputation (being considered a "top" firm)
- Contributions to employees (employment security, wages, etc.)
- Contributions to society (taxes paid, participation in charities, providing a needed product or service, etc.)
- Market leadership (market share)
- Technological leadership (innovations, creativity, etc.)
- Survival (avoiding bankruptcy)
- Personal needs of top management (using the firm for personal purposes, such as providing jobs for relatives)

WHAT ARE STRATEGIES?

A **strategy** of a corporation is a comprehensive plan stating how the corporation will achieve its mission and objectives. It maximizes competitive advantage and minimizes competitive disadvantage. For example, even though Cadbury Schweppes was a major competitor in confectionary and soft drinks, it was not likely to achieve its challenging objective of significantly increasing its profit margin within four years without making a major change in strategy. Management therefore decided to cut costs by closing 33 factories and reducing staff by 10 percent. It also made the strategic decision to concentrate on the confectionary business by divesting its less-profitable Dr. Pepper/Snapple soft drinks unit. Management was also considering acquisitions as a means of building on its existing strengths in confectionary by purchasing either Kraft's confectionary unit or the Hershey Company.

The typical business firm usually considers three types of strategy: corporate, business, and functional.

1. **Corporate strategy** describes a company's overall direction in terms of its general attitude toward growth and the management of its various businesses and product lines. Corporate strategy is composed of directional strategy, portfolio analysis, and parenting strategy. Corporate directional strategy is conceptualized in terms of stability, growth, and retrenchment. Cadbury Schweppes, for example, was following a corporate strategy of retrenchment by selling its marginally profitable soft drink business and concentrating on its very successful confectionary business.

2. **Business strategy** usually occurs at the business unit or product level, and it emphasizes improvement of the competitive position of a corporation's products or services in the specific industry or market segment served by that business unit. Business strategies are composed of *competitive* and *cooperative* strategies. For example, Apple uses a differentiation competitive strategy that emphasizes innovative products with creative design. In contrast, British Airways followed a cooperative strategy by forming an alliance with American Airlines in order to provide global service.

3. **Functional strategy** is the approach taken by a functional area, such as marketing or research and development, to achieve corporate and business unit objectives and strategies by maximizing resource productivity. It is concerned with developing and nurturing a distinctive competence to provide a company or business unit with

a competitive advantage. An example of a marketing functional strategy is Dell Computer's selling directly to the consumer to reduce distribution expenses and increase customer service.

Business firms use all three types of strategy simultaneously. A **hierarchy of strategy** is the grouping of strategy types by level in the organization. This hierarchy of strategy is a nesting of one strategy within another so that they complement and support one another (see **Figure 1.2**). Functional strategies support business strategies, which, in turn, support the corporate strategy(ies).

Just as many firms often have no formally stated objectives, many CEOs have unstated, incremental, or intuitive strategies that have never been articulated or analyzed. Often the only way to spot the implicit strategies of a corporation is to examine not what management says, but what it does. Implicit strategies can be derived from corporate policies, programs approved (and disapproved), and authorized budgets. Programs and divisions favored by budget increases and staffed by managers who are considered to be on the fast track to promotion reveal where the corporation is putting its money and energy.

WHAT ARE POLICIES?

A **policy** is a broad guideline for decision making that links the formulation of strategy with its implementation. Companies use policies to make sure that employees throughout the firm make decisions and take actions that support the corporation's mission, objectives, and strategies. For example, when Cisco decided upon a strategy of growth through acquisitions, it established a policy to consider only companies with no more than 75 employees, 75 percent of whom were engineers. Consider the following company policies:

- **Southwest Airlines.** Offer no meals or reserved seating on airplanes. (This supports Southwest's competitive strategy of having the lowest costs in the industry.)

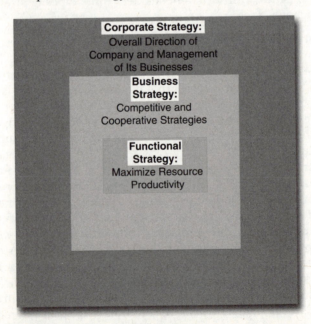

Corporate Strategy:
Overall Direction of
Company and Management
of Its Businesses

Business Strategy:
Competitive and
Cooperative Strategies

Functional Strategy:
Maximize Resource
Productivity

FIGURE 1.2   Hierarchy of Strategy

- **3M.** Researchers should spend 15 percent of their time working on something other than their primary project. (This supports 3M's strong product development strategy.)
- **Intel.** Cannibalize your product line (undercut the sales of your current products) with better products before a competitor does it to you. (This supports Intel's objective of market leadership.)
- **General Electric.** GE must be number one or two wherever it competes. (This supports GE's objective to be number one in market capitalization.)

Policies like these provide clear guidance to managers throughout the organization. (Strategy formulation is discussed in greater detail in Chapters 5, 6, and 7.)

What is Strategy Implementation?

Strategy implementation is the process by which strategies and policies are put into action through the development of programs, budgets, and procedures. This process might involve changes within the overall culture, structure, or management system of the entire organization, or within all of these areas. Except when such drastic corporate-wide changes are needed, however, middle- and lower-level managers typically implement strategy, with review by top management. Sometimes referred to as *operational planning*, strategy implementation often involves day-to-day decisions in resource allocation.

WHAT ARE PROGRAMS?

A **program** is a statement of the activities or steps needed to accomplish a single-use plan. It makes the strategy action oriented. It may involve restructuring the corporation, changing the company's internal culture, or beginning a new research effort. For example, Boeing's strategy to regain industry leadership with its new 787 Dreamliner meant that the company had to increase its manufacturing efficiency if it were to keep the price low. To significantly cut costs, management decided to implement a series of programs:

- Outsource approximately 70 percent of manufacturing.
- Reduce final assembly time to three days (compared to 20 for its 737 plane) by having suppliers build completed plane sections.
- Use new, lightweight composite materials in place of aluminum to reduce inspection time.
- Resolve poor relations with labor unions caused by downsizing and outsourcing.

WHAT ARE BUDGETS USED FOR?

A **budget** is a statement of a corporation's programs in dollar terms. Used in planning and control, it lists the detailed cost of each program. Many corporations demand a certain percentage return on investment (ROI), often called a *hurdle rate*, before management will approve a new program. This ensures that the new program will significantly add to the corporation's profit performance and thus build stockholder value. The budget thus not only serves as a detailed plan of the new strategy in action, it also specifies through pro forma financial statements the expected impact on the firm's financial future. For example, General Electric established an $8 billion budget to invest in new jet engine technology for regional jet airplanes. Management decided that an anticipated growth in regional jets should be the company's target. The program paid off in 2003 when GE won a $3 billion contract to provide jet engines for China's new fleet of 500 regional jets in time for the 2008 Beijing Olympics.[7]

WHAT ARE PROCEDURES?

Procedures, sometimes termed *standard operating procedures (SOP)*, are a system of sequential steps or techniques that describe in detail how a particular task or job is to be done. They typically detail the various activities that must be carried out for completion of a corporation's program. For example, when the home improvement retailer Home Depot wanted to improve its customer service in 2009, management instituted "power hours" on weekdays from 10 a.m. to 2 p.m. when employees were supposed to do nothing but serve customers. They were to stock shelves, unload boxes, and survey inventory at other times. Management also changed Home Depot's performance review process so that store employees were evaluated almost entirely on customer service.[8] (Strategy implementation is discussed in more detail in Chapters 8 and 9.)

What is Evaluation and Control?

Evaluation and control is the process by which corporate activities and performance results are monitored so that actual performance can be compared with desired performance. Managers at all levels use the resulting information to take corrective action and resolve problems. Although evaluation and control is the final major element of strategic management, it also can pinpoint weaknesses in previously implemented strategic plans and thus stimulate the entire process to begin again.

Performance is the end result of activities—the actual outcomes. The practice of strategic management is justified in terms of its ability to improve an organization's performance, typically measured in terms of profits and ROI. For evaluation and control to be effective, managers must obtain clear, prompt, and unbiased information from the people below them in the corporation's hierarchy. Using this information, managers compare what is actually happening with what was originally planned in the formulation stage. For example, when market share (followed by profits) declined at Dell in 2007, Michael Dell, founder, returned to the CEO position and reevaluated his company's strategy and operations. The company's expansion of its computer product line into new types of hardware, such as storage, printers, and televisions, had not worked as planned. In some areas, like televisions and printers, Dell's customization ability did not add much value. In other areas, like services, lower-cost competitors were already established. Michael Dell concluded, "I think you're going to see a more streamlined organization, with a much clearer strategy."[9]

The evaluation and control of performance completes the strategic management model. Based on performance results, management may need to adjust its strategy formulation, implementation, or both. (Evaluation and control are discussed in more detail in Chapter 10.)

Does the Model have a Feedback/Learning Process?

The strategic management model depicted in Figure 1.1 includes a *feedback/learning process* in which information from each element of the process is used to make possible adjustments to each of the previous elements of the process. As the firm or business unit formulates and implements strategies, it must often go back to revise or correct decisions made earlier in the process. In the case of Dell, the personal computer market had matured and by 2007 there were fewer growth opportunities available within the industry. Dell's management needed to reassess the company's environment and find better opportunities to profitably apply its core competencies.

1.4 STRATEGIC DECISION MAKING

The distinguishing characteristic of strategic management is its emphasis on strategic decision making. As organizations grow larger and more complex with more uncertain environments, decisions become increasingly complicated and difficult to make. We propose a strategic decision-making framework that can help members of organizations make these types of decisions.

What Makes a Decision Strategic?

Unlike many other decisions, **strategic decisions** deal with the long-run future of the entire organization and have three characteristics:

1. *Rare*. Strategic decisions are unusual and typically have no precedent to follow.
2. *Consequential*. Strategic decisions commit substantial resources and demand a great deal of commitment from people at all levels.
3. *Directive*. Strategic decisions set precedents for lesser decisions and future actions throughout the organization.[10]

What are Mintzberg's Modes of Strategic Decision Making?

Some strategic decisions are made in a flash by one person (often an entrepreneur or a powerful chief executive officer) who has a brilliant insight and is quickly able to convince others to follow this idea. Other strategic decisions seem to develop out of a series of small incremental choices that over time push the organization more in one direction than another. According to Henry Mintzberg, the most typical **strategic decision-making modes** are entrepreneurial, adaptive, and planning.[11] A fourth mode, logical incrementalism, was later added by Quinn.

- **Entrepreneurial mode.** In this mode of strategic decision making, the strategy is developed by one powerful individual. The focus is on opportunities, and problems are secondary. Strategy is guided by the founder's own vision of direction and is exemplified by large, bold decisions. The dominant goal is growth of the corporation. Amazon.com, founded by Jeff Bezos, is an example of this mode of strategic decision making. The company reflected his vision of using the Internet to market books and more. Although Amazon's clear growth strategy was certainly an advantage of the entrepreneurial mode, Bezos' eccentric management style made it difficult to retain senior executives.
- **Adaptive mode.** Sometimes referred to as "muddling through," this decision-making mode is characterized by reactive solutions to existing problems, rather than a proactive search for new opportunities. Much bargaining concerning priorities of objectives occurs. Strategy is fragmented and is developed to move the corporation forward in incremental steps. Encyclopædia Britannica, Inc., operated successfully for many years in this mode, by continuing to rely on the

door-to-door selling of its prestigious books long after dual career couples made this marketing approach obsolete. Only after it was acquired in 1996 did the company produce electronic versions of its books and change its marketing strategy to television advertising.

- **Planning mode.** This decision-making mode involves the systematic gathering of appropriate information for situation analysis, the generation of feasible alternative strategies, and the rational selection of the most appropriate strategy. This mode includes both the proactive search for new opportunities and the reactive solution of existing problems. IBM under CEO Louis Gerstner is an example of the planning mode. One of Gerstner's first actions as CEO was to convene a two-day meeting on corporate strategy with senior executives. An in-depth analysis of IBM's product line resulted in a strategic decision to invest in providing a complete set of services instead of computer hardware. Since making this strategic decision in 1993, 80 percent of IBM's revenue growth has come from services.

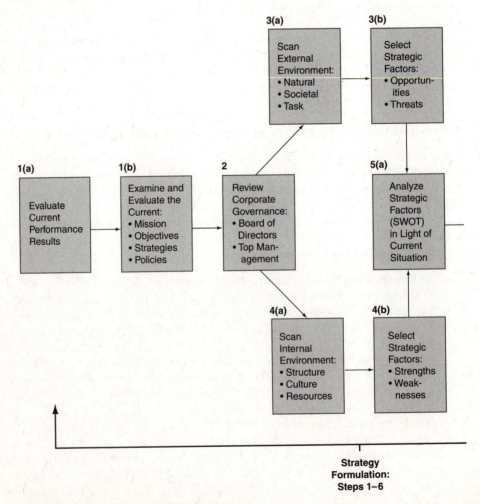

FIGURE 1.3   **Strategic Decision-Making Process**

- **Logical incrementalism.** A fourth decision-making mode, which is a synthesis of the planning, adaptive, and, to a lesser extent, the entrepreneurial modes, was proposed by Quinn. In this mode, top management has a reasonably clear idea of the corporation's mission and objectives, but in its development of strategies, it chooses to use "an interactive process in which the organization probes the future, experiments and learns from a series of partial (incremental) commitments rather than through global formulations of total strategies."[12] Thus, although the mission and objectives are set, the strategy is allowed to emerge out of debate, discussion, and experimentation. This approach appears to be useful when the environment is changing rapidly and when it is important to build consensus and develop needed resources before committing the entire corporation to a specific strategy.

How can Managers make Better Strategic Decisions?

Good arguments can be made for using either the entrepreneurial or adaptive modes (or logical incrementalism) in certain situations. This book proposes, however, that in most situations the planning mode, which includes the basic elements of the strategic management process, is a more rational and thus better way of making strategic decisions. The planning mode is not only more analytical and less political than the other modes are, but also more appropriate for dealing with complex, changing environments. We propose the following eight-step **strategic decision-making process** (which is also illustrated in **Figure 1.3**):

1. **Evaluate current performance results** in terms of (a) return on investment, profitability, and so forth, and (b) the current mission, objectives, strategies, and policies.

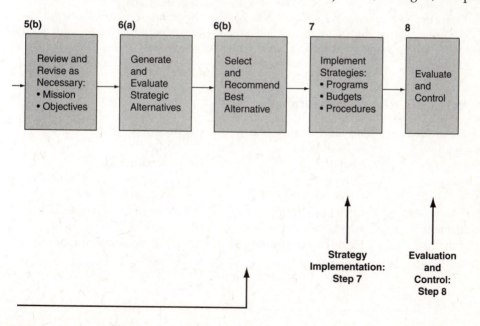

FIGURE 1.3 (continued)

Source: T. L. Wheelen and J. D. Hunger, *Strategic Decision Making Process.* Copyright © 1994 and 1997 by Wheelen and Hunger Associates. Reprinted by permission.

2. **Review corporate governance**, that is, the performance of the firm's board of directors and top management.
3. **Scan the external environment** to locate strategic factors that pose opportunities and threats.
4. **Scan the internal corporate environment** to determine strategic factors that are strengths and weaknesses.
5. **Analyze strategic factors** to (a) pinpoint problem areas, and (b) review and revise the corporate mission and objectives as necessary.
6. **Generate, evaluate, and select the best alternative strategy** in light of the analysis conducted in Step 5.
7. **Implement selected strategies** via programs, budgets, and procedures.
8. **Evaluate implemented strategies** via feedback systems, and the control of activities to ensure their minimum deviation from plans.

This rational approach to strategic decision making has been used successfully by corporations like Warner-Lambert, IBM, Target, General Electric, Avon Products, Bechtel Group, Inc., and Taisei Corporation.

Discussion Questions

1. Why has strategic management become so important to today's corporations?
2. How does strategic management typically evolve in a corporation?
3. What is a learning organization? Is this approach to strategic management better than the more traditional top-down approach in which strategic planning is primarily done by top management?
4. Why are strategic decisions different from other kinds of decisions?
5. When is the planning mode of strategic decision making superior to the entrepreneurial and adaptive modes?

Key Terms (listed in order of appearance)

key strategic questions 2
strategic management 2
phases of development 3
learning organization 3
triggering event 5
environmental scanning 5
external environment 5
internal environment 5
strategy formulation 6
mission 6

mission statement 6
objectives 6
goal 6
strategy 7
corporate strategy 7
business strategy 7
functional strategy 7
hierarchy of strategy 8
policy 8
strategy implementation 9

program 9
budget 9
procedures 10
evaluation and control 10
strategic decisions 11
strategic decision-making modes 11
strategic decision-making process 13

Notes

1. D. Kiley, "Ford's Savior?" *Business Week* (March 16, 2009), pp. 30–34; D. Kiley, "One Ford for the Whole Wide World," *Business Week* (June 15, 2009), pp. 58–59; K. Johnson, "Ford's 2006 Actions May Save Company," *Minneapolis Star Tribune* (December 11, 2008), p. D3; C. Woodyard, "Ford Shares Toyota's Vision," *USA Today* (April 1, 2009), pp. B1, B2.

2. F. W. Gluck, S. P. Kaufman, and A. S. Walleck, "The Four Phases of Strategic Management," *Journal of Business Strategy* (Winter 1982), pp. 9–21.

3. R. A. D'Aveni, *Hypercompetition* (New York: Free Press, 1994).

4. K. G. Smith and C. M. Grimm, "Environmental Variation, Strategic Change and Firm Performance: A Study of Railroad Deregulation," *Strategic Management Journal* (July–August 1987), pp. 363–376; J. A. Nickerson and B. S. Silverman, "Why Firms Want to Organize Efficiently and What Keeps Them From Doing So: Inappropriate Governance, Performance, and Adaptation in a Deregulated Industry," *Administrative Science Quarterly* (September 2003), pp. 433–465.

5. H. Mintzberg, "Planning on the Left Side and Managing on the Right," *Harvard Business Review* (July–August 1976), p. 56.

6. "Time to Break Off a Chunk," *The Economist* (December 15, 2007), pp. 75–76.

7. S. Holmes, "GE: Little Engines That Could," *Business Week* (January 20, 2003), pp. 62–63.

8. J. McGregor, "Putting Home Depot's House in Order," *Business Week* (May 18, 2009), p. 54.

9. L. Lee and P. Burrows, "Is Dell Too Big for Michael Dell?" *Business Week* (February 12, 2007), p. 33.

10. D. J. Hickson, R. J. Butler, D. Cray, G. R. Mallory, and D. C. Wilson, *Top Decisions: Strategic Decision-Making in Organizations* (San Francisco: Jossey-Bass, 1986), pp. 26–42.

11. H. Mintzberg, "Strategy-Making in Three Modes," *California Management Review* (Winter 1973), pp. 44–53.

12. J. B. Quinn, *Strategies for Change: Logical Incrementalism* (Homewood, Ill.: Irwin, 1980), p. 58.

2 CORPORATE GOVERNANCE AND SOCIAL RESPONSIBILITY

Only a few miles from the gleaming skyscrapers of prosperous Minneapolis was a neighborhood littered with shattered glass from stolen cars and derelict houses used by drug lords. During the 1990s, the Hawthorne neighborhood had become a no-man's-land where gun battles terrified local residents and raised the per capita murder rate 70 percent higher than that of New York.

Executives at General Mills became concerned when the murder rate reached a record high in 1996. The company's headquarters was located just five miles away from Hawthorne, then the city's most violent neighborhood. Working with law enforcement, politicians, community leaders, and residents, General Mills spent $2.5 million and donated thousands of employee hours to help clean up Hawthorne. Crack houses were demolished to make way for a new elementary school. Dilapidated houses in the neighborhood's core were rebuilt. General Mills provided grants to help people buy Hawthorne's houses. By 2003, homicides were down 32 percent and robberies had declined 56 percent in Hawthorne.

This story was nothing new for General Mills, a company often listed in *Fortune* magazine's "Most Admired Companies," ranked the third most socially responsible company in a survey conducted by *The Wall Street Journal* and Harris Interactive and fourth in a *Business Week* listing of "most generous corporate donors." Since 2000, the company has annually contributed 5 percent of pretax earnings to a wide variety of social causes. In 2009, for example, the company donated nearly $21 million to nonprofit organizations supporting education, youth nutrition and fitness, arts and culture, and social services plus $70 million in product donations to food banks throughout the nation and company cash contributions. Community performance is even reflected in the performance reviews of top management. For joining with a nonprofit organization and a minority-owned food company to create 150 inner-city jobs, General Mills received *Business Ethics'* annual corporate citizenship award.[1]

Was this the best use of General Mills' time and money? At a time when companies were being pressured to cut costs and outsource jobs to countries with cheaper labor, what do business corporations owe their local communities? Should business firms give away shareholders' money, support social causes, and ask employees to donate their time to the community? Critics argue that this sort of thing is done best by government and not-for-profit charities. Isn't the primary goal of business to maximize profits, not to be a social worker? Shouldn't the board of directors, whose job is to represent the shareholders, have demanded that management focus instead on building net income and earnings per share?

2.1 CORPORATE GOVERNANCE: ROLE OF THE BOARD OF DIRECTORS

A **corporation** is a mechanism established to allow different parties to contribute capital, expertise, and labor for their mutual benefit. The investor or shareholder participates in the profits of the enterprise without taking responsibility for the operations. Management runs the company without being personally responsible for providing the funds. To make this possible, laws have been passed so that shareholders have limited liability and, correspondingly, limited involvement in a corporation's activities. That involvement does include, however, the right to elect directors who have a legal duty to represent the shareholders and protect their interests. As representatives of the shareholders, directors have both the authority and the responsibility to establish basic corporate policies and ensure that they are followed.

The board of directors has, therefore, an obligation to approve all decisions that might affect the long-run performance of the corporation. This means that the corporation is fundamentally governed by the board of directors overseeing top management, with the concurrence of the shareholder. The term **corporate governance** refers to the relationship among these three groups (boards of directors, management, and shareholders) in determining the direction and performance of the corporation.

Over the past decade, shareholders and various interest groups have seriously questioned the role of the board of directors in corporations. They are concerned that outside board members often lack sufficient knowledge, involvement, and enthusiasm to adequately provide guidance to top management. Instances of widespread corruption and questionable accounting practices at Enron, Global Crossing, WorldCom, Tyco, and Qwest, among others, seem to justify their concerns.

The general public has not only become more aware and more critical of the apparent lack of many boards of directors to assume responsibility for corporate activities, but it has also begun to push government to demand accountability. As a result, the board as a "rubber stamp" of the CEO or as a bastion of the "old boy" selection system is being replaced by more active, more professional boards.

What are the Responsibilities of the Board?

Laws and standards defining the responsibilities of boards of directors vary from country to country. For example, board members in Ontario, Canada, face more than 100 provincial and federal laws governing director liability. The United States, however, has no clear national standards or federal laws. Specific requirements of board members (also called directors) vary, depending on the state in which the corporate charter is issued. Nevertheless, a consensus is developing worldwide concerning the major responsibilities of a board. Interviews with 200 directors from eight countries (Canada, Finland, France, Germany, the Netherlands, Switzerland, the United

Kingdom, and Venezuela) revealed strong agreement on the following five **board of directors' responsibilities** listed in order of importance:

1. Setting corporate strategy, overall direction, and mission or vision
2. Succession—hiring and firing the CEO and top management
3. Controlling, monitoring, or supervising top management
4. Reviewing and approving the use of resources
5. Caring for stockholder interests[2]

In addition to the aforementioned duties, directors in the United States must make certain that the corporation is managed in accordance with the laws of the state in which it is incorporated. They must also ensure management's adherence to laws and regulations such as those dealing with the issuance of securities, insider trading, and other conflict-of-interest situations. They must also be aware of the needs and demands of constituent groups in order to achieve a judicious balance among their diverse interests while ensuring the continued functioning of the corporation.

In a legal sense, the board of directors is required to direct the affairs of the corporation but not to manage them. It is charged by law to act with *due care*, that is, to conscientiously carry out its responsibilities. If a director or the board as a whole fails to act with due care and, as a result, the corporation is in some way harmed, the careless director or directors can be held personally liable for the harm done.

What is the Role of the Board in Strategic Management?

How does a board of directors fulfill its many responsibilities? The role of the board in strategic management is to carry out three basic tasks:

- *Monitor.* By acting through its committees, a board can keep abreast of developments both inside and outside the corporation. It can thus bring to management's attention developments it might have overlooked. At a minimum, a board should carry out this task.
- *Evaluate and influence.* A board can examine management's proposals, decisions, and actions; agree or disagree with them; give advice and offer suggestions; and outline alternatives. More active boards do this in addition to monitoring.
- *Initiate and determine.* A board can delineate a corporation's mission and specify strategic options to its management. Only the most active boards take on this task in addition to the previous ones.

Is there a Board of Directors' Continuum?

A board of directors is involved in strategic management to the extent that it carries out the three tasks of monitoring, evaluating and influencing, and initiating and determining. The **board of directors' continuum** as shown in **Figure 2.1** depicts the possible degree of involvement (from low to high) in strategic management. Boards can range from phantom boards with no real involvement to catalyst boards with a very high degree of involvement. Research does suggest that active board involvement in strategic management is positively related to a corporation's financial performance and its credit rating.

Highly involved boards tend to be very active. They take their tasks of monitoring, evaluating and influencing, and initiating and determining very seriously; they advise

←─────── **DEGREE OF INVOLVEMENT IN STRATEGIC MANAGEMENT** ───────→

Low
(Passive)

High
(Active)

Phantom	Rubber Stamp	Minimal Review	Nominal Participation	Active Participation	Catalyst
Never knows what to do, if anything; no degree of involvement.	Permits officers to make all decisions. It votes as the officers recommend on action issues.	Formally reviews selected issues that officers bring to its attention.	Involved to a limited degree in the performance or review of selected key decisions, indicators, or programs of management.	Approves, questions, and makes final decisions on mission, strategy, policies, and objectives. Has active board committees. Performs fiscal and management audits.	Takes the leading role in establishing and modifying the mission, objectives, strategy, and policies. It has a very active strategy committee.

FIGURE 2.1   **Board of Directors' Involvement in Strategic Management**

Source: T. L. Wheelen and J. D. Hunger, *Board of Directors Continuum.* Copyright © 1994 by Wheelen and Hunger Associates. Reprinted by permission.

when necessary and keep management alert. As depicted in Figure 2.1, their heavy involvement in strategic management places them in the active participation or even catalyst positions. For example, a 2008 global survey of directors by McKinsey & Company found that 43 percent had high to very high influence in creating corporate value. Together with top management, these highly involved boards considered global trends and future scenarios and developed plans.[3] Some corporations with actively participating boards are Target, Medtronic, Best Western, Service Corporation International, Bank of Montreal, Mead Corporation, Rolm and Haas, Whirlpool, 3M, Apria Healthcare, General Electric, Pfizer, and Texas Instruments.

As a board becomes less involved in the affairs of the corporation, it moves farther to the left on the continuum (see Figure 2.1). On the far left are passive phantom or rubber stamp boards that typically never initiate or determine strategy unless a crisis occurs. In these situations, the CEO also serves as Chairman of the Board and works to keep board members under his or her control by giving them the "mushroom treatment" (i.e., throw manure on them and keep them in the dark!).

Generally, the smaller the corporation, the less active is its board of directors in strategic management. The board tends to be dominated by directors who are also owner-managers of the company. Other directors are usually friends or family members. As the corporation grows and sells stock to finance growth, however, the board becomes more active in terms of roles and responsibilities.

Who are Members of a Board of Directors?

The boards of most publicly owned corporations are composed of both inside and outside directors. **Inside directors** (sometimes called *management directors*) are typically officers or executives employed by the corporation. **Outside directors** may be executives of other firms but are not employees of the board's corporation. Although there is no clear evidence that a high proportion of outsiders on a board improves corporate performance, investors are willing to pay a premium for a corporation's stock if its board contains a majority of outsiders. There is currently a U.S. trend to both increase the number of outsiders and reduce the size of the board. The board of directors of a typical large U.S. corporation has an average of ten directors, of whom eight are outsiders; whereas, Japanese boards, in contrast, contain 12 insiders and only two outsiders. The typical small U.S. corporation has four to five members, of whom only one or two are outsiders.

People who favor a high proportion of outsiders state that outside directors are less biased and more likely to evaluate management's performance objectively than inside directors. This is the main reason why the U.S. Securities and Exchange Commission (SEC) requires that a majority of directors on the board be independent outsiders. The SEC also requires that all listed companies staff their audit, compensation, and nominating/corporate governance committees entirely with independent, outside members. This view is in agreement with **agency theory**, which states that problems arise in corporations because the agents (top management) are not willing to bear responsibility for their decisions unless they own a substantial amount of stock in the corporation. The theory suggests that a majority of a board needs to be from outside the firm so that top management is prevented from acting selfishly to the detriment of the shareholders. Outsiders tend to be more objective and critical of corporate activities.

In contrast, those who prefer inside directors over outside directors contend that outside directors are less effective than insiders because the outsiders are less likely to have the necessary interest, availability, or competency. This view is in agreement with **stewardship theory**, which states that because of their long tenure with the corporation, insiders (senior executives) tend to identify with the corporation and its success. Rather than use the firm for their own ends, these executives are thus most interested in guaranteeing the continued life and success of the corporation. Outside directors, however, may serve on so many boards that they spread their time and interest too thinly to actively fulfill their responsibilities. For example, the average board member of a U.S. Fortune 500 firm serves on three boards. In addition, the term *outsider* may be too simplistic; some outsiders are not truly objective and should be considered more as insiders than outsiders. Such outsiders may be *affiliated directors* who handle the legal or insurance work for the company, retired executives of the company, and family members of the founder of the firm.

The majority of outside directors are active or retired CEOs and chief operating officers (COOs) of other corporations. Others are academicians, attorneys, consultants, former government officials, major shareholders, and bankers. Given that approximately 66 percent of the outstanding stock in the largest U.S. and U.K. corporations is now owned by institutional investors, such as mutual funds and pension plans, these investors are taking an increasingly active role in board membership and activities.[4] In Germany, bankers are represented on almost every board—primarily because they own large blocks of stock in German corporations. In Denmark, Sweden, Belgium, and Italy, however, investment companies assume this role.

Boards of directors have been working to increase the number of women, minorities, and nonnationals serving on boards. Korn/Ferry International reports that of the *Fortune 1000* largest U.S. firms, 85 percent had at least one woman director in 2006 (compared to 69% in 1995), comprising 15 percent of total directors. Approximately one-half of the boards in Europe included a female director, comprising 9 percent of total directors.

Korn/Ferry's survey also revealed that 76 percent of the U.S. boards had at least one ethnic minority in 2006 (African American, 47%; Latino, 19%; Asian, 10%) as director compared to only 47 percent in 1995, comprising around 14 percent of total directors.[5] Only 33 percent of U.S. boards had an international director, whereas, most European boards reported one or more nonnational directors.

Outside directors serving on the boards of large *Fortune 1000* U.S. corporations annually earned on average $58,217 in cash plus an average of $75,499 in stock options. Most of the companies (63%) paid their outside directors an annual retainer plus a fee for every meeting attended. Directors serving on the boards of small companies usually received much less compensation (around $10,000).

Why are Interlocking Directorates Useful?

CEOs often nominate chief executives (as well as board members) from other firms to membership on their own boards in order to create an interlocking directorate. A *direct* **interlocking directorate** occurs when two firms share a director or when an executive of one firm sits on the board of a second firm. An *indirect interlock* occurs when two corporations have directors who also serve on the board of a third firm, such as a bank.

Although the Clayton Act and the Banking Act of 1933 prohibit interlocking directorates by U.S. companies competing in the same industry, interlocking continues to occur in almost all corporations, especially large ones. Interlocking occurs because large firms have a significant impact on other corporations; and these other corporations, in turn, have some control over the firm's inputs and marketplace. Interlocking directorates are also a useful method for gaining both inside information about an uncertain environment and objective expertise about potential strategies and tactics. Family-owned corporations, however, are less likely to have interlocking directorates than corporations with highly dispersed stock ownership, probably because family-owned corporations do not like to dilute their corporate control by adding outsiders to boardroom discussions. Nevertheless, there is some evidence to indicate that well-interlocked corporations are better able to survive in a highly competitive environment.

How are People Nominated and Elected to Boards?

Traditionally, the CEO of the corporation decided whom to invite to board membership and merely asked the shareholders for approval through the proxy statement. Because board members nominated by the CEO often feel that they should go along with any proposals the CEO makes, there is an increasing tendency for a special board committee to nominate new outside board members for election by the stockholders. Ninety-seven percent of large U.S. corporations use nominating committees to identify potential directors. This practice is less common in Europe where only 60 percent of boards use nominating committees.[6] There is also increasing pressure for the direct shareholder nomination of directors.

A survey of directors of U.S. corporations revealed the following criteria in a good director:

- Willing to challenge management when necessary (95%)
- Special expertise important to the company (67%)
- Available outside meetings to advise management (57%)
- Expertise on global business issues (41%)

- Understands the firm's key technologies and processes (39%)
- Brings external contacts that are potentially valuable to the firm (33%)
- Has detailed knowledge of the firm's industry (31%)
- Has high visibility in his or her field (31%)
- Is accomplished at representing the firm to stakeholders (18%)

How are Boards Organized?

The size of the board is determined by the corporation's charter and its bylaws in compliance with state laws. Although some states require a minimum number of board members, most corporations have quite a bit of discretion in determination of board size. The average size of boards of large, publicly owned firms in the United States is 10, but varies elsewhere from 16 in Germany to 14 in Japan, and 10 in the United Kingdom.

Approximately 70 percent of top executives of the U.S. publicly held corporations hold the dual designation of Chairman and CEO. (Only 5% of the firms in the United Kingdom have a combined Chair/CEO.)[7] The combined Chair/CEO position is being increasingly criticized because of the potential for conflict of interest. The CEO is supposed to concentrate on strategy, planning, external relations, and responsibility to the board. The Chair's responsibility is to ensure that the board and its committees perform their functions as stated in its charter. Critics of combining the two offices in one person ask how the board can properly oversee top management if the Chair also comprises top management. They recommend that outside directors elect a **lead director**—an outside director who would conduct the annual evaluation of the CEO. The Chair and CEO roles are separated by law in Germany, the Netherlands, and Finland. Of those U.S. companies combining the Chair and CEO positions, 96 percent had a lead director in 2007, up from only 32 percent in 2002. Although research is mixed regarding the impact of the combined Chair/CEO position on overall corporate financial performance, firm stock price and credit ratings both respond negatively to announcements of CEOs also assuming the Chair position.

The most effective boards accomplish much of their work through committees. Although the committees do not have legal duties, unless detailed in the bylaws, most committees are granted full power to act with the authority of the board between board meetings. Typical standing committees (in order of prevalence) are the audit, compensation, nominating, corporate governance, stock options, director compensation, and executive committees.

What is the Impact of Sarbanes–Oxley?

In response to the many corporate scandals uncovered since 2000, the U.S. Congress passed the **Sarbanes–Oxley Act** in June 2002. This act was designed to protect shareholders from the excesses and failed oversight that characterized failures at Enron, Tyco, World Com, Adelphia Communications, Qwest, and Global Crossing, among other prominent firms. Several key elements of Sarbanes–Oxley were designed to formalize greater board independence and oversight. For example, the act required that all directors serving on the audit committee be independent of the firm and receive no fees other than for services as a director. Additionally, boards may no longer grant loans to corporate officers. The act also established formal procedures for individuals (known as "whistle-blowers") to report incidents of questionable accounting or auditing. Firms are prohibited from retaliating against anyone reporting wrongdoing. Both the CEO and CFO must certify the corporation's financial information. The act banned auditors from providing both external and internal audit services to the same company. The bill also required that firms identify whether they have a "financial expert" serving on the audit committee who is independent from management. As a result of Sarbanes–Oxley, the SEC required that the audit, nominating, and compensation committees be staffed entirely by outside directors.

What are the Trends in Boards of Directors?

The role of the board of directors in the strategic management of the corporation is likely to be more active in the future. Although neither the composition of boards nor the board leadership structure has been consistently linked to firm financial performance, better governance does lead to higher credit ratings and stock price. Some of today's trends that are likely to continue include (1) increasing number and power of institutional investors (pension funds, etc.) and other outsiders on the board, (2) larger stock ownership by directors and executives, (3) increasing board diversity, (4) less CEOs also serving as Chairman of the Board, and (5) greater willingness of the board to help shape strategy and balance the economic goal of profitability with the needs of society.

2.2   CORPORATE GOVERNANCE: ROLE OF TOP MANAGEMENT

The top management function is usually performed by the CEO of the corporation in coordination with the COO (Chief Operating Officer) or President, Executive Vice President, and Vice Presidents of divisions and functional areas. Even though strategic management involves everyone in the organization, the board of directors holds top management primarily responsible for the strategic management of the firm.

What are the Responsibilities of Top Management?

Top management responsibilities, especially those of the CEO, involve getting things accomplished through and with others in order to meet the corporate objectives. Top management's job is thus multidimensional and is oriented toward the welfare of the total organization. The CEO, in particular, must successfully handle two responsibilities crucial to the effective strategic management of the corporation: (1) provide executive leadership and a strategic vision and (2) manage the strategic planning process.

WHAT ARE EXECUTIVE LEADERSHIP AND STRATEGIC VISION?

Executive leadership is the directing of activities toward the accomplishment of corporate objectives. Executive leadership is important because it sets the tone for the entire corporation. People in an organization want to have a sense of mission, but only top management is in the position to specify and communicate to the workforce a *strategic vision* of what the company is capable of becoming. Top management's enthusiasm (or lack of it) about the corporation tends to be contagious.

Chief executive officers with a clear strategic vision are often perceived to be dynamic and charismatic leaders. They have many of the characteristics of *transformational leaders*—leaders who provide change and movement in an organization by providing a vision for that change. For instance, the positive attitudes characterizing many well-known industrial leaders—such as Bill Gates at Microsoft, Anita Roddick at The Body Shop, Steve Jobs at Apple Computer, Richard Branson at Virgin, and Phil Knight at Nike—energized their respective corporations. They are able to command respect and influence strategy formulation and implementation because they tend to have three key characteristics:

1. *The CEO articulates a strategic vision* for the corporation. The CEO envisions the company not as it currently is, but as it can become. Because the CEO's vision puts activities and conflicts in a new perspective, it gives renewed meaning to everyone's work activities and enables employees to see beyond the details of their own jobs to the functioning of the total corporation.
2. *The CEO presents a role* for others to identify with and to follow. The CEO sets an example in terms of behavior and dress. The CEO's attitudes and values concerning the corporation's purpose and activities are clear-cut and constantly communicated in words and deeds.
3. *The CEO not only communicates high performance standards, but also shows confidence in the followers' abilities to meet these standards.* No leader ever improved performance by setting easily attainable goals that provided no challenge. The CEO must be willing to follow through by coaching people.

HOW DOES TOP MANAGEMENT MANAGE THE STRATEGIC PLANNING PROCESS?

As business corporations adopt more of the characteristics of the learning organization, strategic planning initiatives can come from any part of an organization. A survey of 156 large corporations throughout the world revealed that in two-thirds of the firms, strategies were first proposed in the business units and sent to headquarters for approval.[8] However, unless top management encourages and supports the planning process, strategic management is not likely to result. In most corporations, top management must initiate and manage the strategic planning process. It may do so by first asking business units and functional areas to propose strategic plans for themselves, or it may begin by drafting an overall corporate plan within which the units can then build their own plans. Other organizations engage in *concurrent* strategic planning in which all the units of the organization draft plans for themselves after they have been provided with the overall mission and objectives of the organization.

Many large organizations have a *strategic planning staff* charged with supporting both top management and the business units in the strategic planning process. This planning staff typically consists of fewer than ten people, headed by a Director of Corporate Development or Chief Strategy Officer. The staff's major responsibilities are to (1) identify and analyze company-wide strategic issues, and suggest corporate strategic alternatives to top management and (2) work as facilitators with business units to guide them through the strategic planning process.

2.3 SOCIAL RESPONSIBILITIES AND ETHICS IN STRATEGIC DECISION MAKING

Should strategic decision makers be responsible only to shareholders or should they have broader responsibilities? The concept of **social responsibility** proposes that a private corporation has responsibilities to society that extend beyond making a profit. Strategic decisions often affect more than just the corporation. A decision to retrench by closing some plants and discontinuing product lines, for example, affects not only the firm's workforce but also communities where the plants are located and those customers who have no other source of the discontinued product. This brings into consideration the question of the appropriateness of certain missions, objectives, and strategies of business corporations. Some businesspeople believe profit maximization is the primary goal of their firm, whereas concerned interest groups argue that other goals should have a priority, such as the hiring of minorities and women or community development. Strategic managers must be able to deal with these conflicting interests to formulate a viable strategic plan in an ethical manner.

What are the Responsibilities of a Business Firm?

What are the responsibilities of a business firm and how many of these responsibilities must strategic managers fulfill? Milton Friedman and Archie Carroll offer two contrasting views of the responsibilities of business firms to society.

WHAT IS FRIEDMAN'S TRADITIONAL VIEW OF BUSINESS RESPONSIBILITY?

Milton Friedman, in urging a return to a laissez-faire worldwide economy, that is, one with a minimum of government regulation, argues against the concept of social responsibility. If a businessperson acts "responsibly" by cutting the price of the firm's product to prevent inflation, or by making expenditures to reduce pollution, or by hiring the hard-core unemployed, that person, according to Friedman, is spending the stockholders' money for a general social interest. Even if the businessperson has shareholder permission or encouragement to do so, he or she is still acting from motives other than economic and may, in the long run, cause harm to the very society the firm is trying to help. By taking on the burden of these social costs, the business becomes less efficient—either prices go up to pay for the increased costs or investment in new activities and research is postponed. These results negatively, perhaps fatally, affect the long-term efficiency of a business. Friedman thus referred to the social responsibility of business as a "fundamentally subversive doctrine" and stated that "there is one and only one social responsibility of business—to use its resources and engage in activities designed to increase its profits so long as it stays within the rules of the game, which is to say, engages in open and free competition without deception or fraud."[9]

WHAT ARE CARROLL'S FOUR RESPONSIBILITIES OF BUSINESS?

Archie Carroll proposes that the managers of business organizations have four responsibilities: economic, legal, ethical, and discretionary.[10] These responsibilities are displayed in **Figure 2.2** and are defined as follows:

1. **Economic** responsibilities are to produce goods and services of value to society so that the firm may repay its creditors and shareholders.
2. **Legal** responsibilities are defined by governments in laws that management is expected to obey.
3. **Ethical** responsibilities are to follow the generally held beliefs about how one should act in a society. For example, society generally expects firms to work with the employees and the community in planning for layoffs, even though there may

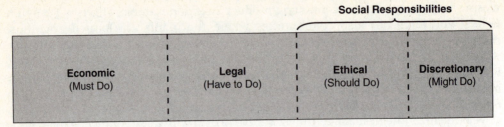

FIGURE 2.2 **Responsibilities of Business**

Source: Adapted from A. B. Carroll, "A Three Dimensional Conceptual Model of Corporate Performance," *Academy of Management Review* (October 1979), p. 499. Reprinted with permission.

be no law requiring this. The affected people can get very upset if an organization's management fails to act according to generally prevailing ethical values.

4. **Discretionary** responsibilities are the purely voluntary obligations a corporation assumes, for example, philanthropic contributions, training the hard-core unemployed, and providing day-care centers. The difference between ethical and discretionary responsibilities is that few people expect an organization to fulfill discretionary responsibilities, whereas many expect an organization to fulfill ethical ones.

Carroll lists these four responsibilities in order of priority. A business firm must first make a profit to satisfy its economic responsibilities. To continue in existence, it must follow the laws, thus fulfilling its legal responsibilities. To this point Carroll and Friedman are in agreement. Carroll, however, goes further by arguing that business managers have responsibilities beyond economic and legal.

Once the two basic responsibilities are satisfied, according to Carroll, the firm should look to fulfilling its social responsibilities. Social responsibility, therefore, includes both ethical and discretionary, but not economic and legal responsibilities. A firm can fulfill its ethical responsibilities by doing those things that society tends to value but has not yet put into law. Once ethical responsibilities are satisfied, a firm can focus on discretionary responsibilities—purely voluntary actions that society has not yet decided are necessary.

The discretionary responsibilities of today may become the ethical responsibilities of tomorrow. The provision of day-care facilities is, for example, moving rapidly from a discretionary to an ethical responsibility. Carroll suggests that to the extent that business corporations fail to acknowledge discretionary or ethical responsibilities, society, through government, will act, making them legal responsibilities. This may be done by government, moreover, without regard to an organization's economic responsibilities. As a result, the organization may have greater difficulty in earning a profit than it would have had in assuming voluntarily some ethical and discretionary responsibilities.

Both Friedman and Carroll argue their positions based on the impact of socially responsible actions on a firm's profits. Friedman says that socially responsible actions hurt a firm's efficiency. Carroll proposes that a lack of social responsibility results in an increase in government regulations, thus reducing a firm's efficiency. Although past evidence has been mixed, research now suggests that socially responsible actions may have a positive effect on a firm's financial performance through an enhanced reputation with consumers, local communities, and others. Being known as a socially responsible firm may provide a company with *social capital*, the goodwill of key stakeholders, that can be used for competitive advantage.[11]

Corporations are increasingly being evaluated on criteria other than economic. For example, Dow Jones & Company, a leading provider of global business news and information, developed a *sustainability index* that considers environmental and social factors in addition to economic.

Who are Corporate Stakeholders?

The concept that business must be socially responsible sounds appealing until one asks, "Responsible to whom?" A corporation's task environment includes a large number of groups with interest in the activities of a business organization. These groups are called **stakeholders** because they are groups that affect or are affected by the achievement of the firm's objectives. Should a corporation be responsible only to some of these groups, or does business have an equal responsibility to all of them?

In any one strategic decision, the interests of one stakeholder group can conflict with another. For example, a business firm's decision to use only recycled materials in its manufacturing process may have a positive effect on environmental groups but a negative effect on shareholder dividends. Which group's interests should have priority?

To answer this question, the corporation may need to craft an **enterprise strategy**—an overarching strategy that explicitly articulates the firm's ethical relationship with its stakeholders. This requires not only that management clearly state the firm's key ethical values, but also understand its societal context, and undertakes stakeholder analysis to identify the concerns and abilities of each stakeholder.[12] One approach to stakeholder analysis is to first categorize stakeholders into *primary stakeholders*, those who have a direct connection with the corporation and sufficient power to directly affect corporate activities, and *secondary stakeholders*, those who have only an indirect stake in the corporation, but who are also affected by corporate activities. Then estimate the effect on each stakeholder group from any particular strategic alternative. What seems at first to be the best decision because it appears to be the most profitable may actually result in the worst set of consequences to the corporation.

What is the Role of Ethics in Decision Making?

Ethics is defined as the consensually accepted standards of behavior for an occupation, trade, or profession. There is some evidence that ethics are often ignored in the workplace. For example, a survey by the Ethics Resource Center of 1,324 employees of 747 U.S. companies found that 48 percent of these employees had engaged in one or more unethical and/or illegal actions during the past year.[13] Some people justify their seemingly unethical positions by arguing that there is no one absolute code of ethics and that morality is relative. Simply put, **moral relativism** claims that morality is relative to some personal, social, or cultural standard and that there is no method for deciding whether one decision is better than another. Although this argument may make some sense in some instances, moral relativism could enable a person to justify almost any sort of decision or action, so long as it is not declared illegal.

Following Carroll's work, if business people do not act ethically, government will be forced to pass laws regulating their actions – with the usual result of increasing costs. For self-interest, if for no other reason, managers should be more ethical in their decision making. One way to do that is by encouraging codes of ethics.

A **code of ethics** specifies how an organization expects its employees to behave while on the job. Developing codes of ethics can be a useful way to promote ethical behavior. Such codes are currently being used by over half of American business corporations. A code of ethics (1) clarifies company expectations of employee conduct in various situations and (2) makes clear that the company expects its people to recognize the ethical dimensions in their decisions and actions. A company that wants to improve its employees' ethical behavior should not only develop a comprehensive code of ethics, but also communicate the code in its training programs, in its performance appraisal system, in policies and procedures, and through its own actions.

A starting point for developing a code of ethics is to consider the three basic approaches to ethical behavior:

- **Utilitarian approach.** This approach proposes that actions and plans should be judged by their consequences. People should therefore behave in such a way that will produce the greatest benefit to society and produce the least harm or the lowest cost.
- **Individual rights approach.** This approach proposes that human beings have certain fundamental rights that should be respected in all decisions. A particular decision or behavior should be avoided if it interferes with the rights of others.
- **Justice approach.** This approach proposes that decision makers be equitable, fair, and impartial in the distribution of costs and benefits to individuals and groups. It follows the principles of *distributive justice* (people who are similar on relevant dimensions such as job seniority should be treated in the same way) and *fairness* (liberty should be equal for all persons). The justice approach can also include the concepts of *retributive justice* (punishment should be proportional to the "crime") and *compensatory justice* (wrongs should be compensated in proportion to the offense).

Ethical problems can be solved by asking the following three questions regarding an act or decision:

1. *Utility.* Does it optimize the satisfactions of all stakeholders?
2. *Rights.* Does it respect the rights of the individuals involved?
3. *Justice.* Is it consistent with the canons of justice?[14]

Discussion Questions

1. When does a corporation need a board of directors?
2. Who should and should not serve on a board of directors? What of environmentalists or union leaders?
3. What recommendations would you make to improve corporate governance?
4. Do you agree with economist Milton Friedman that social responsibility is a "fundamentally subversive doctrine" that will only hurt a business corporation's long-term efficiency?
5. Is there a relationship between corporate governance and social responsibility?

Key Terms (listed in order of appearance)

corporation *17*
corporate governance *17*
board of directors'
     responsibilities *18*
board of directors'
     continuum *18*
inside directors *19*
outside directors *19*

agency theory *20*
stewardship theory *20*
interlocking directorate *21*
lead director *22*
Sarbanes–Oxley Act *22*
top management
     responsibilities *23*
executive leadership *23*

social responsibility *24*
stakeholders *27*
enterprise strategy *27*
ethics *27*
moral relativism *27*
code of ethics *28*

Notes

1. *2009 Annual Report*, General Mills, Inc., Minneapolis, Minn., p. 17; M. Conlin, J. Hempel, J. Tanzer, and D. Poole, "The Corporate Donors," *Business Week* (December 1, 2003), pp. 92–96; I. Sager, "The List: Angels in the Boardroom," *Business Week* (July 7, 2003), p. 12.
2. A. Demb and F. F. Neubauer, "The Corporate Board: Confronting the Paradoxes," *Long Range Planning* (June 1992), p. 13.
3. A. Chen, J. Osofsky, and E. Stephenson, "Making the Board More Strategic: A McKinsey Global Survey," *McKinsey Quarterly* (March 2008), pp. 1–10.
4. D. R. Dalton, M. A. Hitt, S. T. Certo, and C. M. Dalton, "The Fundamental Agency Problem and Its Mitigation," Chapter One in *Academy of Management Annals*, edited by J. F. Westfall and A. F. Brief (London: Routledge, 2007).
5. *33rd Annual Board of Directors Study* (New York: Korn/Ferry International, 2007), p. 11; T. Neff and J. H. Daum, "The Empty Boardroom," *Strategy + Business* (Summer 2007), pp. 57–61.
6. *33rd Annual Board of Directors Study* (New York: Korn/Ferry International, 2007), p. 17 and *30th Annual Board of Directors Study Supplement: Governance Trends of the Fortune 1000* (New York: Korn/Ferry International, 2004), p. 5.
7. Dalton, Hitt, Certo, and Dalton, "The Fundamental Agency Problem."; P. Coombes

and S. C-Y Wong, "Chairman and CEO—One Job or Two?" *McKinsey Quarterly* (2004, No. 2), pp. 43–47.
8. M. C. Mankins and R. Steele, "Stop Making Plans, Start Making Decisions," *Harvard Business Review* (January 2006), pp. 76–84.
9. M. Friedman, "The Social Responsibility of Business Is to Increase Its Profits," *New York Times Magazine* (September 13, 1970), pp. 30, 126–127; and *Capitalism and Freedom* (Chicago: University of Chicago Press, 1963), p. 133.
10. A. B. Carroll, "A Three-Dimensional Conceptual Model of Corporate Performance," *Academy of Management Review* (October 1979), pp. 497–505.
11. P. S. Adler and S. W. Kwon, "Social Capital: Prospects for a New Concept," *Academy of Management Journal* (January 2002), pp. 17–40. Also called "moral capital" in P. C. Godfrey, "The Relationship Between Corporate Philanthropy and Shareholder Wealth: A Risk Management Perspective," *Academy of Management Review* (October 2005), pp. 777–799.
12. W. E. Stead and J. G. Stead, *Sustainable Strategic Management* (Armonk, N.Y.: M. E. Sharpe, 2004), p. 41.
13. M. Hendricks, "Well, Honestly!" *Entrepreneur* (December 2006), pp. 103–104.
14. G. F. Cavanagh, *American Business Values*, 3rd ed. (Upper Saddle River, N.J.: Prentice Hall, 1990), pp. 186–199.

3

ENVIRONMENTAL SCANNING AND INDUSTRY ANALYSIS

Few, if any, companies were prepared when the world's economy went into a major recession in 2008. Many responded to the downturn by focusing only on short-term survival. The exception was Intel Corporation. Instead of cancelling all long-term plans, CEO Paul Otellini proposed in early 2009 that the company invest $7 billion to upgrade its U.S. manufacturing plants. This upgrade was to help revive sales in the firm's mature PC business while guiding the company into new growth markets. Otellini envisioned a promising opportunity to diversify with a new family of microprocessors called Atom for any product needing processing power and access to the Internet, from a web-connected television or a cash register to new types of mobile computing devices. Competitors like Qualcomm and Texas Instruments were using a rival chip architecture, created by ARM Holdings, that needed very little battery power. With the growth in laptop computers, battery usage and heat were becoming key considerations in selling PCs. Intel needed to make heavy investments so that Atom could become as energy-efficient as ARM's microprocessors. Otherwise, device makers might buy from Intel's competitors. Otellini knew that the economy would eventually recover and he wanted Intel to be properly positioned for future growth in new markets. According to Qualcomm CEO Paul Jacobs, "It's a race to see who will get there first."[1]

Intel is an example of a firm that refused to be daunted by a poor economy in order to take advantage of environmental trends to create a new product. A changing environment can, however, also hurt a company. Many pioneering companies have gone out of business because of their failure to adapt to environmental change or, even worse, by failing to create change. For example, leading manufacturers of vacuum tubes failed to make the change to transistors and consequently lost this market. Eastman Kodak, the pioneer and market leader of chemical-based film photography, is currently struggling to make its transition to the newer digital technology. The same may soon be true of auto manufacturers looking for substitutes for the gasoline engine. Failure to adapt is, however, only one side of the coin. The Intel example shows how a changing environment can create new opportunities at the same time it destroys old ones. The lesson is simple: To be successful over time, an organization needs to be in tune with its external environment. There must be a strategic fit between what the environment wants and what the corporation has to offer, as well as between what the corporation needs and what the environment can provide.

3.1 ENVIRONMENTAL SCANNING

Before an organization can begin strategy formulation, it must scan the external environment to identify possible opportunities and threats and its internal environment for strengths and weaknesses. **Environmental scanning** is the monitoring, evaluating, and disseminating of information from the external and internal environments to key people within the corporation. It is a tool that a corporation uses to avoid strategic surprize and ensure long-term health. Research has found a positive relationship between environmental scanning and profits.

What External Environmental Variables should be Scanned?

In undertaking environmental scanning, strategic managers must first be aware of the many variables within a corporation's natural, societal, and task environments. The **natural environment** includes physical resources, wildlife, and climate that are an inherent part of existence on Earth. These factors form an ecological system of inter-related life. The **societal environment** is mankind's social system that includes general forces that do not directly touch on the short-run activities of the organization that can, and often do, influence its long-run decisions.

These forces, shown in **Figure 3.1**, are as follows:

- **Economic forces** regulate the exchange of materials, money, energy, and information.
- **Technological forces** generate problem-solving inventions.
- **Political–legal forces** allocate power and provide constraining and protecting laws and regulations.
- **Sociocultural forces** regulate the values, mores, and customs of society.

The **task environment** includes those elements or groups that directly affect the corporation and, in turn, are affected by it. These include governments, local communities, suppliers, competitors, customers, creditors, employees, shareholders, labor unions, special-interest groups, and trade associations. A corporation's task environment can be thought of as the industry within which it operates. **Industry analysis** refers to an in-depth examination of key factors within a corporation's task environment. The natural, societal, and task environments must be monitored so that strategic factors that are likely to have a strong impact on corporate success or failure can be detected.

WHAT SHOULD BE SCANNED IN THE NATURAL AND SOCIETAL ENVIRONMENTS?

The natural environment includes physical resources, wildlife, and climate that are an inherent part of existence on Earth. The concept of *environmental sustainability* argues that a firm's ability to continuously renew itself for long-term success and survival is dependent not only on the greater economic and social system of which it is a part, but also on the natural ecosystem in which the firm is embedded.[2] *Global warming* means that aspects of the natural environment, such as sea level, weather, and climate, are becoming increasingly uncertain and difficult to predict. Management must therefore

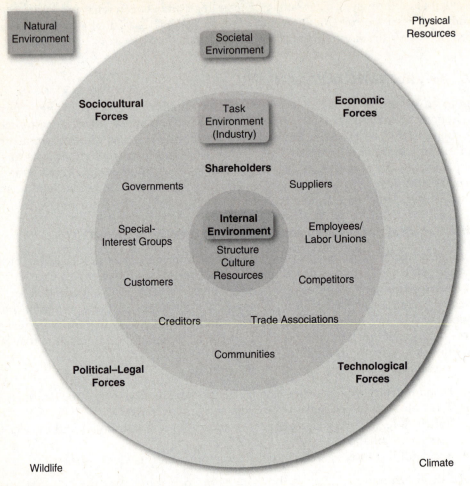

FIGURE 3.1 Environmental Variables

not only scan the natural environment for possible strategic factors, but also include in its strategic decision-making processes the impact of its activities on the natural environment.

The number of possible strategic factors in the societal environment is very high. The number becomes enormous when we realize that, generally speaking, each country in the world can be represented by its own unique set of societal forces—some of which are very similar to neighboring countries and some very different.

How Can STEEP Analysis Be Used to Monitor Natural and Societal Environmental Trends? As noted in **Table 3.1**, large corporations categorize the societal environment in any one geographic region into multiple categories and focus their scanning in each category on trends with corporate-wide relevance. By including ecological trends from the natural environment, this scanning can be called **STEEP Analysis**, the scanning of Sociocultural, Technological, Economic, Ecological, and Political–legal environmental

Table 3.1 Some Important Variables in the Societal Environment			
Economic	**Technological**	**Political–Legal**	**Sociocultural**
GDP trends	Total government spending for R&D	Antitrust regulations	Lifestyle changes
Interest rates	Total industry spending for R&D	Environmental protection laws	Career expectations
Money supply	Focus of technological efforts	Global warming legislation	Consumer activism
Inflation rates	Patent protection	Immigration laws	Rate of family formation
Unemployment levels	New products	Tax laws	Growth rate of population
Wage/price controls	New developments in technology transfer from lab to marketplace	Special incentives	Age distribution of population
Devaluation/ revaluation	Productivity Improvements through automation	Foreign trade regulations	Regional shifts in population
Energy alternatives	Internet availability	Attitudes toward foreign companies	Life expectancies
Energy availability and cost	Telecommunication infrastructure	Laws on hiring and promotion	Birthrates
Disposable and discretionary income	Computer hacking activity	Stability of government	Pension plans
Currency markets		Outsourcing regulation	Health care
Global financial system		Foreign "sweat shops"	Level of education
			Unionization

forces. (It may also be called *PESTEL Analysis* for Political, Economic, Sociocultural, Technological, Ecological, and Legal forces.) Obviously, trends in any one area may be very important to firms in one industry but less important to those in others.

Demographic trends are part of the *sociocultural* aspect of the societal environment. Even though the world's population is growing, from 3.71 billion people in 1970 to 6.82 billion in 2010 to 8.72 billion by 2040, not all regions will grow equally. With faster growth, developing nations will continue to have more young than old people, but it will be the reverse in the slower-growth industrialized nations. The demographic bulge caused by the baby boom in the 1950s continues to affect market demand in many industries. This group of 77 million people now in their 50s and 60s is the largest age-group in all developed countries, especially in Europe and Japan. Companies with an eye on the future can find many opportunities to offer products and services to the growing number of "woofies" (well-off old folks—defined as people over 50 with money to spend).[3] Anticipating the needs of seniors for prescription drugs is one reason why the Walgreen Company is opening a new corner pharmacy every 19 hours!

Changes in the *technological* part of the societal environment can also have a great impact on multiple industries. For example, improvements in computer micro-processors have not only led to the widespread use of home computers, but also to better automobile engine performance in terms of power and fuel economy through the use of microprocessors to monitor fuel injection.

Trends in the *economic* part of the societal environment can have an obvious impact on business activity. For example, an increase in interest rates means fewer sales of major home appliances because a rising interest rate tends to be reflected in higher mortgage rates. Because higher mortgage rates increase the cost of buying a house, the demand for new and used houses tends to fall. Because most major home appliances are sold when people change houses, a reduction in house sales soon translates into a decline in sales of refrigerators, stoves, and dishwashers and reduced profits for everyone in that industry.

Trends in the *ecology* of the natural environment can be driven by climate change and can have a huge impact on a societal environment and multiple industries. Freshwater availability is becoming increasingly important in countries undergoing droughts. For example, PepsiCo and Coca-Cola have been criticized for allegedly depleting groundwater in India.

Trends in the *political–legal* part of the societal environment have a significant impact on business firms. For example, periods of strict enforcement of U.S. antitrust laws directly affect corporate growth strategy. As large companies find it more difficult to acquire another firm in the same or in a related industry, they are typically driven to diversify into unrelated industries. In Europe, the formation of the European Union has led to an increase in merger activity across national boundaries.

What Are International Societal Considerations?   Each country or group of countries in which a company operates presents a unique societal environment with a different set of economic, technological, political–legal, and sociocultural variables for the company to face. This is especially an issue for a **multinational corporation (MNC)**, a company having significant manufacturing and marketing operations in multiple countries.

International societal environments vary so widely that a corporation's internal environment and strategic management process must be very flexible. Cultural trends in Germany, for example, have resulted in the inclusion of worker representatives in corporate strategic planning. Differences in societal environments strongly affect the ways in which an MNC conducts its marketing, financial, manufacturing, and other functional activities. For example, the existence of regional associations like the European Union, the North American Free Trade Zone, the Central American Free Trade Zone, the Association of Southeast Asian Nations, and Mercosur in South America has a significant impact on the competitive "rules of the game" for both the MNCs operating within and those that want to enter these areas.

To account for the many differences among societal environments from one country to another, Table 3.1 would need to be changed to include such variables as currency convertibility, climate, outsourcing capability, and regional associations under the Economic category; natural resource availability, transportation network, and communication infrastructure under the Technological category; form of govern-ment, regulations on foreign ownership, and terrorist activity under the Political–legal category; and language, social institutions, and attitudes toward human rights and foreigners under the Sociocultural category.

Before a company plans its strategy for a particular international location, it must scan the particular country's societal environment in question for opportunities and threats and compare them to its own organizational strengths and weaknesses.

WHAT SHOULD BE SCANNED IN THE TASK ENVIRONMENT?

As shown in **Figure 3.2**, a corporation's scanning of the environment should include analyses of all the relevant elements in the task environment. These analyses take the form of individual reports written by various people in different parts of the firm. At Procter & Gamble (P&G), for example, each quarter, people from each of the brand management teams work with key people from the sales and market research departments to research and write a "competitive activity report" on each of the product categories in which P&G competes. People in purchasing write similar reports concerning new developments in the industries that supply P&G. These and other reports are then summarized and transmitted up the corporate hierarchy for top management to use in strategic decision making. If a new development is reported regarding a particular product category, top management may then send memos to people throughout the organization to watch for and report on developments in related product areas. The many reports resulting from these scanning efforts, when boiled down to their essentials, act as a detailed list of external strategic factors.

How can Managers Identify External Strategic Factors?

Companies often respond differently to the same environmental changes because of differences in the ability of managers to recognize and understand external strategic

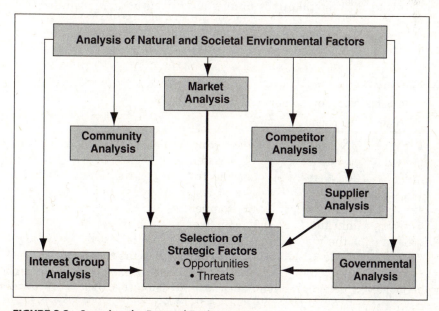

FIGURE 3.2   Scanning the External Environment

issues and factors. Few firms can successfully monitor all important external factors. Even though managers agree that strategic importance determines what variables are consistently tracked, they sometimes miss or choose to ignore crucial new developments. Personal values of a corporation's managers and the success of current strategies are likely to bias both their perception of what is important to monitor in the external environment and their interpretations of what they perceive. This is known as *strategic myopia:* the willingness to reject unfamiliar as well as negative information. If a firm needs to change its strategy, it might not be gathering the appropriate external information to change strategies successfully.

One way to identify and analyze developments in the external environment is to use the **issues priority matrix**, provided in **Figure 3.3**:

1. Identify a number of likely trends emerging in the natural, societal, and task environments. These are strategic environmental issues—those important trends that, if they happen, will determine what various industries will look like in the near future.
2. Assess the probability of these trends actually occurring, from low to medium to high.
3. Attempt to ascertain the likely impact (from low to high) of each of these trends on the corporation.

A corporation's external strategic factors are the key environmental trends that are judged to have both a medium to high probability of occurrence and a medium to high probability of impact on the corporation. The issues priority matrix can then be used to help managers decide which environmental trends should be merely scanned (low priority) and which should be monitored as strategic factors (high priority). Those environmental trends judged to be a corporation's strategic factors are then categorized as potential opportunities and threats and are included in strategy formulation.

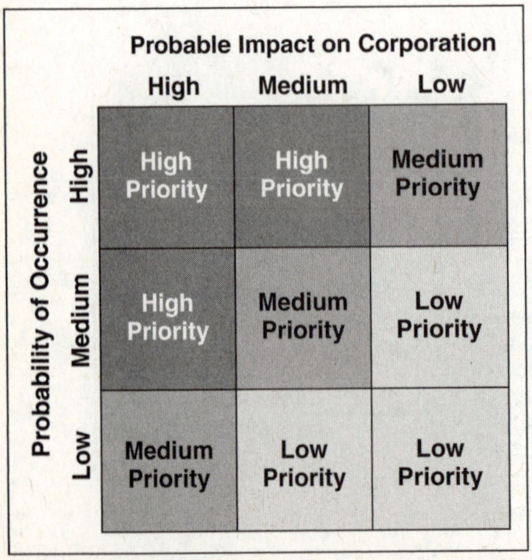

	Probable Impact on Corporation		
	High	**Medium**	**Low**
High	High Priority	High Priority	Medium Priority
Medium	High Priority	Medium Priority	Low Priority
Low	Medium Priority	Low Priority	Low Priority

Probability of Occurrence

FIGURE 3.3 Issues Priority Matrix

Source: Adapted from L. L. Lederman, "Foresight Activities in the U.S.A.: Time for a Re-Assessment?" *Long Range Planning* (June 1984), p. 46. Copyright © 1984 by Pergamon Press, Ltd. Reprinted by permission.

3.2 INDUSTRY ANALYSIS: ANALYZING THE TASK ENVIRONMENT

An **industry** is a group of firms producing a similar product or service, such as financial services or soft drinks. An examination of the important stakeholder groups, such as suppliers and customers, in the task environment of a particular corporation is a part of industry analysis.

What is Michael Porter's Approach to Industry Analysis?

Michael Porter, an authority on competitive strategy, contends that a corporation is most concerned with the intensity of competition within its industry. Basic competitive forces, which are depicted in **Figure 3.4**, determine the intensity level. "The collective strength of these forces," he contends, "determines the ultimate profit potential in the industry, where profit potential is measured in terms of long-run return on invested capital."[4] The stronger each of these forces is, the more companies are limited in their ability to raise prices and earn greater profits. Although Porter mentions only five forces, a sixth—other stakeholders—is added here to reflect the power that governments, local communities, and other groups from the task environment wield over industry activities.

Using the model in Figure 3.4, a strong force can be regarded as a threat because it is likely to reduce profits. In contrast, a weak force can be viewed as an opportunity because it may allow the company to earn greater profits. In the short run, these forces act as constraints on a company's activities. In the long run, however, it may be possible

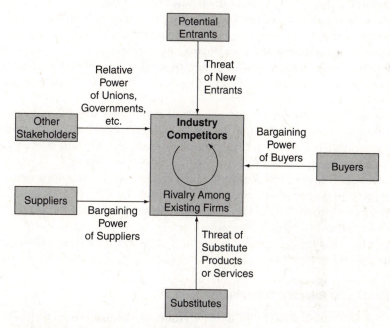

FIGURE 3.4   Forces Driving Industry Competition

Source: Adapted/reprinted with permission of The Free Press, an imprint of Simon & Schuster, from *Competitive Strategy: Techniques for Analyzing Industries and Competitors* by Michael E. Porter. Copyright © 1980 by The Free Press.

for a company, through its choice of strategy, to change the strength of one or more of the forces to the company's advantage.

In carefully scanning its industry, the corporation must assess the importance to its success of each of the following six forces: threat of new entrants, rivalry among existing firms, threat of substitute products, bargaining power of buyers, bargaining power of suppliers, and relative power of other stakeholders.[5]

WHAT IS THE THREAT OF NEW ENTRANTS?

New entrants are newcomers to an existing industry. They typically bring new capacity, a desire to gain market share, and substantial resources. Therefore, they are threats to an established corporation. The threat of entry depends on the presence of entry barriers and the reaction that can be expected from existing competitors. An **entry barrier** is an obstruction that makes it difficult for a company to enter an industry. For example, no new domestic automobile companies have been successfully established in the United States since the 1930s because of the high capital requirements to build production facilities and develop a dealer distribution network. Some of the possible barriers to entry are the following:

- **Economies of Scale.** Scale economies in the production and sale of microprocessors, for example, gave Intel a significant cost advantage over any new rival.
- **Product Differentiation.** Corporations like Procter & Gamble and General Mills, which manufacture products like Tide and Cheerios, create high entry barriers through their high levels of advertising and promotion.
- **Capital Requirements.** The need to invest huge financial resources in manufacturing facilities in order to produce large commercial airplanes creates a significant barrier to entry to any new competitor for Boeing and Airbus.
- **Switching Costs.** Once a software program like Excel or Word becomes established in an office, office managers are very reluctant to switch to a new program because of the high training costs.
- **Access to Distribution Channels.** Small entrepreneurs often have difficulty obtaining supermarket shelf space for their goods because large retailers charge for space on their shelves and give priority to the established firms who can pay for the advertising needed to generate high customer demand.
- **Cost Disadvantages Independent of Size.** Microsoft's development of the first widely adopted operating system (MS-DOS) for the IBM-type personal computer gave it a significant advantage over potential competitors. Its introduction of Windows helped to cement that advantage.
- **Government Policy.** Governments can limit entry into an industry through licensing requirements by restricting access to raw materials, such as offshore oil drilling sites.

WHAT IS RIVALRY AMONG EXISTING FIRMS?

Rivalry is the amount of direct competition in an industry. In most industries, corporations are mutually dependent. A competitive move by one firm can be expected to have a noticeable effect on its competitors and thus may cause retaliation or counterefforts. For example, the entry by direct marketing companies such as Dell and Gateway into a PC industry previously dominated by IBM, Apple, and Compaq increased the level of competitive activity to such an extent that any price reduction or new product introduction is now quickly followed by similar moves from other PC makers. According to Porter, intense rivalry is related to the presence of the following factors:

- **Number of Competitors.** When competitors are few and roughly equal in size, such as in the auto and major home appliance industries, they watch each other carefully to make sure that any move by another firm is matched by an equal countermove.
- **Rate of Industry Growth.** Any slowing in passenger traffic tends to set off price wars in the airline industry because the only path to growth is to take sales away from a competitor.
- **Product or Service Characteristics.** A product can be unique, with many qualities differentiating it from others of its kind or it may be a *commodity*, a product like gasoline, whose characteristics are the same, regardless of who sells it.
- **Amount of Fixed Costs.** Because airlines must fly their planes on a schedule regardless of the number of paying passengers for any one flight, they offer cheap standby fares whenever a plane has empty seats.
- **Capacity.** If the only way a manufacturer can increase capacity is in a large increment by building a new plant (as in the paper industry), it will run that new plant at full capacity to keep its unit costs as low as possible—thus producing so much that the selling price falls throughout the industry.
- **Height of Exit Barriers.** Exit barriers keep a company from leaving an industry. The brewing industry, for example, has a low percentage of companies that leave the industry because breweries are specialized assets with few uses except for making beer.
- **Diversity of Rivals.** Rivals that have very different ideas of how to compete are likely to cross paths often and unknowingly challenge each other's position. This happens often in retailing.

WHAT IS THE THREAT OF SUBSTITUTE PRODUCTS OR SERVICES?

Substitute products are those products that appear to be different but can satisfy the same need as another product. According to Porter, "Substitutes limit the potential returns of an industry by placing a ceiling on the prices firms in the industry can profitably charge."[6] To the extent that switching costs are low, substitutes may have a strong effect on an industry. Tea can be considered a substitute for coffee. If the price of coffee goes up high enough, coffee drinkers will slowly begin switching to tea. The price of tea thus puts a price ceiling on the price of coffee. Sometimes a difficult task, the identification of possible substitute products or services means searching for products or services that can perform the same function, even though they may not appear to be easily substitutable.

WHAT IS THE BARGAINING POWER OF BUYERS?

Buyers affect an industry through their ability to force down prices, bargain for higher quality or more services, and play competitors against each other. A buyer or distributor is powerful if some of the following factors hold true:

- A buyer purchases a large proportion of the seller's product or service (e.g., oil filters purchased by a major automaker).
- A buyer has the potential to integrate backward by producing the product itself (e.g., a newspaper chain could make its own paper).
- Alternative suppliers are plentiful because the product is standard or undifferentiated (e.g., motorists can choose among many gas stations).
- Changing suppliers costs very little (e.g., office supplies are sold by many vendors).
- The purchased product represents a high percentage of a buyer's costs, thus providing an incentive to shop around for a lower price (e.g., gasoline purchased for resale by convenience stores makes up half their costs but very little of their profits).
- A buyer earns low profits and is thus very sensitive to costs and service differences (e.g., grocery stores have very small margins).
- The purchased product is unimportant to the final quality or price of a buyer's products or services and thus can be easily substituted without adversely affecting the final product (e.g., electric wire bought for use in lamps).

WHAT IS THE BARGAINING POWER OF SUPPLIERS?

Suppliers can affect an industry through their ability to raise prices or reduce the quality of purchased goods and services. A supplier or supplier group is powerful if some of the following factors apply:

- The supplier industry is dominated by a few companies, but it sells to many (e.g., the petroleum industry).
- Its product or service is unique or it has built up switching costs (e.g., word processing software).
- Substitutes are not readily available (e.g., electricity).
- Suppliers are able to integrate forward and compete directly with their present customers (e.g., a microprocessor producer like Intel could easily make PCs).
- A purchasing industry buys only a small portion of the supplier group's goods and services and is thus unimportant to the supplier (e.g., sales of lawn mower tires are less important to the tire industry than are sales of auto tires).

WHAT IS THE RELATIVE POWER OF OTHER STAKEHOLDERS?

A sixth force should be added to Porter's list to include a variety of stakeholder groups from the task environment. Some of these other stakeholders are governments (if not explicitly included elsewhere), local communities, creditors (if not included with suppliers), trade associations, special-interest groups, shareholders, and complementors. A *complementor* is a company (e.g., Microsoft) or an industry whose product works well with a firm's (e.g., Intel's) product and without which the product would lose much of its value.

The importance of these stakeholders varies by industry. For example, environmental groups in Maine, Michigan, Oregon, and Iowa successfully fought to pass bills outlawing disposable bottles and cans, and thus deposits for most drink containers are now required. This effectively raised costs across the board, with the most impact on the marginal producers who could not internally absorb all of these costs.

Do Industries Evolve Over Time?

Most industries evolve over time through a series of stages from growth through maturity to eventual decline. The strength of each of the six competitive forces described in the preceding section varies according to the stage of industry evolution. The industry life cycle is useful for explaining and predicting trends among the six forces that drive industry competition. For example, when an industry is new, people often buy the product regardless of price because it fulfills a unique need. This usually occurs in a **fragmented industry** in which no firm has large market share and each firm serves only a small piece of the total market in competition with others (e.g., cleaning services). As new competitors enter the industry, prices drop as a result of competition. Companies use the experience curve (discussed in Chapter 4) and economies of scale to reduce costs faster than their competitors. Companies integrate to reduce costs even further by acquiring their suppliers and distributors. Competitors try to differentiate their products from one another's to avoid the fierce price competition common to a maturing industry.

By the time an industry enters maturity, products tend to become more like commodities. This is now a **consolidated industry**—dominated by a few large firms, each of which struggles to differentiate its products from the competitors. As buyers become more sophisticated over time, they base their purchasing decisions on better information. Products become more like commodities in which price becomes a dominant concern given a minimum level of quality and features, and profit margins decline. The automobile, petroleum, and major home appliance industries are current examples of mature, consolidated industries, each controlled by a few large competitors.

As an industry moves through maturity toward possible decline, the growth rate of its products' sales slows and may even begin to decrease. To the extent that exit barriers are low, firms will begin converting their facilities to alternative uses or will sell them to another firm. The industry tends to consolidate around fewer but larger competitors. The tobacco industry is an example of an industry currently in decline.

How are International Industries Categorized?

World industries vary on a continuum from multidomestic to global (see **Figure 3.5**).[7] A **multidomestic industry** is a collection of essentially domestic industries, like retailing and insurance, in which products or services are tailored specifically for a particular country. The activities in a subsidiary of an MNC in this type of industry are essentially independent of the activities of the MNC's subsidiaries in other countries.

Multidomestic ⟵	⟶ *Global*
Industry in which companies tailor their products to the specific needs of consumers in a particular country.	Industry in which companies manufacture and sell the same products, with only minor adjustments made for individual countries around the world.
• Retailing	• Automobiles
• Insurance	• Tires
• Banking	• Television sets

FIGURE 3.5   Continuum of International Industries

In each country, the MNC tailors its products or services to the very specific needs of consumers in that particular country. A **global industry**, in contrast, operates world-wide, with MNCs making only small adjustments for country-specific circumstances. A global industry is one in which the activities of an MNC in one country are significantly affected by its activities in other countries. MNCs produce products or services in various locations throughout the world and sell them all over the world, making only minor adjustments for specific country requirements. Examples of global industries are commercial aircraft, television sets, semiconductors, copiers, automobiles, watches, and tires. The largest industrial corporations in the world in terms of dollar sales are, for the most part, MNCs operating in global industries.

The factors that tend to determine whether an industry will be primarily multidomestic or primarily global are (1) the *pressure for coordination* within the MNCs operating in that industry and (2) the *pressure for local responsiveness* on the part of individual country markets. To the extent that the pressure for coordination is strong and the pressure for local responsiveness is weak for MNCs within a particular industry, that industry will tend to become global. In contrast, when the pressure for local responsiveness is strong and the pressure for coordination is weak for MNCs in an industry, that industry will tend to become multidomestic. Between these two extremes lie a number of industries with varying characteristics of both multidomestic and global industries. These are regional industries, in which MNCs primarily coordinate their activities within regions, such as the Americas or Asia.

What is a Strategic Group?

A **strategic group** is a set of business units or firms that "pursue similar strategies with similar resources."[8] Categorizing firms in any one industry into a set of strategic groups is very useful to strategic managers as a way of better understanding the competitive environment. Because a corporation's structure and culture tend to reflect the kinds of strategies it follows, companies or business units belonging to a particular strategic group within the same industry tend to be strong rivals and more similar to each other than to competitors in other strategic groups within the same industry. For example, although McDonald's and Olive Garden are a part of the same restaurant industry, they have different missions, objectives, and strategies and thus belong to different strategic groups. They generally have very little in common and pay little attention to each other when planning competitive actions. Burger King and Hardee's, however, have a great deal in common with McDonald's in terms of their similar strategy of producing a high volume of low-price meals targeted for sale to the average family. Consequently they are strong rivals and are organized to operate in a similar fashion.

Strategic groups in a particular industry can be mapped by plotting the market positions of industry competitors on a two-dimensional graph using two strategic variables as the vertical and horizontal axes (see **Figure 3.6**). *First*, select two broad characteristics, such as price and menu, that differentiate the companies in an industry from one another. *Second*, plot the firms using these two characteristics as the dimensions. *Third*, draw a circle around those companies that are closest to one another as one strategic group, varying the size of the circle in proportion to the group's share

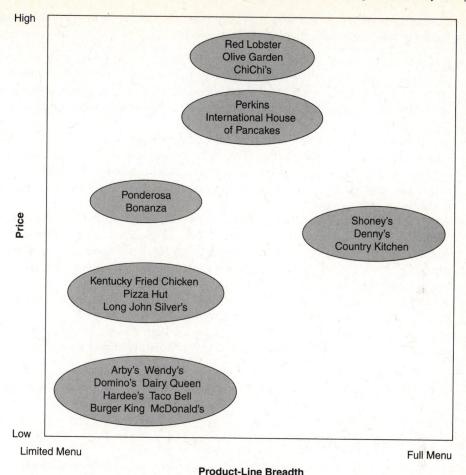

FIGURE 3.6   Mapping Strategic Groups in the U.S. Restaurant Chain Industry

of total industry sales. Name each strategic group in the restaurant industry with an identifying title, such as quick fast food or buffet-style service. Other dimensions, such as quality and degree of vertical integration, can also be used in additional graphs of the restaurant industry to show how the various firms in the industry compete.

What are Strategic Types?

In analyzing the level of competitive intensity within a particular industry or strategic group, it is useful to characterize the various competitors for predictive purposes. A **strategic type** is a category of firms based on a common strategic orientation and a combination of structure, culture, and processes consistent with that strategy. According to Miles and Snow, competing firms within a single industry can be categorized on the basis of their general strategic orientation into one of four basic types: defenders, prospectors, analyzers, and reactors.[9] This distinction helps explain why companies facing similar situations behave differently and why they continue to do so over a long period of time. These general types have the following characteristics:

- **Defenders** are companies with a limited product line that *focus on improving the efficiency of their existing operations.* This cost orientation makes them unlikely to innovate in new areas. An example would be Dean Foods, a company specializing in making low-cost imitations of leading products marketed by supermarkets and drug stores.
- **Prospectors** are companies with fairly broad product lines that *focus on product innovation and market opportunities.* This sales orientation makes them somewhat inefficient. They tend to emphasize creativity over efficiency. PepsiCo, with its "shotgun approach" (ready, fire, aim) to new product introduction is a good example of a prospector.
- **Analyzers** are companies that *operate in at least two different product-market areas, one stable and one variable.* In the stable areas, efficiency is emphasized; in the variable areas, innovation is emphasized. With its many consumer products in multiple markets and careful approach to product development ("ready, aim, fire"), Procter & Gamble is a typical analyzer.
- **Reactors** are companies that *lack a consistent strategy-structure-culture relationship.* Their (often ineffective) responses to environmental pressures tend to be piecemeal strategic changes. By allowing Target to take the high end of the discount market and Wal-Mart the low end, Kmart was left with no identity and no market of its own.

Dividing the competition into these four categories enables the strategic manager not only to monitor the effectiveness of certain strategic orientations, but also to develop scenarios of future industry developments (discussed later in this chapter).

What is Hypercompetition?

Hypercompetition describes an industry undergoing an ever-increasing level of environmental uncertainty in which competitive advantage is only temporary. For example, industries that once were multidomestic (like major home appliances) are becoming global. New flexible, aggressive, innovative competitors are moving into established markets to rapidly erode the advantages of large, previously dominant firms. Distribution channels vary from country to country and are being altered daily through the use of sophisticated information systems. Closer relationships with suppliers are being forged to reduce costs, increase quality, and gain access to new technology. According to D'Aveni, "Market stability is threatened by short product life cycles, short product design cycles, new technologies, frequent entry by unexpected outsiders, repositioning by incumbents, and tactical redefinitions of market boundaries as diverse industries merge."[10] Companies learn to quickly imitate the successful strategies of market leaders, and it becomes harder to sustain any competitive advantage for long.

In hypercompetitive industries such as computers, competitive advantage comes from an up-to-date knowledge of environmental trends and competitive activity coupled with a willingness to risk a current advantage for a possible new advantage. Companies must be willing to cannibalize their own products (replacing popular products before competitors do so) in order to sustain their competitive advantage.

Table 3.2 Industry Matrix					
Key Success Factors	**Weight**	**Company A Rating**	**Company A Weighted Score**	**Company B Rating**	**Company B Weighted Score**
1	2	3	4	5	6
Totals	**1.00**				

Source: T. L. Wheelen and J. D. Hunger, *Industry Matrix.* Copyright © 1997, 2001, and 2005 by Wheelen and Hunger Associates. Reprinted by permission.

What is the Value of an Industry Matrix?

Within any industry there usually are certain variables—key success factors—that a company's management must understand in order to be successful. **Key success factors** are those variables that can affect significantly the overall competitive positions of companies within any particular industry. They typically vary from industry to industry and are crucial to determining a company's ability to succeed within that industry. They are usually determined by the economic and technological characteristics of the industry and by the competitive weapons on which the firms in the industry have built their strategies.

An **industry matrix** summarizes the key success factors that face a particular industry. As shown in **Table 3.2**, the matrix gives a weight for each factor based on how important that factor is to the future of the industry. The matrix also specifies how well various competitors in the industry are responding to each factor.

To generate an industry matrix using two industry competitors (called A and B), complete the following steps for the industry being analyzed:

- In **Column 1** (*Key Success Factors*), list the 8 to 10 factors that appear to determine current and expected success in the industry.
- In **Column 2** (*Weight*), assign a weight to each factor from **1.0** (*Most Important*) to **0.0** (*Not Important*) based on that factor's probable impact on the overall industry's current and future success. (*All weights must sum to 1.0 regardless of the number of factors.*)
- In **Column 3** (*Company A Rating*), examine a particular company within the industry—for example, Company A. Assign a rating to each factor from **5** (*Outstanding*) to **1** (*Poor*) based on how well that company is currently dealing with each key success factor.

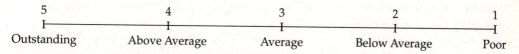

5	4	3	2	1
Outstanding	Above Average	Average	Below Average	Poor

- In **Column 4** (*Company A Weighted Score*), multiply the weight in **Column 2** for each factor times its rating in **Column 3** to obtain that factor's weighted score for Company A.

- In **Column 5** (*Company B Rating*), examine a second company within the industry—in this case, Company B. Assign a rating to each factor from **5** (*Outstanding*) to **1** (*Poor*) based on Company B's current response to each particular factor.
- In **Column 6** (*Company B Weighted Score*), multiply the weight in **Column 2** for each factor times its rating in **Column 5** to obtain that factor's weighted score for Company B.
- Finally, add the weighted scores for all the factors in **Columns 4** and **6** to determine the total weighted scores for companies A and B. *The **total weighted score** indicates how well each company is responding to current and expected key success factors in the industry's environment.* An average company should have a total weighted score of 3.0.

The industry matrix can be expanded to include all the major competitors within an industry simply by adding two additional columns for each additional competitor.

3.3 COMPETITIVE INTELLIGENCE

Much external environmental scanning is done on an informal and individual basis. Information is obtained from a variety of sources, such as customers, suppliers, bankers, consultants, publications, personal observations, subordinates, superiors, and peers. For example, R&D scientists and engineers can learn about new products and competitors' ideas at professional meetings; someone from the purchasing department may uncover valuable bits of information about a competitor by speaking with supplier representatives. A study of product innovation found that 77 percent of all product innovations in the scientific instruments and 67 percent in semiconductors and printed circuit boards were initiated by the customer in the form of inquiries and complaints.[11] In these industries, the sales force and service departments must be especially vigilant.

Competitive intelligence is a formal program of gathering information on a company's competitors. Sometimes called *business intelligence,* this is one of the fastest growing fields in strategic management. Close to 80 percent of large U.S. corporations currently report having at least a modest level of competitive intelligence activities. According to a survey of 141 large American corporations, spending on competitive intelligence activities was rising from $1 billion in 2007 to $10 billion by 2012.[12]

Most corporations rely on outside organizations to provide them with environmental data. Firms such as A. C. Nielsen Co. provide subscribers with bimonthly data on brand share, retail prices, percentages of stores stocking an item, and percentages of stock-out stores. Strategists can use these data to spot regional and national trends as well as to assess market share. "Information brokers" such as MarketResearch.com, LexisNexis, and Finsbury Data Services sell information on market conditions, government regulations, competitors, and new products. Company and industry profiles are generally available from Hoover's On-Line Web site at www.hoovers.com. Many business corporations have established their own in-house libraries and computerized information systems to deal with the growing mass of available information.

Some companies, however, choose to use industrial espionage or other intelligence-gathering techniques to get their information straight from their competitors. According to a survey by the American Society for Industrial Security, PricewaterhouseCoopers, and the U.S. Chamber of Commerce, Fortune 1000 companies lost an estimated $59 billion in one year alone due to the theft of trade secrets.[13] By hiring current or former competitors' employees or using private contractors, some firms attempt to steal trade secrets, technology, business plans, and pricing strategies. For example, Avon Products hired private investigators to retrieve documents (some of them shredded) that Mary Kay Corporation had thrown away in a public dumpster.

To combat the increasing theft of company secrets, the U.S. government passed the Economic Espionage Act in 1996. The law makes it illegal (with fines up to $5 million and 10 years in jail) to steal any material that a business has taken "reasonable efforts" to keep secret, and if the material derives its value from not being known. The Society of Competitive Intelligence Professionals at www.scip.org urges strategists to stay within the law and to act ethically when searching for information. The society states that illegal activities are foolish because the vast majority of worthwhile competitive intelligence is available publicly via annual reports, Web sites, and libraries.

3.4   FORECASTING

Environmental scanning provides reasonably hard data on the present situation and current trends, but intuition and luck are needed to accurately predict if these trends will continue. The resulting forecasts are, however, usually based on a set of assumptions that may or may not be valid.

Why can Assumptions be Dangerous?

Faulty underlying assumptions are the most frequent cause of forecasting errors. Nevertheless many managers who formulate and implement strategic plans rarely consider that their success is based on a series of assumptions. Many long-range plans are simply based on projections of the current situation. For example, few people in 2007 expected the price of oil (light, sweet crude, also called West Texas intermediate) to rise above $80 per barrel and were extremely surprised to see the price approach $150 by July 2008, especially since the price had been around $20 per barrel in 2002. Sales of large cars plummeted as demand for fuel-efficient autos escalated. In another example, many banks made a number of questionable mortgages based on the assumption that U.S. housing prices would continue to rise as they had in the past. When housing prices fell in 2007, these "sub-prime" mortgages were almost worthless—causing a number of banks to sell out or fail in 2008.

What Forecasting Techniques are Available?

Various techniques are used to forecast future situations, and each has its proponents and critics. The most popular forecasting technique is **extrapolation**—the extension of present trends into the future. Trend extrapolation rests on the assumption that the world is reasonably consistent and changes slowly in the short run. Approaches of this type include time-series methods, which attempt to carry a series of historical events forward into the future. The basic problem with extrapolation is that a historical trend is based on a series of patterns or relationships among so many different variables that a change in any one can drastically alter the future direction of the trend. As a rule of thumb, the further into the past one can find relevant data supporting the trend, the more confidence one can have in the prediction.

Brainstorming and statistical modeling are also popular forecasting techniques. *Brainstorming* is a nonquantitative approach in which ideas are proposed without first mentally screening them and without criticism by others. All that is required is the presence of people with some knowledge of the situation to be predicted. Ideas tend to build on previous ideas until a consensus is reached. This is a good technique to use with operating managers who have more faith in "gut feeling" than in quantitative "number-crunching" techniques. *Expert opinion* is a nonquantitative technique in which experts in a particular area attempt to forecast likely developments. This type of forecast is based on the ability of a knowledgeable person(s) to construct probable future developments based on the interaction of key variables. One application, developed by the RAND Corporation, is the *Delphi technique*, in which separated experts independently assess the likelihoods of specified events. *Statistical modeling* is a quantitative technique that attempts to discover causal or at least explanatory factors that link two or more time series together. Examples of statistical modeling are regression analysis and other econometric methods. Although very useful in the grasping of historic trends, statistical modeling, like trend extrapolation, is based on historical data. As the patterns of relationships change, the accuracy of the forecast deteriorates.

Scenarios are focused descriptions of different likely futures presented in a narrative fashion. Scenario writing appears to be the most widely used forecasting technique after trend extrapolation. The scenario thus may be merely a written description of some future state, in terms of key variables and issues, or it may be generated in combination with other forecasting techniques.

An *industry scenario* is a forecasted description of a particular industry's likely future. It is a scenario that is developed by analyzing the probable impact of future societal forces on key groups in a particular industry. The process may operate as follows:[14]

1. Examine possible shifts in the natural and societal variables globally.
2. Identify uncertainties in each of the six forces of the task environment (e.g., potential entrants, competitors, likely substitutes, buyers, suppliers, and other key stakeholders).
3. Make a range of plausible assumptions about future trends.
4. Combine assumptions about individual trends into internally consistent scenarios.
5. Analyze the industry situation that would prevail under each scenario.
6. Determine the sources of competitive advantage under each scenario.
7. Predict competitors' behavior under each scenario.
8. Select those scenarios that are either most likely to occur or are most likely to have a strong impact on the future of the company. Use these scenarios as assumptions in strategy formulation.

3.5 SYNTHESIS OF EXTERNAL FACTORS—EFAS

After strategists have scanned the natural, societal, and task environments and identified a number of likely external factors for their particular corporation, they may want to refine their analysis of these factors using a form such as the one given in **Table 3.3**. Using an EFAS (**External Factors Analysis Summary**) **Table** is one way to organize the external factors into the generally accepted categories of opportunities and threats as well as to analyze how well a particular company's management (rating) is responding to these specific factors in light of the perceived importance (weight) of these factors to the company.

Table 3.3 External Factor Analysis Summary (EFAS) Table for Maytag

External Factors	Weight	Rating	Weighted Score	Comments
1	**2**	**3**	**4**	**5**
Opportunities				
• Economic integration of European Union	0.20	4	0.80	Acquisition of Hoover
• Demographics favor quality appliances	0.10	5	0.50	Maytag quality
• Economic development of Asia	0.05	1	0.05	Low Maytag presence
• Opening of Eastern Europe	0.05	2	0.10	Will take time
• Trend to superstores	0.10	2	0.20	Maytag weak in this channel
Threats				
• Increasing government regulations	0.10	4	0.40	Well positioned
• Strong U.S. competition	0.10	4	0.40	Well positioned
• Whirlpool and Electrolux strong globally	0.15	3	0.45	Hoover weak globally
• New product advances	0.05	1	0.05	Questionable
• Japanese appliance companies	0.10	2	0.20	Only Asian presence is Australia
Totals	**1.00**		**3.15**	

Notes:

1. List opportunities and threats (5–10 each) in Column 1.

2. Weight each factor from 1.0 (Most Important) to 0.0 (Not Important) in Column 2 based on that factor's probable impact on the company's strategic position. **The total weights must sum to 1.00.**

3. Rate each factor from 5.0 (Outstanding) to 1.0 (Poor) in Column 3 based on the company's response to that factor.

4. Multiply each factor's weight times its rating to obtain each factor's weighted score in Column 4.

5. Use Column 5 (comments) for rationale used for each factor.

6. Add the weighted scores to obtain the *total weighted score* for the company in Column 4. This figure tells how well the company is responding to the factors in its external environment.

Source: Thomas L. Wheelen. Copyright © 1982, 1985, 1987, 1988, 1989, 1990, 1991, 1998, and every year after that. Kathryn E. Wheelen solely owns all of (Dr.) Thomas L. Wheelan's copyright materials. Kathryn E. Wheelen requires written reprint permission for each book that this material is to be printed in. Thomas L. Wheelen and J. David Hunger, copyright © 1991–first year "External Factor Analysis Summary" (EFAS) appeared in this text (5th ed.). Reprinted by permission of the copyright holder.

To generate an EFAS Table, complete the following steps for the company being analyzed:

- In **Column 1** (***External Factors***), list the 8 to 10 most important opportunities and threats facing the company.
- In **Column 2** (***Weight***), assign a weight to each factor from **1.0** (*Most Important*) to **0.0** (*Not Important*) based on that factor's probable impact on a particular company's current strategic position. The higher the weight, the more important this factor is to

the current and future success of the company. (*All weights must sum to 1.00 regardless of the number of factors.*)

- In **Column 3** (*Rating*), assign a rating to each factor from **5** (*Outstanding*) to **1** (*Poor*) based on the company's current response to that particular factor. Each rating is a judgment regarding how well the company is currently dealing with each external factor.

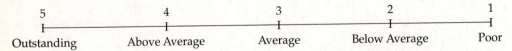

| 5 | 4 | 3 | 2 | 1 |
| Outstanding | Above Average | Average | Below Average | Poor |

- In **Column 4** (*Weighted Score*), multiply the weight in **Column 2** for each factor times its rating in **Column 3** to obtain that factor's weighted score.
- In **Column 5** (*Comments*), note why a particular factor was selected and/or how its weight and rating were estimated.
- Finally, add the weighted scores for all the external factors in **Column 4** to determine the total weighted score for the particular company. The **total weighted score** indicates how well a particular company is responding to current and expected factors in its external environment. The score can be used to compare the firm to other firms in its industry. *The total weighted score for an average firm in an industry is always 3.0.*

As an example of this procedure, Table 3.3 includes a number of external factors for Maytag Corporation as of 1995 with corresponding weights, ratings, and weighted scores provided.

Discussion Questions

1. Discuss how a development in a corporation's societal environment can affect the corporation through its task environment.
2. According to Porter, what determines the level of competitive intensity in an industry?
3. According to Porter's discussion of industry analysis, is Pepsi Cola a substitute for Coca-Cola?
4. How can a decision maker identify strategic factors in the corporation's external environment?
5. Compare and contrast trend extrapolation with the writing of scenarios as forecasting techniques.

Key Terms (listed in order of appearance)

Notes

1. C. Edwards and P. Burrows, "Intel Tries to Invest Its Way Out of a Rut," *Business Week* (April 27, 2009), pp. 44–46.
2. W. E. Stead and J. G. Stead, *Sustainable Strategic Management* (Armonk, N.Y.: M.E. Sharp, 2004), p. 6.
3. J. Wyatt, "Playing the Woofie Card," *Fortune* (February 6, 1995), pp. 130–132.
4. M. E. Porter, *Competitive Strategy* (New York: The Free Press, 1980), p. 3.
5. This summary of the forces driving competitive strategy is taken from Porter, *Competitive Strategy,* pp. 7–29.
6. Ibid., p. 23.
7. M. E. Porter, "Changing Patterns of International Competition," *California Management Review* (Winter 1986), pp. 9–40.
8. K. J. Hatten and M. L. Hatten, "Strategic Groups, Asymmetrical Mobility Barriers, and Contestability," *Strategic Management Journal* (July–August 1987), p. 329.
9. R. E. Miles and C. C. Snow, *Organizational Strategy, Structure, and Process* (New York: McGraw-Hill, 1978).
10. R. A. D'Aveni, *Hypercompetition* (New York: The Free Press, 1994), pp. xii–xiv.
11. E. Von Hipple, *Sources of Innovation* (New York: Oxford University Press, 1988), p. 4.
12. "Competitive Intelligence Spending 'to Rise Tenfold' in 5 Years," *Daily Research News* (June 19, 2007).
13. E. Iwata, "More U.S. Trade Secrets Walk Out Door with Foreign Spies," *USA Today* (February 13, 2003), pp. B1, B2.
14. This process of scenario development is adapted from M. E. Porter, *Competitive Advantage* (New York: The Free Press, 1985), pp. 448–470.

4 INTERNAL SCANNING: ORGANIZATIONAL ANALYSIS

On January 10, 2008, a new automobile from Tata Motors was introduced to the world at the Indian Auto Show in New Delhi. Called the *People's Car*, the new auto was planned to sell for $2,500 (including taxes) in India. Even though many manufacturers were hoping to introduce cheap small cars into India and other developing nations, Tata Motors seemed to have significant advantages that other companies lacked. India's low labor costs meant that Tata could engineer a new model for 20 percent of the $350 million it would cost in developed nations. A factory worker in Mumbai earned just $1.20 per hour, less than auto workers earned in China. The company would save about $900 per car by skipping equipment that the United States, Europe, and Japan required for emissions control. The People's Car did not have features like antilock brakes, air bags, or support beams to protect passengers in case of a crash. The dashboard contained just a speedometer, fuel gauge, and oil light. It lacked a radio, reclining seats, or power steering. It came with a small 650 cc engine that generated only 70 horsepower, but obtained 50–60 miles per gallon. The car's suspension system used old technology that was cheap but resulted in a rougher ride than in more expensive cars. More importantly, Tata Motors would save money by using an innovative distribution strategy. Instead of selling completed cars to dealers, Tata planned to supply kits that would then be assembled by the dealers. By eliminating large, centralized assembly plants, Tata could cut the car's retail price by 20 percent.

Although Tata Motors intended to initially sell the People's Car in India and then offer it in other developing markets, management felt that they could build a car that would meet U.S. or European specifications for around $6,000—still a low price for an automobile. Given that Tata Motors was able to acquire Jaguar and Land Rover from Ford later in the year, other auto companies had to admit that Tata was on its way to becoming a major competitor in the industry.[1]

4.1 RESOURCE-BASED VIEW OF THE FIRM

Scanning and analyzing the external environment for opportunities and threats is not enough to provide an organization a competitive advantage. Strategic managers must also look within the corporation itself to identify internal strategic factors—those critical *strengths* and *weaknesses* that are likely to determine if the firm will be able to take advantage of opportunities while avoiding threats. This internal scanning, often referred to as **organizational analysis**, is concerned with identifying and developing an organization's resources.

What are Core and Distinctive Competencies?

Resources are an organization's assets and are thus its basic building blocks. They include *tangible assets*, such as plant, equipment, finances, and location; *human assets*, in terms of the number of employees and their skills; and *intangible assets*, such as technology, culture, and reputation. **Capabilities** refer to a corporation's ability to exploit its resources. They consist of business processes and routines that manage the interaction among resources to turn inputs into outputs. For example, a company's marketing capability can be based on the interaction among its marketing specialists, distribution channels, and sales people. A capability is functionally based and is resident in a particular function. Thus, there are marketing capabilities, manufacturing capabilities, and human resource management capabilities. When these capabilities are constantly being updated and reconfigured to make them more adaptive to an uncertain environment, they are called *dynamic capabilities*.

A **competency** is the cross-functional integration and coordination of capabilities. For example, a competency in new product development in one division of a corporation may be the consequence of integrating MIS capabilities, marketing capabilities, R&D capabilities, and production capabilities within the division. A **core competency** is a collection of competencies that cross divisional boundaries, is widespread within the corporation, and is something that a corporation can do exceedingly well. Thus new product development would be a core competency if it goes beyond one division. For example, a core competency of Avon Products is its expertise in door-to-door selling. FedEx has a core competency in its application of information technology to all of its operations. A company must constantly reinvest in a core competency or risk its becoming a *core rigidity*, that is, a strength that over time matures and becomes a weakness. Although it is typically not an asset in the accounting sense, a core competency is a very valuable resource—it does not "wear out" with use. In general, the more core competencies are used, the more refined they get and the more valuable they become. When core competencies are superior to those of the competition, they are called **distinctive competencies**. General Electric, for example, is well known for its distinctive competency in management development. Its executives are sought out by other companies hiring top managers.

Barney, in his **VRIO framework** of analysis, proposes four questions to evaluate a firm's competencies:

1. *Value*: Does it provide competitive advantage?
2. *Rareness*: Do no other competitors possess it?
3. *Imitability*: Is it costly for others to imitate?
4. *Organization*: Is the firm organized to exploit the resource?

If the answer to these questions is *yes* for a particular competency, it is considered to be a strength and thus a distinctive competency.[2]

How do Resources Determine Competitive Advantage?

Proposing that a company's sustained competitive advantage is primarily determined by its resource endowments, Grant presents a five-step, resource-based approach to strategy analysis:

1. Identify and classify the firm's resources in terms of strengths and weaknesses.
2. Combine the firm's strengths into specific capabilities and core competencies.
3. Appraise the profit potential of these capabilities and competencies in terms of their potential for sustainable competitive advantage and the ability to harvest the profits resulting from their use. Are there any distinctive competencies?
4. Select the strategy that best exploits the firm's capabilities and competencies relative to external opportunities.
5. Identify resource gaps and invest in upgrading weaknesses.[3]

What Determines the Sustainability of an Advantage?

The ability of a firm to use its resources, capabilities, and competencies to develop a competitive advantage through distinctive competencies does not mean it will be able to sustain it. Two basic characteristics determine the sustainability of a firm's distinctive competencies: durability and imitability.

Durability is the rate at which a firm's underlying resources, capabilities, or core competencies depreciate or become obsolete. For example, new technology can make a company's distinctive competency obsolete or irrelevant. As people shift from PCs to a wide array of devices like iPhones, Blackberries, and Kindles, Microsoft's distinctive competency in operating systems becomes less relevant.

Imitability is the rate at which a firm's underlying resources, capabilities, or core competencies can be duplicated by others. Competitors' efforts may range from reverse engineering to hiring employees from the competitor to outright patent infringement. It is relatively easy to learn and imitate another company's distinctive competency if it comes from *explicit knowledge*, that is, knowledge that can be easily articulated and communicated. This is the type of knowledge that competitive intelligence activities can quickly identify and communicate. *Tacit knowledge*, in contrast, is knowledge that is *not* easily communicated because it is deeply rooted in employee experience or in a corporation's culture. A distinctive competency can be easily imitated to the extent that it is transparent, transferable, and replicable:

- **Transparency.** It is the speed with which other firms can understand the relationship of resources and capabilities supporting a successful firm's strategy. For example, Gillette's competitors could never understand how the Sensor or Mach 3 razor was produced simply by taking one apart. Gillette's Sensor razor design was very difficult to copy, partially because the manufacturing equipment needed to produce it was so expensive and complicated.
- **Transferability.** It is the ability of competitors to gather the resources and capabilities necessary to support a competitive challenge. For example, it may be very difficult for a winemaker to duplicate a French winery's key resources of land and climate, especially if the imitator is located in Iowa.

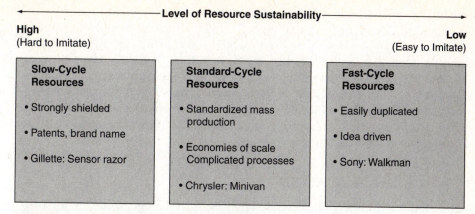

FIGURE 4.1   Continuum of Resource Sustainability

Source: Suggested by J. R. Williams, "How Sustainable Is Your Competitive Advantage?" *California Management Review* (Spring 1992), p. 33.

- **Replicability.** It is the ability of competitors to use duplicated resources and capabilities to imitate the other firm's success. For example, although many companies have copied P&G's brand management system, most have been unable to duplicate the company's success.

A *continuum of resource sustainability* is composed of an organization's resources and capabilities characterized by their durability and imitability (i.e., they aren't transparent, transferable, or replicable). This continuum is depicted in **Figure 4.1**. At one extreme are slow-cycle resources, which are sustainable because they are shielded by patents, geography, strong brand names, and the like. These resources and capabilities are distinctive competencies because they provide a sustainable competitive advantage. Gillette's razor technology is a good example of a product built around slow-cycle resources. The other extreme includes fast-cycle resources, which face the highest imitation pressures because they are based on a concept or technology that can be easily duplicated, such as Sony's Walkman. To the extent that a company has fast-cycle resources, the primary way it can compete successfully is through increased speed from lab to marketplace. Otherwise, it has no real sustainable competitive advantage.

4.2   BUSINESS MODELS

When analyzing a company, it is helpful to learn what sort of business model it is following. This is especially important when analyzing Internet-based companies. A **business model** is a company's method for making money in the current business environment. It includes the key structural and operational characteristics of a firm—how it earns revenue and makes a profit.

The simplest business model is to provide a good or service that can be sold so that revenues exceed costs and expenses. Other models can be much more complicated. Some of the many possible business models are provided here. The *Customer Solutions Model* is one in which a company like IBM makes money not by selling products, but by selling its expertise as consultants. In the *Multi-Component System*, a company like Gillette sells razors at break-even in order to sell higher-margin razor blades. In the

Advertising Model, a company like Google offers free Web services to users in order to expose them to the advertising that pays the bills. Financial planners, mutual funds, and realtors use the *Switchboard Model*, in which a firm acts as an intermediary to connect multiple sellers to multiple buyers for a fee. In the *Efficiency Model*, a company like Dell or Wal-Mart waits until a product or service becomes standardized and then enters the market with a low-priced, low-margin product appealing to the mass market. This is contrasted with the *Time Model*, in which a firm like Sony uses product R&D to be the first to enter a market with a new innovation. Once others enter the market with process R&D and lower prices, it's time to move on.[4]

4.3 VALUE-CHAIN ANALYSIS

A **value chain** is a linked set of value-creating activities beginning with basic raw materials coming from suppliers, to a series of value-added activities involved in producing and marketing a product or service, and ending with distributors getting the final goods into the hands of the ultimate consumer. **Figure 4.2** is an example of a typical value chain for a manufactured product. The focus of value-chain analysis is to examine the corporation in the context of the overall chain of value-creating activities, of which the firm may only be a small part.

Industry Value-Chain Analysis

The value chains of most industries can be split into two segments: upstream and downstream halves. In the petroleum industry, for example, upstream refers to oil exploration, drilling, and moving the crude oil to the refinery; whereas, downstream refers to refining the oil plus the transporting and marketing of gasoline and refined oil to distributors and gas station retailers. Even though most large oil companies are completely integrated, they often vary in the amount of expertise they have at each part of the value chain. Amoco, for example, had its greatest expertise downstream in marketing and retailing. British Petroleum, in contrast, was more dominant in upstream activities like exploration. The merger of these two firms combined their core competencies and created a stronger overall firm.

In analyzing the complete value chain of a product, note that even if a firm operates up and down the entire industry chain, it usually has an area of primary expertise where its primary activities lie. A company's *center of gravity* is the part of the chain that is most important to the company and the point where its greatest expertise and capabilities, its core competencies, lie. According to Galbraith, a company's center of gravity is usually the point at which the company started.[5] After a firm successfully establishes itself at this point by obtaining a competitive advantage, one of its first strategic moves is to move forward or backward along the value chain in order to reduce costs, guarantee access to key raw materials, or guarantee distribution. This process is called *vertical integration*.

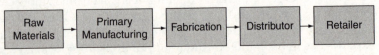

FIGURE 4.2 Typical Value Chain for a Manufactured Product

Corporate Value-Chain Analysis

Each corporation has its internal value chain of activities. Porter proposes that a manufacturing firm's *primary activities* usually begin with inbound logistics (raw materials handling and warehousing), go through an operations process in which a product is manufactured, and continue to outbound logistics (warehousing and distribution), marketing and sales, and finally to service (installation, repair, and sale of parts). Several *support activities*, such as procurement (purchasing), technology development (R&D), human resource management, and firm infrastructure (accounting, finance, and strategic planning), ensure that the primary value-chain activities operate effectively and efficiently. Each of a company's product lines has its own distinctive value chain. Because most corporations make several different products or services, an internal analysis of the firm involves analyzing a series of different value chains.

The systematic examination of individual value activities can lead to a better understanding of a corporation's strengths and weaknesses—thus identifying any core or distinctive competencies. According to Porter, "Differences among competitor value chains are a key source of competitive advantage."[6] Corporate value-chain analysis involves the following steps:

1. *Examine each product line's value chain in terms of the various activities involved in producing that product or service.* Which activities can be considered strengths (competencies) or weaknesses?

2. *Examine the "linkages" within each product line's value chain. Linkages* are the connections between the way one value activity (e.g., marketing) is performed and the cost of performance of another activity (e.g., quality control). In seeking ways for a corporation to gain competitive advantage in the marketplace, the same function can be performed in different ways with different results. For example, quality inspection of 100 percent of output by the workers themselves instead of the usual 10 percent by quality control inspectors might increase production costs, but that increase could be more than offset by the savings obtained from reducing the number of repair people needed to fix defective products and increasing the amount of time devoted by salespeople to selling instead of exchanging already-sold, but defective, products.

3. *Examine the potential synergies among the value chains of different product lines or business units.* Each value element, such as advertising or manufacturing, has an inherent economy of scale in which activities are conducted at their lowest possible cost per unit of output. If a particular product is not being produced at a high-enough level to reach economies of scale in distribution, another product could be used to share the same distribution channel. This is a way to achieve economies of scope (defined later in the chapter).

4.4 SCANNING INTERNAL RESOURCES AND CAPABILITIES

The simplest way to begin an analysis of a corporation's value chain is by carefully examining its traditional functional areas for strengths and weaknesses. Functional resources include not only the financial, physical, and human assets in each area, but also the ability of the people in each area to formulate and implement the necessary functional objectives, strategies, and policies. The capabilities include the knowledge of analytical concepts and procedural techniques common to each area and the ability of the people in each area to use them effectively. If used properly, these capabilities serve as strengths to carry out value-added activities and support strategic decisions. In addition to the usual business functions of marketing, finance, R&D, operations, human resources, and information systems, we also discuss structure and culture as key parts of a business corporation's value chain.

What are the Typical Organizational Structures?

Although an almost infinite variety of structural forms are possible, certain basic types predominate in modern complex organizations. **Figure 4.3** illustrates three basic structures: simple, functional, and divisional. Generally speaking, each structure tends to support some corporate strategies over others.

- **Simple structure** has no functional or product categories and is appropriate for a small, entrepreneur-dominated company with one or two product lines that operates in a reasonably small, easily identifiable market niche. Employees tend to be generalists and jacks-of-all-trades.
- **Functional structure** is appropriate for a medium-sized firm with several product lines in one industry. Employees tend to be specialists in the business functions important to that industry, such as manufacturing, marketing, finance, and human resources.
- **Divisional structure** is appropriate for a large corporation with many product lines in several related industries. Employees tend to be functional specialists organized according to product/market distinctions. General Motors, for example, groups its various product lines into the separate divisions of Chevrolet, Buick, and Cadillac. Management attempts to find some synergy among divisional activities through the use of committees and horizontal linkages.
- **Strategic business units (SBUs)** are a recent modification to the divisional structure. SBUs are divisions or groups of divisions composed of independent product-market segments that are given primary responsibility and authority for the management of their own functional areas. An SBU may be of any size or level, but it must have (1) a unique mission, (2) identifiable competitors, (3) an external market focus, and (4) control over its business functions. The idea is to decentralize on the basis of strategic elements rather than on the basis of size, product characteristics, or span of control and to create horizontal linkages among units previously kept separate. For example, rather than organize products on the basis of packaging technology like frozen foods, canned foods, and bagged foods, General Foods organized its products into SBUs on the basis of consumer-oriented menu segments: breakfast food, beverage, main meal, dessert, and pet foods.
- **Conglomerate structure** is appropriate for a large corporation with many product lines in several unrelated industries. A variant of the divisional structure, the conglomerate structure (sometimes called a holding company) is typically an assemblage of legally independent firms (subsidiaries) operating under one corporate umbrella but controlled through the subsidiaries' boards of directors. The unrelated nature of the subsidiaries prevents any attempt at gaining synergy among them. One example of a conglomerate is Berkshire Hathaway.

I. Simple Structure

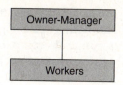

II. Functional Structure

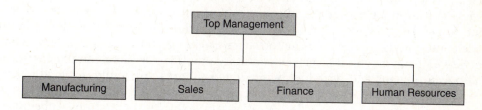

III. Divisional Structure *

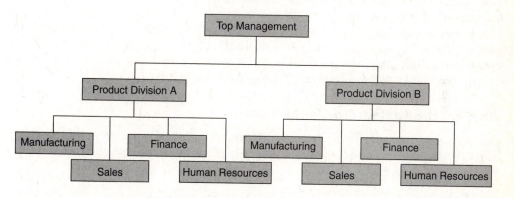

*Conglomerate structure and strategic business units (SBUs) are variations of the divisional structure.

FIGURE 4.3   Basic Structures of Corporations

If the current basic structure of a corporation does not easily support a strategy under consideration, top management must decide whether the proposed strategy is feasible or if the structure should be changed to a more advanced one such as the matrix or network. (Advanced structural designs are discussed in Chapter 8.)

What is Corporate Culture?

Corporate culture is the collection of beliefs, expectations, and values learned and shared by a corporation's members and transmitted from one generation of employees to another. The term *corporate culture* generally reflects the values of the founder(s) and the mission of the firm. It gives a company a sense of identity. The culture includes the dominant orientation of the company, such as R&D at HP, high productivity at Nucor, customer service at Nordstrom, innovation at Google, or product quality at BMW. Like structure, if an organization's culture is compatible with a new strategy, it is an internal strength. But if the corporate culture is not compatible with the proposed strategy, it is a serious weakness.

Corporate culture has two distinct attributes: intensity and integration. **Cultural intensity** (or depth) is the degree to which members of a unit accept the norms, values, or other culture content associated with the unit. Organizations with strong norms promoting a particular value, such as quality at BMW, have intensive cultures, whereas new firms (or those in transition) have weaker, less intensive cultures. Employees of a company with an intensive culture tend to exhibit consistency in behavior, that is, they tend to act similarly over time. **Cultural integration** (or breadth) is the extent to which units throughout an organization share a common culture. Organizations with a pervasive dominant culture, such as a military unit, may be hierarchically controlled and power oriented and have highly integrated cultures. All employees tend to hold the same cultural values and norms. In contrast, a company that is structured into diverse units by functions or divisions usually exhibits some strong subcultures (e.g., R&D versus manufacturing) and an overall weaker corporate culture.

Corporate culture shapes the behavior of people in the corporation. Because these cultures have a powerful influence on the behavior of managers at all levels, they can strongly affect a corporation's ability to shift its strategic direction. A strong culture should not only promote survival, but also create the basis for a superior competitive position by increasing motivation and facilitating coordination and control. To the extent that a distinctive competency is tacit knowledge embedded in an organization's culture, it will be very hard for a competitor to duplicate it.

What are the Strategic Marketing Issues?

The marketing manager is the company's primary link to the customer and the competition. The manager must therefore be especially concerned with the firm's market position and marketing mix.

WHAT ARE MARKET POSITION AND SEGMENTATION?

Market position refers to the selection of specific areas for marketing concentration and can be expressed in terms of market, product, and geographical locations. Through market research, corporations are able to practice **market segmentation**—tailoring products for specific market niches.

WHAT IS MARKETING MIX?

The marketing mix is the particular combination of key variables under the corporation's control that it can use to affect demand and gain competitive advantage. These variables are product, place, promotion, and price. Within each of these four variables are several subvariables, listed in **Table 4.1**, that should be analyzed in terms of their effects on divisional and corporate performance.

Table 4.1 Marketing Mix Variables			
Product	**Place**	**Promotion**	**Price**
Quality	Channels	Advertising	List price
Features	Coverage	Personal selling	Discounts
Options	Locations	Sales promotion	Allowances
Style	Inventory	Publicity	Payment periods
Brand name	Transport		Credit terms
Packaging			
Sizes			
Services			
Warranties			
Returns			

Source: Philip Kotler, *Marketing Management: Analysis, Planning, and Control,* 4th ed. (Upper Saddle River, N.J.: Prentice Hall, 1980), p. 89. Reprinted by permission of Pearson Education, Inc.

WHAT IS THE PRODUCT LIFE CYCLE?

One of the most useful concepts in marketing insofar as strategic management is concerned is that of the product life cycle. As depicted in **Figure 4.4**, the **product life cycle** is a graph showing time plotted against the dollar sales of a product as it moves from introduction through growth and maturity to decline. This concept enables a marketing

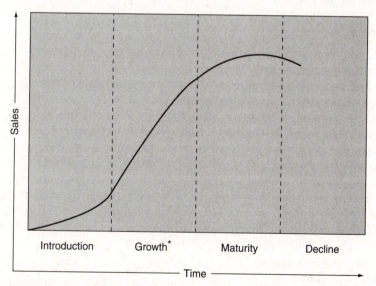

FIGURE 4.4   The Product Life Cycle

*The right end of the Growth stage is often called Competitive Turbulence because of price and distribution competion that shakes out the weaker competitors. For further information, see C. R. Wasson, *Dynamic Competitive Strategy and Product Life Cycles*, 3rd ed. (Austin, TCX.: Austin Press, 1978).

manager to examine the marketing mix of a particular product or group of products in terms of its position in its life cycle.

WHY IS BRANDING IMPORTANT?

A *brand* is a name given to a company's product which identifies that item in the mind of the consumer. Over time and with proper advertising, a brand connotes various characteristics in the consumers' minds. For example, Ivory suggests "pure" soap. A brand can thus be an important corporate resource. According to *Business Week*, the value of the Coca-Cola brand is worth $65.3 billion.[7]

A *corporate brand* is a type of brand in which the company's name serves as the brand. The value of a corporate brand, like Walt Disney, is that it typically stands for consumers' impressions of a company and can thus be extended onto products not currently offered—regardless of the company's actual expertise.

What are the Strategic Financial Issues?

The financial manager must ascertain the best sources, uses, and control of funds. Cash must be raised from internal or external sources and allocated for different uses. The flow of funds in the operations of the organization must be monitored. To the extent that a corporation is involved in international activities, currency fluctuations must be dealt with to ensure that profits aren't wiped out by the rise or fall of the dollar versus the yen, euro, and other currencies. Benefits, in the form of returns, repayments, or products and services, must be given to the sources of outside financing. All these tasks must be handled in a way that complements and supports overall corporate strategy.

WHAT IS FINANCIAL LEVERAGE?

The mix of externally generated short-term and long-term funds in relation to the amount and timing of internally generated funds should be appropriate to the corporate objectives, strategies, and policies. The concept of **financial leverage** (the ratio of total debt to total assets) helps describe the use of debt (versus equity) to finance the company's programs from outside. Financing company activities by selling bonds or notes instead of through issuing stock boosts earnings per share: The interest paid on the debt reduces taxable income, but fewer stockholders share the profits. The debt, however, does raise the firm's break-even point above what it would have been if the firm had been financed from internally generated funds only. High leverage may therefore be perceived as a corporate strength in times of prosperity and ever-increasing sales or as a weakness in times of a recession and falling sales because leverage magnifies the effect of an increase or decrease in dollar sales on earnings per share.

WHAT IS CAPITAL BUDGETING?

Capital budgeting is the analyzing and ranking of possible investments in fixed assets such as land, buildings, and equipment in terms of the additional outlays and additional receipts that will result from each investment. A good finance department will be able to prepare such capital budgets and rank them on the basis of some accepted criteria or *hurdle rate* (e.g., years to pay back investment, rate of return, or time to break-even point) for the purpose of strategic decision making.

What are the Strategic Research and Development (R&D) Issues?

The R&D manager is responsible for suggesting and implementing a company's technological strategy in light of its corporate objectives and policies. The manager's job therefore involves (1) choosing among alternative new technologies to use within the corporation, (2) developing methods of embodying the new technology in new products and processes, and (3) deploying resources so that the new technology can be successfully implemented.

WHAT ARE R&D INTENSITY, TECHNOLOGICAL COMPETENCE, AND TECHNOLOGY TRANSFER?

The company must make available the resources necessary for effective research and development. A company's **R&D intensity** (its spending on R&D as a percentage of sales revenue) is a principal means of gaining market share in global competition. The amount spent on R&D often varies by industry. For example, the computer software and drug industries spend an average of 13.2 percent and 11.5 percent, respectively, of their sales dollar for R&D. A good rule of thumb for R&D spending is that a corporation should spend at a rate "normal" for that particular industry.

Simply spending money on R&D or new projects does not mean, however, that the money will produce useful results. A company's R&D unit should be evaluated for **technological competence**, the proper management of technology, in both the development and the use of innovative technology. Not only should the corporation make a consistent research effort (as measured by reasonably constant corporate expenditures that result in usable innovations), it should also be proficient in managing research personnel and integrating their innovations into its day-to-day operations. A company should also be proficient in **technology transfer**, the process of taking a new technology from the laboratory to the marketplace. For example, Xerox Corporation has been criticized because it failed to take advantage of various innovations (such as the mouse and the graphical user interface for personal computers) developed originally in its sophisticated Palo Alto Research Center.

WHAT IS THE R&D MIX?

Research and development includes basic, product, and engineering or process R&D. *Basic R&D* focuses on theoretical problem areas and is typically undertaken by scientists in well-equipped laboratories. The best indicators of a company's capability in this area are its patents and research publications. *Product R&D* concentrates on marketing and is concerned with product or product-packaging improvements. The best measurements of ability in this area are the number of successful new products introduced and the percentage of total sales and profits coming from products introduced within the past five years. *Engineering or process R&D* is concerned with engineering and concentrates on improving quality control, design specifications, and production equipment. A company's capability in this area can be measured by consistent reductions in unit manufacturing costs and product defects. Most corporations have a mix of basic, product, and process R&D, which varies by industry, company, and product line. The **R&D mix** is the balance of the three types of research. The mix should be appropriate to the strategy being considered and to each product's life cycle. For example, it is generally accepted that product R&D normally dominates the early stages of a product's life cycle (when the product's optimal form and features are still being debated), whereas process R&D becomes especially important in the later stages (when the product's design is fixed and the emphasis is on reducing costs and improving quality).

WHAT IS THE IMPACT OF TECHNOLOGICAL DISCONTINUITY ON STRATEGY?

The R&D manager must determine when to abandon present technology and when to develop or adopt new technology. According to Richard Foster of McKinsey and Company, **technological discontinuity** is the displacement of one technology by another. It is a frequent and strategically important phenomenon. Such a discontinuity occurs when a new technology does not simply enhance the current technology but actually substitutes for that technology to yield better performance. For each technology within a given field or industry, according to Foster, the plotting of product performance against research effort and expenditures on a graph results in an S-shaped curve. He describes the process depicted in **Figure 4.5** as follows:

> Early in the development of the technology a knowledge base is being built and progress requires a relatively large amount of effort. Later, progress comes more easily. And then, as the limits of that technology are approached, progress becomes slow and expensive. That is when R&D dollars should be allocated to technology with more potential. That is also—not so incidentally—when a competitor who has bet on a new technology can sweep away your business or topple an entire industry.[8]

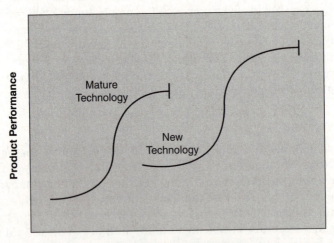

In the corporate planning process, it is generally assumed that incremental progress in technology will occur. But past developments in a given technology cannot be extrapolated into the future, because every technology has its limits. The key to competitiveness is to determine when to shift resources to a technology with more potential.

FIGURE 4.5 Technological Discontinuity

Source: P. Pascarella, "Are You Investing in the Wrong Technology?" *Industry Week* (July 25, 1983), p. 38. Copyright © 1983 Penton/IPC. All rights reserved. Reprinted by permission.

Christensen explains in *The Innovator's Dilemma* why established market leaders are typically reluctant to move in a timely manner to a new technology. Their reluctance to switch technologies (even when the firm is aware of the new technology and may have even invented it!) is because the resource allocation process in most companies gives priority to those projects (typically based on the old technology) with the greatest likelihood of generating a good return on investment—those projects appealing to the firm's current customers (whose products are also based on the characteristics of the old technology). The new technology is generally riskier and of little appeal to the current customers of established firms. Products derived from the new technology are more expensive and do not meet the customers' requirements—requirements based on the old technology. New entrepreneurial firms are typically more interested in the new technology because it is one way to appeal to a developing market niche in a market currently dominated by established companies. Even though the new technology may be more expensive to develop, it offers performance improvements in areas that are attractive to this small niche, but of no consequence to the customers of the established competitors.[9]

What are the Strategic Operations Issues?

The primary task of the operations (manufacturing or service) manager is to develop and operate a system that will produce the required number of products or services, with a certain quality, at a given cost, within an allotted time. Many of the key concepts and techniques popularly used in manufacturing can be applied to service businesses. In general terms, manufacturing can be intermittent or continuous. In *intermittent systems* (job shops), the item is normally processed sequentially, but the work and sequence of the process vary. At each location, the tasks determine the details of processing and the time required for them. In contrast, *continuous systems* are those laid out as lines on which products can be continuously assembled or processed—an example is an automobile assembly line.

The type of manufacturing system that a corporation uses determines divisional or corporate strategy. It makes no sense, for example, to plan to increase sales by saturating the market with low-priced products if the company's manufacturing process was designed as an intermittent job shop system that produces one-time-only products to a customer's specifications. Conversely, a plan to produce several specialty products might not be economically feasible if the manufacturing process was designed to be a mass-producing, continuous system using low-skilled labor or special-purpose robots.

WHAT IS THE EXPERIENCE CURVE?

A conceptual framework that many large corporations have used successfully is the experience curve (originally called the learning curve). The **experience curve** suggests that unit production costs decline by some fixed percentage (commonly 20–30%) each time the total accumulated volume of production (in units) doubles. The actual percentage varies by industry and is based on many variables: the amount of time it takes a person to learn a new task, economies of scale, product and process improvements, and lower raw materials cost, among others. For example, in an industry with an 85 percent experience curve, a corporation might expect a 15 percent reduction in costs for every doubling of volume. The total costs per unit can be expected to drop from $100 when the total production is 10 units to $85 ($100 × 85%) when production increases to 20 units and to $72.25 ($85 × 85%) when it reaches 40 units. Achieving these results often means investing in R&D and assets, resulting in higher fixed costs and less flexibility. Nevertheless, the manufacturing strategy is to build capacity ahead of demand in order to achieve the lower unit costs that develop from the experience curve. On the basis of some future point on the experience curve, the product or service should be priced very low to preempt competition and increase market demand. The resulting high number of units sold and high market share should result in high profits, based on the low unit costs.

Management commonly uses the experience curve to estimate the production costs of (1) a product never before made with the present techniques and processes or (2) current products produced by newly introduced techniques or processes. The concept was first applied in the airframe industry and can be applied in the service industry as well. Although many firms have used experience curves extensively, an unquestioning acceptance of the industry norm (such as 80% for the airframe industry or 70% for integrated circuits) is risky. The experience curve of the industry as a whole might not hold true for a particular company for a variety of reasons.

WHAT IS FLEXIBLE MANUFACTURING?

The use of large mass-production facilities to take advantage of experience-curve economies has been criticized. The use of computer-assisted design and computer-assisted manufacturing (CAD/CAM) and robot technology allows learning times to be shorter and products to be economically manufactured in small, customized batches. **Economies of scope** (in which the manufacturing activities of the common parts of various products are combined to gain economies even though small numbers of each product are made) replace **economies of scale** (in which unit costs are reduced by making large numbers of the same product) in flexible manufacturing. **Flexible manufacturing** permits the low-volume output of custom-tailored products at relatively low unit costs through economies of scope. It is thus possible to have the cost advantages of continuous systems with the customer-oriented advantages of intermittent systems.

What are the Strategic Human Resource Issues?

The primary task of the manager of human resources is to improve the match between individuals and jobs. A good HRM department should know how to use attitude surveys and other feedback devices to assess employees' satisfaction with their jobs and with the corporation as a whole. HRM managers should also use job analysis to obtain job description information about what each job needs to accomplish in terms of quality and quantity. Up-to-date job descriptions are essential not only for proper employee selection, appraisal, training, and development; wage and salary administration; and labor negotiations, but also for summarizing the corporate-wide human resources in terms of employee-skill categories. Just as a company must know the number, type, and quality of its manufacturing facilities, it must also know the kinds of people it employs and the skills they possess. IBM, Procter & Gamble, and Hewlett-Packard, for example, use employee profiles to ensure that they have the right mix of talents for implementing their planned strategies.

HOW SHOULD TEAMS BE USED?

Human resource managers should know about work options, such as part-time work, job sharing, flextime, extended leaves, contract work, and the proper use of teams. Over two-thirds of large U.S. companies are successfully using **autonomous** *(self-managing)* **work teams** in which a group of people work together without a supervisor to plan, coordinate, and evaluate their work. Northern Telecom found productivity and quality to increase with autonomous work teams to such an extent that it was able to reduce the number of quality inspectors by 40 percent.

As a way to move a product more quickly through its development stage, companies like Motorola, Chrysler, NCR, Boeing, and General Electric have begun using **cross-functional work teams**. Instead of developing products in a series of steps—beginning with a request from sales, which leads to design, to engineering and to purchasing, and finally to manufacturing (often resulting in customer rejection of a costly product)—companies are tearing down the traditional walls separating departments so that people from each discipline can get involved in projects early on. In a process called *concurrent engineering*, the once-isolated specialists now work side by side and compare notes constantly in an effort to design cost-effective products with features customers want.

Virtual teams are groups of geographically and/or organizationally dispersed coworkers that are assembled using a combination of telecommunications and information technologies to accomplish an organizational task. Internet, intranet, and extranet systems combine with other new technologies such as desktop video conferencing and collaborative software to create a new workplace in which teams of workers are no longer restrained by geography, time, or organizational boundaries. More than 60 percent of professional employees now work in virtual teams.[10]

HOW IMPORTANT ARE UNION RELATIONS?

If the corporation is unionized, a good human resource manager should be able to work closely with the union. Even though union membership had dropped to only 12.1 percent of the U.S. workforce by 2007, compared to 24 percent in 1973, it still included 15.7 million people. To save jobs, U.S. unions are increasingly willing to support new strategic initiatives and employee involvement programs. Outside the United States, however, the average proportion of unionized workers among major industrialized nations is around 50 percent. A significant issue for unions is the increasing use of temporary workers, often part-time employees who earn low wages and few benefits. Over 90 percent of U.S. and European firms use temporary workers in some capacity; 43 percent use them in professional and technical functions.

HOW IMPORTANT IS DIVERSITY?

Human diversity is the mix in the workplace of people from different races, cultures, and backgrounds. Realizing that the demographics are changing toward an increasing percentage of minorities and women in the U.S. workforce, companies are now concerned with hiring and promoting people without regard to ethnic background. Research has found that an increase in racial diversity leads to an increase in firm performance.[11] Good human resource managers should be working to ensure that people are treated fairly on the job and not harassed by prejudiced coworkers or managers.

An organization's human resources are especially important in today's world of global communication and transportation systems. Competitors around the world copy advances in technology almost immediately. Because people are not as willing to move to other companies in other countries, the only long-term resource advantage remaining to corporations operating in the industrialized nations may lie in the area of skilled human resources.

What are the Strategic Information Technology Issues?

The primary task of the manager of information technology is to design and manage the flow of information in an organization in ways that improve productivity and decision making. Information must be collected, stored, and synthesized in such a manner that it can answer important operating and strategic questions.

A corporation's information technology can be a strength or a weakness in all three elements of strategic management. Not only can it aid in environmental scanning and in controlling a company's many activities, it can also be used as a strategic weapon in gaining competitive advantage. For example, by allowing customers to directly access its package-tracking database via its Web site instead of having to ask a human operator, Fed Ex improved its customer service and saved up to $2 million annually—providing it an advantage over its rival, UPS.

A current trend in corporate information systems is the increasing use of the Internet for marketing, intranets for internal communication, and extranets for logistics and distribution. An *intranet* is an information network within an organization that also has access to the external worldwide Internet. Intranets typically begin as ways to provide employees with company information such as lists of product prices, fringe benefits, and company policies. An *extranet* is an information network within an organization that is available to key suppliers and customers. The key issue in building an extranet is the creation of "fire walls" to block extranet users from accessing the firm's or other users' confidential data. Once this is accomplished, companies can allow employees, customers, and suppliers to access information and conduct business on the Internet in a completely automated manner. By connecting these groups, companies hope to obtain a competitive advantage by reducing the time needed to design and bring new products to market, slashing inventories, customizing manufacturing, and entering new markets. Many companies are now using wikis, blogs, RSS (really simple syndication), social networks (e.g., MySpace and Facebook), podcasts, and mash-ups through company Web sites to forge tighter links with customers and suppliers and engage employees more successfully.

The expansion of the marketing-oriented Internet into intranets and extranets is making significant contributions to organizational performance through supply chain management. **Supply chain management** is the forming of networks for sourcing raw materials, manufacturing products or creating services, storing and distributing the goods, and delivering them to customers. Companies who are known to be exemplars in supply-chain management, such as Wal-Mart, Dell Computer, and Toyota, spend only 4 percent of their revenues on supply chain costs compared to 10 percent by the average firm.

4.5 SYNTHESIS OF INTERNAL FACTORS—IFAS

Once strategists have scanned the internal organizational environment and identified factors for their corporation, they may wish to summarize their analysis of these factors using a form such as the one given in **Table 4.2**. This **IFAS (Internal Factor Analysis Summary) Table** is one way to organize the internal factors into the generally accepted categories of strengths and weaknesses and to analyze how well a particular company's management is responding to these specific factors in light of the perceived importance of these factors to the company.

Table 4.2 Internal Factor Analysis Summary (IFAS) Table for Maytag

Internal Factors	Weight	Rating	Weighted Score	Weighted Comments
1	2	3	4	5
Strengths				
• Quality Maytag culture	0.15	5	0.75	Quality key to success
• Experienced top management	0.05	4	0.20	Know appliances
• Vertical integration	0.10	4	0.40	Dedicated factories
• Employee relations	0.05	3	0.15	Good, but deteriorating
• Hoover's international orientation	0.15	3	0.45	Hoover name in cleaners
Weaknesses				
• Process-oriented R&D	0.05	2	0.10	Slow on new products
• Distribution channels	0.05	2	0.10	Superstores replacing small dealers
• Financial position	0.15	2	0.30	High debt load
• Global positioning	0.20	2	0.40	Hoover weak outside the New Zealand, U.K., and Australia
• Manufacturing facilities	0.05	4	0.20	Investing now
Totals	**1.00**		**3.05**	

Notes:

1. List strengths and weaknesses (5–10 each) in Column 1.

2. Weight each factor from 1.0 (Most Important) to 0.0 (Not Important) in Column 2 based on that factor's probable impact on the company's strategic position. **The total weights must sum to 1.00.**

3. Rate each factor from 5 (Outstanding) to 1 (Poor) in Column 3 based on the company's response to that factor.

4. Multiply each factor's weight times its rating to obtain each factor's weighted score in Column 4.

5. Use Column 5 (comments) for rationale used for each factor.

6. Add the weighted scores to obtain the *total weighted score* for the company in Column 4. This figure tells how well the company is responding to the factors in its internal environment.

Source: Thomas L. Wheelen, Copyright © 1982, 1985, 1987, 1988, 1989, 1990, 1991, 1995, and every year after that Kathryn E. Wheelen solely owns all of (Dr.) Thomas L. Wheelen's copyright materials. Kathryn E. Wheelen requires written reprint permission for each book that this material is to be printed in. Thomas L. Wheelen and J. David Hunger, copyright © 1991–first year "Internal Factor Analysis Summary (IFSA) appeared in this text (5th ed.) Reprinted by permission of the copyright holder.

To use the IFAS Table, complete the following steps for the company being analyzed:

- In **Column 1 (*Internal Factors*)**, list the 8 to 10 most important strengths and weaknesses facing the company.
- In **Column 2 (*Weight*)**, assign a weight to each factor from **1.0** (*Most Important*) to **0.0** (*Not Important*) based on that factor's probable impact on a particular company's current strategic position. The higher the weight, the more important this factor is to the current and future success of the company. (*All weights must sum to 1.0 regardless of the number of strategic factors.*)
- In **Column 3 (*Rating*)**, assign a rating to each factor from **5** (*Outstanding*) to **1** (*Poor*) based on management's current response to that particular factor. Each rating is a judgment regarding how well the company's management is currently managing each internal factor.

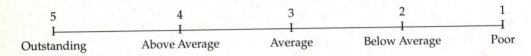

5	4	3	2	1
Outstanding	Above Average	Average	Below Average	Poor

- In **Column 4 (*Weighted Score*)**, multiply the weight in **Column 2** for each factor times its rating in **Column 3** to obtain that factor's weighted score.
- In **Column 5 (*Comments*)**, note why a particular factor was selected and/or how its weight and rating were estimated.
- Finally, add the weighted scores for all the internal factors in **Column 4** to determine the total weighted score for that particular company. The **total weighted score** indicates how well a particular company is managing current and expected factors in its internal environment. The score can be used to compare that firm to other firms in its industry. ***The total weighted score for an average firm in an industry is always 3.0.***

As an example of this procedure, Table 4.2 includes a number of internal factors for Maytag Corporation as of 1995 with corresponding weights, ratings, and weighted scores provided.

Discussion Questions

1. What is the relevance of the resource-based view of a firm to strategic management in a global environment?
2. How can value-chain analysis help identify a company's strengths and weaknesses?
3. In what ways can a corporation's structure and culture be internal strengths or weaknesses?
4. What are the pros and cons of management's using the experience curve to determine strategy?
5. How might a firm's management decide whether it should continue to invest in current known technology or in new, but untested technology? What factors might encourage or discourage such a shift?

Key Terms (listed in order of appearance)

organizational analysis 53
resources 53
capabilities 53
competency 53
core competency 53
distinctive competency 53
VRIO framework 53
durability 54
imitability 54
business model 55
value chain (industry and
   corporate) 56
simple structure 58
functional structure 58

divisional structure 58
strategic business units 58
conglomerate structure 58
corporate culture 59
cultural intensity 60
cultural integration 60
market position 60
market segmentation 60
product life cycle 61
financial leverage 62
capital budgeting 62
R&D intensity 63
technological competence 63
technology transfer 63

R&D mix 63
technological discontinuity 64
experience curve 65
economies of scope 66
economies of scale 66
flexible manufacturing 66
autonomous work teams 67
cross-functional
   work teams 67
virtual teams 67
human diversity 67
supply chain management 68
IFAS Table 69

Notes

1. D. Welch and N. Lakshman, "My Other Car Is a Tata," *Business Week* (January 14, 2008), pp. 33–34; "The New People's Car," *Economist* (March 28, 2009), pp. 73–74.

2. J. B. Barney, *Gaining and Sustaining Competitive Advantage* (Reading, Mass.: Addison-Wesley, 1997), pp. 145–164. Barney's VRIO questions are very similar to those proposed by G. Hamel and S. K. Prahalad in their book, *Competing for the Future* (Boston: Harvard Business School Press, 1994) on pages 202–207 in which they state that to be distinctive, a competency must (a) provide customer value, (b) be competitor unique, and (c) be extendable to develop new products and/or markets.

3. R. M. Grant, "The Resource-Based Theory of Competitive Advantage: Implications for Strategy Formulation," *California Management Review* (Spring 1991), pp. 114–135.

4. C. A. de Kluyver and J. A. Pearce II, *Strategy: A View from the Top* (Upper Saddle River, NJ: Prentice Hall, 2003), pp. 63–66.

5. J. R. Galbraith, "Strategy and Organization Planning," *The Strategy Process: Concepts, Contexts, and Cases*, 2nd ed., edited by H. Mintzberg and J. B. Quinn (Englewood Cliffs, N.J.: Prentice Hall, 1991), pp. 315–324.

6. M. Porter, *Competitive Advantage: Creating and Sustaining Superior Performance* (New York: Free Press, 1985), p. 36.

7. D. Kiley, B. Helm, L. Lee, G. Edmundson, C. Edwards, and M. Scott, "Best Global Brands," *Business Week* (August 6, 2007), pp. 56–64.

8. P. Pascarella, "Are You Investing in the Wrong Technology?" *Industry Week* (July 25, 1983), p. 37.

9. C. M. Christensen, *The Innovator's Dilemma* (Boston: Harvard Business School Press, 1997).

10. C. B. Gibson and J. L. Gibbs, "Unpacking the Concept of Virtuality: The Effects of Geographic Dispersion, Electronic Dependence, Dynamic Structure, and National Diversity on Team Innovation," *Administrative Science Quarterly* (September 2006), pp. 451–495.

11. O. C. Richard, B. P. S. Murthi, and K. Ismail, "The Impact of Racial Diversity on Intermediate and Long-Term Performance: The Moderating Role of Environmental Context," *Strategic Management Journal* (December 2007), pp. 1213–1233; G. Colvin, "The 50 Best Companies for Asians, Blacks, and Hispanics," *Fortune* (July 19, 1999), pp. 53–58.

STRATEGY FORMULATION: SITUATION ANALYSIS AND BUSINESS STRATEGY

Midamar Corporation is a family-owned company in Cedar Rapids, Iowa, which has carved out a growing niche for itself in the world food industry: supplying food prepared according to strict religious standards. The company specializes in halal foods, which are produced and processed according to Islamic law for sale to Muslims. Why did it focus on this type of food? According to owner-founder Bill Aossey, "It's a big world, and you can only specialize in so many places." Although halal foods are not as widely known as kosher foods (processed according to Judaic law), its market is growing along with Islam, the world's fastest-growing religion. Midamar purchases halal-certified meat from Midwestern companies certified to conduct halal processing. Certification requires practicing Muslims schooled in halal processing to slaughter the livestock and to oversee meat and poultry processing.

Aossey is a practicing Muslim who did not imagine such a vast market when he founded his business in 1974. "People thought it would be a passing fad," remarked Aossey. The company has grown to the point where it now exports halal-certified beef, lamb, and poultry to hotels, restaurants, and distributors in 30 countries throughout Asia, Africa, Europe, and North America. Its customers include McDonald's, Pizza Hut, and KFC. McDonald's, for example, uses Midamar's turkey strips as a bacon-alternative in a breakfast product recently introduced in Singapore.

Midamar is successful because its chief executive formulated a strategy designed to give it an advantage in a very competitive industry. It is an example of a differentiation focus competitive strategy in which a company focuses on a particular target market to provide a differentiated product or service. This strategy is one of the business competitive strategies discussed in this chapter.

5.1 SITUATIONAL (SWOT) ANALYSIS

Strategy formulation is often referred to as strategic planning or long-range planning and is concerned with developing a corporation's mission, objectives, strategies, and policies. It begins with situation analysis: the process of finding a strategic fit between external opportunities and internal strengths while working around external threats and internal weaknesses. **SWOT** is an acronym used to describe the particular strengths, weaknesses, opportunities, and threats that are strategic factors for a company. Over the years, SWOT analysis has proven to be the most widely used and enduring analytical technique in strategic management. SWOT analysis should result not only in the identification of a corporation's distinctive competencies, the particular capabilities and resources a firm possesses, and the superior way in which they are used, but also in the identification of opportunities that the firm is not currently able to take advantage of due to a lack of appropriate resources.

SWOT analysis, by itself, is not a panacea. Some of the primary criticisms of SWOT analysis are:

- It generates lengthy lists.
- It uses no weights to reflect priorities.
- It uses ambiguous words and phrases.
- The same factor can be placed in two categories (e.g., a strength may also be a weakness).
- There is no obligation to verify opinions with data or analysis.
- It only requires a single level of analysis.
- There is no logical link to strategy implementation.[1]

What Is a Strategic Factors Analysis Summary Matrix?

The EFAS and IFAS Tables have been developed to deal with many of the criticisms of SWOT analysis. When used together, they are a powerful analytical set of tools for strategic analysis. The **SFAS (Strategic Factors Analysis Summary) Matrix** summarizes a corporation's strategic factors by combining the external factors from the EFAS Table with the internal factors from the IFAS Table. The EFAS and IFAS examples of Maytag Corporation in Tables 3.3 and 4.2 provide a list of 20 internal and external factors. These are too many factors for most people to use in strategy formulation. The SFAS Matrix requires the strategic decision maker to condense these strengths, weaknesses, opportunities, and threats into ten or fewer strategic factors. This is done by reviewing each of the weights for the individual factors in the EFAS and IFAS Tables. The highest weighted EFAS and IFAS factors should appear in the SFAS Matrix.

As shown in **Figure 5.1**, you can create an SFAS Matrix by following these steps:

1. In **Column 1 (*Strategic Factors*)**, list the most important EFAS and IFAS items. After each factor, indicate whether it is a strength (**S**), weakness (**W**), opportunity (**O**), or threat (**T**).
2. In **Column 2 (*Weight*)**, enter the weights for all of the internal and external strategic factors. As with the EFAS and IFAS Tables presented earlier, the *weight column must still total 1.00*. This means that the weights calculated earlier for EFAS and IFAS will probably have to be adjusted.
3. In **Column 3 (*Rating*)**, enter the ratings of how the company's management is responding to each of the strategic factors. These ratings will probably (but not always) be the same as those listed in the EFAS and IFAS Tables.
4. In **Column 4 (*Weighted Score*)**, calculate the weighted scores as done earlier for EFAS and IFAS.

TABLE 4.2   Internal Factor Analysis Summary (IFAS): Maytag as Example

Internal Factors	Weight	Rating	Weighted Score	Comments
	1	2	3	4	5
Strengths				
• Quality Maytag culture	.15	5	.75	Quality key to success
• Experienced top management	.05	4	.20	Know appliances
• Vertical integration	.10	4	.40	Dedicated factories
• Employee relations	.05	3	.15	Good, but deteriorating
• Hoover's international orientation	.15	3	.45	Hoover name in cleaners
Weaknesses				
• Process-oriented R&D	.05	2	.10	Slow on new products
• Distribution channels	.05	2	.10	Superstores replacing small dealers
• Financial position	.15	2	.30	High debt load
• Global positioning	.20	2	.40	Hoover weak outside the New Zealand, U.K., and Australia
• Manufacturing facilities	.05	4	.20	Investing now
Totals	**1.00**		**3.05**	

TABLE 3.3   External Factor Analysis Summary (EFAS): Maytag as Example

External Factors	Weight	Rating	Weighted Score	Comments
	1	2	3	4	5
Opportunities				
• Economic integration of European Union	.20	4	.80	Acquisition of Hoover
• Demographics favor quality appliances	.10	5	.50	Maytag quality
• Economic development of Asia	.05	1	.05	Low Maytag presence
• Opening of Eastern Europe	.05	2	.10	Will take time
• Trend to superstores	.10	2	.20	Maytag weak in this channel
Threats				
• Increasing government regulations	.10	4	.40	Well positioned
• Strong U.S. competition	.10	4	.40	Well positioned
• Whirlpool and Electrolux strong globally	.15	4	.45	Hoover weak globally
• New product advances	.05	1	.05	Questionable
• Japanese appliance companies	.10	2	.20	Only Asian presence is Australia
Totals	**1.00**		**3.15**	

[1] Strategic Factors (Select the most important opportunities/threats from the EFAS, Table 3-3, and the most important strengths and weaknesses from the IFAS, Table 4-2)	[2] Weight	[3] Rating	[4] Weighted Score	[5] Duration Short	Intermediate	Long	[6] Comments
• Quality Maytag culture (S)	.10	5	.5			X	Quality key to success
• Hoover's international orientation (S)	.10	3	.3		X		Name recognition
• Financial position (W)	.10	2	.2		X		High debt
• Global positioning (W)	.15	2	.3			X	Only in New Zealand, U.K., and Australia
• Economic integration of European Union (O)	.10	4	.4			X	Acquisition of Hoover
• Demographics favor quality (O)	.10	5	.5		X		Maytag quality
• Trend to superstores (O + T)	.10	2	.2	X			Weak in this channel
• Whirlpool and Electrolux (T)	.15	3	.45	X			Dominate industry
• Japanese appliance companies (T)	.10	2	.2			X	Asian presence
Totals	**1.00**		**3.05**				

FIGURE 5.1   Strategic Factors Analysis Summary (SFAS) Matrix

Source: Thomas L. Wheelen, Copyright © 1982, 1985, 1987, 1988, 1989, 1990, 1991, 1992, and every year after that. Kathryn E. Wheelen solely owns all of (Dr.) Thomas L. Wheelen's copyright materials. Kathryn E. Wheelen requires written reprint permission for each book that this materials is to be printed in Thomas L. Wheelen and J. David Hunger, Copyright © 1991–first year "Stategic Factor Analysis Summary" (SFAS) appeared in this text (5th ed). Reprinted by permission of the copyright holders.

Notes:

1. List each of the strategic factors developed in your IFAS and EFAS Tables in Column 1.
2. Weight each factor from 1.0 (Most Important) to 0.0 (Not Important) in Column 2 based on that factor's probable impact on the company's strategic position. **The total weights must sum to 1.00.**
3. Rate each factor from 5 (Outstanding) to 1 (Poor) in Column 3 based on the company's response to that factor.
4. Multiply each factor's weight times its rating to obtain each factor's weighted score in Column 4.
5. For duration in Column 5, check appropriate column (short term—less than 1 year; intermediate—1 to 3 years; long term—over 3 years).
6. Use Column 6 (comments) for rationale used for each factor.
7. Add the weighted scores to obtain the *total weighted score* for the company in Column 4. This figure tells how well the company is dealing with its strategic factors.

5. In **Column 5 (*Duration*)**, indicate *short term* (less than one year), *intermediate term* (one to three years), or *long term* (three years and beyond).
6. In **Column 6 (*Comments*)**, repeat or revise your comments for each strategic factor from the previous EFAS and IFAS Tables. *The total weighted score for the average firm in an industry is always 3.0.*

The resulting SFAS Matrix is a listing of the firm's external and internal strategic factors in one table. The SFAS Matrix includes only the most important factors and provides the basis for strategy formulation.

What Is the Value of a Propitious Niche?

One desired outcome of analyzing strategic factors is identifying a propitious niche where an organization could use its distinctive competence to take advantage of a particular opportunity. A **propitious niche** is a company's specific competitive role that is so well suited to the firm's internal and external environment that other corporations are not likely to challenge or dislodge it.

Finding such a niche is not always easy. A firm's management must be always looking for *strategic windows*, that is, unique market opportunities available only for a limited time. The first one through a strategic window can occupy a propitious niche and discourage competition (if the firm has the required internal strengths). One company that successfully found a propitious niche is Frank J. Zamboni & Company, the manufacturer of the machines that smooth the ice at skating and hockey rinks. Frank Zamboni invented the unique tractor-like machine in 1949, and no one has found a substitute for it. Before the machine was invented, people had to clean and scrape the ice by hand to prepare the surface for skating. Now hockey fans look forward to intermissions just to watch "the Zamboni" slowly drive up and down the ice rink turning rough, scraped ice into a smooth mirror surface. So long as the Zamboni Company is able to produce the machines in the quantity and quality desired at a reasonable price, it's not worth another company's time to go after Frank Zamboni & Company's propitious niche.

5.2   REVIEW OF MISSION AND OBJECTIVES

A corporation must reexamine its current mission and objectives before it can generate and evaluate alternative strategies. Problems in performance can derive from an inappropriate mission statement that is too narrow or too broad. If the mission does not provide a common thread (a unifying theme) for a corporation's businesses, managers may be unclear about where the company is heading. Objectives and strategies might be in conflict with each other. To the detriment of the corporation as a whole, divisions might be competing against one another rather than against outside competition.

A company's objectives can also be inappropriately stated. They can either focus too much on short-term operational goals or be so general that they provide little real guidance. There may be a gap between planned and achieved objectives. When such a gap occurs, either the strategies have to be changed to improve performance or the objectives need to be adjusted downward to be more realistic. Consequently objectives should be constantly reviewed to ensure their usefulness. This is what happened at Boeing when management decided to change its primary objective from being the largest in the industry to being the most profitable. This had a significant effect on its strategies and policies. Following its new objective, the company cancelled its policy of competing with Airbus on price and abandoned its commitment to maintaining a manufacturing capacity that could produce more than half a peak year's demand for airplanes.

5.3 GENERATING ALTERNATIVE STRATEGIES USING A TOWS MATRIX

Thus far we have discussed how a firm uses SWOT analysis to assess its situation. SWOT can also be used to generate a number of possible alternative strategies. The **TOWS** (SWOT backwards) **Matrix** illustrates how the external opportunities and threats facing a particular corporation can be matched with that company's internal strengths and weaknesses to result in four sets of possible strategic alternatives (see **Figure 5.2**). This is a good way to use brainstorming to create alternative strategies that might not otherwise be considered. It forces strategic managers to create various kinds of growth as well as retrenchment strategies. It can be used to generate corporate as well as business and functional strategies.

To generate a TOWS Matrix for a particular company or business unit, refer to the EFAS Table for external factors (Table 3.3) and the IFAS Table for internal factors (Table 4.2). Then take the following steps:

1. In the Opportunities**(O)** block, list the external opportunities available in the company's or business unit's current and future environment from the EFAS Table.
2. In the Threats**(T)** block, list the external threats facing the corporation now and in the future from the EFAS Table.

INTERNAL FACTORS (IFAS) EXTERNAL FACTORS (EFAS)	Strengths (S) List 5–10 *internal* strengths here	Weaknesses (W) List 5–10 *internal* weaknesses here
Opportunities (O) List 5–10 *external* opportunities here	**SO Strategies** Generate strategies here that use **strengths** to take **advantage** of **opportunities**	**WO Strategies** Generate strategies here that take **advantage** of **opportunities** by **overcoming weaknesses**
Threats (T) List 5–10 *external* threats here	**ST Strategies** Generate strategies here that use **strengths** to **avoid threats**	**WT Strategies** Generate strategies here that **minimize weaknesses** and **avoid threats**

FIGURE 5.2 TOWS Matrix

Source: Reprinted from *Long Range Planning* 15, no. 2 (1982), Weihrich "The TOWS Matrix—A Tool For Situational Analysis," p. 60. Copyright © 1982 with permission of Elsevier and Hans Weihrich.

3. In the Strengths **(S)** block, list the current and future strengths for the corporation from the IFAS Table.
4. In the Weaknesses**(W)** block, list the current and future weaknesses for the corporation from the IFAS Table.
5. Generate a series of possible strategies for the corporation under consideration based on particular combinations of the four sets of strategic factors:
   - **SO Strategies** are generated by thinking of ways a corporation could choose to use its strengths to take advantage of opportunities.
   - **ST Strategies** consider a corporation's strengths as a way to avoid threats.
   - **WO Strategies** attempt to take advantage of opportunities by overcoming weaknesses.
   - **WT Strategies** are basically defensive and primarily act to minimize weaknesses and avoid threats.

5.4 BUSINESS STRATEGIES

Business strategy focuses on improving the competitive position of a company's or business unit's products or services within the specific industry or market segment that the company or business unit serves. Business strategy can be *competitive* (battling against all competitors for advantage) or *cooperative* (working with one or more competitors to gain advantage against other competitors) or both. Business strategy asks how the company or its units should compete or cooperate in a particular industry.

What Are Competitive Strategies?

Competitive strategy creates a defendable position in an industry so that a firm can outperform competitors. It raises the following questions:

- Should we compete on the basis of low cost (and thus price), or should we differentiate our products or services on some basis other than cost, such as quality or service?
- Should we compete head-to-head with our major competitors for the biggest but most sought-after share of the market, or should we focus on a niche in which we can satisfy a less sought-after but also profitable segment of the market?

Michael Porter proposes two "generic" competitive strategies for outperforming other corporations in a particular industry: lower cost and differentiation.[2] These strategies are called generic because they can be pursued by any type or size of business firm, even by not-for-profit organizations.

- **Lower cost strategy** is the ability of a company or a business unit to design, produce, and market a comparable product more efficiently than its competitors.
- **Differentiation strategy** is the ability to provide unique and superior value to the buyer in terms of product quality, special features, or after-sale service.

Porter further proposes that a firm's competitive advantage in an industry is determined by its *competitive scope*, that is, the breadth of the target market of the company or business unit. Before using one of the two generic competitive strategies (lower cost or differentiation), the firm or unit must choose the range of product varieties it will produce, the distribution channels it will employ, the types of buyers it will serve, the geographic areas in which it will sell, and the array of related industries in which it will also compete. This should reflect an understanding of the firm's unique resources. Simply put, a company or business unit can choose a *broad target* (i.e., aim at the middle of the mass market) or a *narrow target* (i.e., aim at a market niche). Combining these two types of target markets with the two competitive strategies results in the four variations of generic strategies as depicted in **Figure 5.3**. When the lower cost and differentiation strategies have a broad (mass market) target, they are simply called *cost leadership* and *differentiation*. When they are focused on a market niche (narrow target), however, they are called *cost focus* and *differentiation focus*.

Cost leadership is a low-cost competitive strategy that aims at the broad mass market and requires "aggressive construction of efficient-scale facilities, vigorous pursuit of cost reductions from experience, tight cost and overhead control, avoidance of marginal customer accounts, and cost minimization in areas like R&D, service, sales force, advertising, and so on."[3] Because of its lower costs, the cost leader is able to charge a lower price for its products than its competitors and still make a satisfactory profit. Some companies successfully following this strategy are Wal-Mart, McDonald's, Dell, Alamo car rental, Aldi grocery stores, Southwest Airlines, and Timex watches. Having a low-cost position also gives a company or business unit a defense against rivals. Its lower costs allow it to continue to earn profits during times of heavy competition. Its high market share means that it will have high bargaining power relative to its suppliers (because it buys in large quantities). Its low price will also serve as a barrier to entry because few new entrants will be able to match the leader's cost advantage. As a result, cost leaders are likely to earn above-average returns on investment.

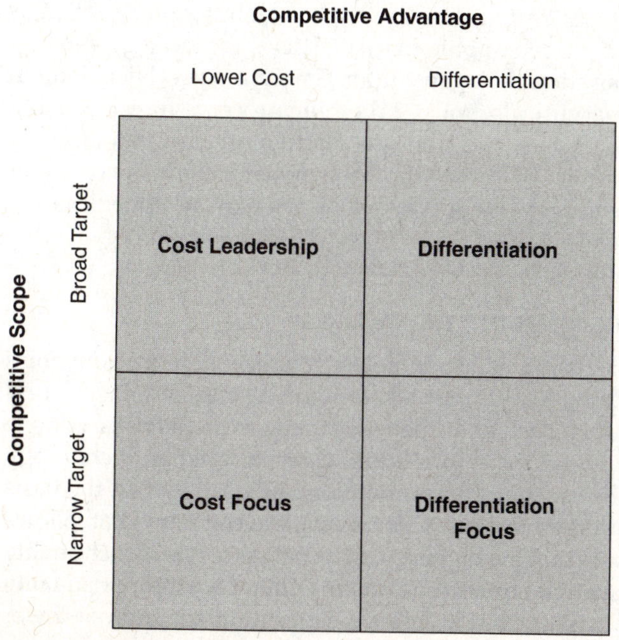

FIGURE 5.3 Porter's Generic Competitive Strategies

Source: Reprinted with permission of The Free Press, a division of Simon & Schuster, from *The Competitive Advantage of Nations* by Michael E. Porter. Copyright © 1990 by Michael E. Porter, p. 39.

Differentiation is aimed at the broad mass market and involves the creation of a product or service that is perceived throughout its industry as unique. The company or business unit may then charge a premium for its product. This specialty can be associated with design or brand image, technology, features, dealer network, or customer service. Differentiation is a viable strategy for earning above-average returns in a specific business because the resulting brand loyalty lowers customers' sensitivity to price. Increased costs can usually be passed on to the buyers. Buyer loyalty also serves as an entry barrier—new firms must develop their own distinctive competence to differentiate their products in some way in order to compete successfully. Examples of companies that have successfully used a differentiation strategy are Walt Disney Productions, Procter & Gamble, Nike, Apple Computer, and BMW automobiles. Research does suggest that a differentiation strategy is more likely to generate higher profits than a low-cost strategy because differentiation creates a better entry barrier. A low-cost strategy is more likely, however, to generate increases in market share.

Cost focus is a lower cost competitive strategy that focuses on a particular buyer group or geographic market and attempts to serve only this niche, to the exclusion of others. In using cost focus, the company or business unit seeks a cost advantage in its target segment. A good example of this strategy is Potlach Corporation, a manufacturer of toilet tissue. Rather than compete directly against Procter & Gamble's Charmin, Potlach makes the house brands for Albertson's, Safeway, Jewel, and many other grocery store chains. It matches the quality of the well-known brands, but keeps costs low by eliminating advertising and promotion expenses. As a result, Spokane-based Potlach makes 92 percent of the private label bathroom tissue and one-third of all bathroom tissue sold in western U.S. grocery stores. The cost focus strategy is valued by those who believe that a company or business unit that focuses its efforts is better able to serve its narrow strategic target more *efficiently* than can its competitors. It does, however, require a trade-off between profitability and overall market share.

Differentiation focus is a differentiation strategy that concentrates on a particular buyer group, product line segment, or geographic market. This is the strategy successfully followed by Midamar Corporation, Morgan Motor Car Company, Nickelodeon cable channel, Orphagenix pharmaceuticals, and local ethnic grocery stores. In using differentiation focus, the company or business unit seeks differentiation in a targeted market segment. This strategy is valued by those who believe that a company or a unit that focuses its efforts is better able to serve the special needs of a narrow strategic target more *effectively* than can its competitors.

WHAT RISKS ARE ASSOCIATED WITH COMPETITIVE STRATEGIES?

No specific competitive strategy is guaranteed to achieve success, and some companies that have successfully implemented one of Porter's competitive strategies have found that they could not sustain the strategy. Each of the generic strategies has its risks. For one thing, cost leadership can be imitated by competitors, especially when technology changes. Differentiation can also be imitated by competition, especially when the basis for differentiation becomes less important to buyers. For example, a company that follows a differentiation strategy must ensure that the higher price it charges for its higher quality is not priced too far above the competition or else customers will not see the extra quality as worth the extra cost. Focusers may be able to achieve better differentiation or lower cost in market segments, but they may also lose to broadly targeted competitors when the segment's uniqueness fades or demand disappears.

WHAT ARE THE ISSUES IN COMPETITIVE STRATEGIES?

Porter argues that to be successful, a company or business unit must achieve one of the generic competitive strategies. Otherwise, the company or business unit is *stuck in the middle* of the competitive marketplace with no competitive advantage and is doomed to below-average performance. A classic example of a company that found itself stuck in the middle was Kmart. The company spent a lot of money trying to imitate both Wal-Mart's low-cost strategy and Target's quality differentiation strategy—only to end up in bankruptcy with no clear competitive advantage. Although some studies do support Porter's argument that companies tend to sort themselves into either lower cost or differentiation strategies and that successful companies emphasize only one strategy, other research suggests that some combination of the two competitive strategies may also be successful.

The Toyota and Honda auto companies are often presented as examples of successful firms able to achieve both of these generic competitive strategies. Thanks to advances in technology, a company may be able to design quality into a product or service in such a way that it can achieve both high quality and high market share—thus lowering costs. Although Porter agrees that it is possible for a company or a business unit to achieve low cost and differentiation simultaneously, he continues to argue that this state is often temporary.[4] Porter does admit, however, that many different kinds of potentially profitable competitive strategies exist. Although there is generally room for only one company to successfully pursue the mass-market cost leadership strategy (because it is so dependent on achieving dominant market share), there is room for an almost unlimited number of differentiation and focus strategies (depending on the range of possible desirable features and the number of identifiable market niches).

WHAT IS THE RELATIONSHIP BETWEEN INDUSTRY STRUCTURE AND COMPETITIVE STRATEGY?

Although each of Porter's generic competitive strategies may be used in any industry, in some instances certain strategies are more likely to succeed than others. In a fragmented industry, for example, in which many small and medium-size local companies compete for relatively small shares of the total market, focus strategies will likely predominate. Fragmented industries are typical for products in the early stages of their life cycle and for products that are adapted to local tastes. If few economies are to be gained through size, no large firms will emerge and entry barriers will be low, allowing a stream of new entrants into the industry; Chinese restaurants, veterinary care, used-car sales, ethnic grocery stores, and funeral homes are examples. If a company can overcome the limitations of a fragmented market, however, it can reap the benefits of a cost leadership or differentiation strategy.

As an industry matures, fragmentation is overcome and the industry tends to become a consolidated industry dominated by a few large companies. Although many industries begin by being fragmented, battles for market share and creative attempts to overcome local or niche market boundaries often increase the market share of a few companies. After product standards become established for minimum quality and features, competition shifts to a greater emphasis on cost and service. Slower growth, overcapacity, and knowledgeable buyers combine to put a premium on a firm's ability to achieve cost leadership or differentiation along the dimensions most desired by the market. R&D shifts from product to process improvements. Overall product quality improves and costs are reduced significantly. This is the type of industry in which cost leadership and differentiation tend to be combined to various degrees. A firm can no longer gain high market share simply through low price. The buyers are more sophisticated and demand a certain minimum level of quality for the price paid. The same is true for firms emphasizing high quality. Either the quality must be high enough and valued by the customer enough to justify the higher price or the price must be dropped (through lowering costs) to compete effectively with the lower-priced products. Hewlett-Packard, for example, spent years restructuring its computer business in order to cut Dell's cost advantage from 20 percent to just 10 percent. This consolidation is taking place worldwide in the automobile, airline, and home appliance industries.

HOW DOES HYPERCOMPETITION AFFECT COMPETITIVE STRATEGY?

In his book *Hypercompetition*, D'Aveni proposes that it is becoming increasingly difficult to sustain a competitive advantage for very long. "Market stability is threatened by short product life cycles, short product design cycles, new technologies, frequent entry by unexpected outsiders, repositioning by incumbents, and tactical redefinitions of market boundaries as diverse industries merge."[5] Consequently a company or business unit must constantly work to improve its competitive advantage. It is not enough to be just the lowest cost competitor. Through continuous improvement programs, competitors are usually working to lower their costs as well. Firms must find new ways to not only reduce costs further, but also add value to the product or service being provided.

D'Aveni contends that when industries become hypercompetitive, they tend to go through escalating stages of competition. Firms initially compete on cost and quality until an abundance of high-quality, low-price goods result. This occurred in the U.S. major home appliance industry by 1980. In a second stage of competition, the competitors move into untapped markets. Others usually imitate these moves until the moves become too risky or expensive. This epitomized the major home appliance industry during the 1980s and 1990s as North American and European firms moved first into each other's markets and then into Asia and South America. They were soon followed by Asian firms expanding into Europe and the Americas.

According to D'Aveni, firms then raise entry barriers to limit competitors. Economies of scale, distribution agreements, and strategic alliances now make it all but impossible for a new firm to enter the major home appliance industry. After the established players have entered and consolidated all new markets, the next stage is for the remaining firms to attack and destroy the strongholds of other firms. Maytag's inability to hold onto its North American stronghold led to its acquisition by Whirlpool in 2006. Eventually, according to D'Aveni, the remaining large global competitors work their way to a situation of perfect competition in which no one has any advantage and profits are minimal.

According to D'Aveni, as industries become hypercompetitive, there is no such thing as a sustainable competitive advantage. Successful strategic initiatives in this type of industry typically last only months to a few years. Also, the only way a firm in this kind of dynamic industry can sustain any competitive advantage is through a continuous series of multiple short-term initiatives aimed at replacing a firm's current successful products with the next generation of products before the competitors can do so. Intel and Microsoft take this approach in the hypercompetitive computer industry.

What Are Competitive Tactics?

A **tactic** is a specific operating plan detailing how a strategy is to be implemented in terms of when and where it is to be put into action. By their nature, tactics are narrower in their scope and shorter in their time horizon than are strategies. Tactics may therefore be viewed (like policies) as a link between the formulation and implementation of strategy. Some of the tactics available to implement competitive strategies are those dealing with timing (when) and market location (where).

WHAT ARE TIMING TACTICS?

A **timing tactic** deals with *when* a company implements a strategy. The first company to manufacture and sell a new product or service is called the *first mover* (or pioneer). Some of the advantages of being a first mover are that the company is able to establish a reputation as a leader in the industry, move down the learning curve to assume the cost leader position, and earn temporarily high profits from buyers who value the product or service very highly. Being a first mover does, however, have its disadvantages. These disadvantages are, conversely, advantages enjoyed by late mover firms. *Late movers* are those firms that enter the market only after product demand has been established. They may be able to imitate others' technological advances (and thus keep R&D costs low), minimize risks by waiting until a new market is established, and take advantage of the natural inclination of the first mover to ignore market segments.

WHAT ARE MARKET LOCATION TACTICS?

A **market location tactic** deals with *where* a company implements a strategy. A company or business unit can implement a competitive strategy either offensively or defensively. An *offensive tactic* attempts to take market share from an established competitor. It usually takes place in an established competitor's market location. A *defensive tactic*, in contrast, attempts to keep a competitor from taking away one's market share. It usually takes place within a company's current market position as a defense against possible attack by a rival.[6]

Offensive Tactics. Some of the methods used to attack a competitor's position are:

- **Frontal Assault.** The attacking firm goes head-to-head with its competitor. It matches the competitor in every category from price to promotion to distribution channel. To be successful, the attacker must not only have superior resources, but it must also be willing to persevere. This is what Kimberly-Clark did when it introduced Huggies disposable diapers against P&G's market-leading Pampers. This tactic is generally very expensive and may serve to awaken a sleeping giant, depressing profits for all in the industry.
- **Flanking Maneuver.** Rather than going straight for a competitor's position of strength with a frontal assault, a firm may attack a part of the market where the competitor is weak. Texas Instruments, for example, avoided competing directly with Intel by developing microprocessors for consumer electronics, cell phones, and medical devices instead of computers. To be successful, the flanker must be patient and willing to carefully expand out of the relatively undefended market niche or else face retaliation by an established competitor.

- **Encirclement.** Usually evolving from a frontal assault or flanking maneuver, encirclement occurs as an attacking company or business unit encircles the competitor's position in terms of products or markets or both. The encircler has greater product variety (a complete product line ranging from low to high price) or serves more markets (it dominates every secondary market), or both. Oracle is using this strategy in its battle against market leader SAP for enterprise resource planning (ERP) software by "surrounding" the latter with acquisitions. To be successful, the encircler must have the wide variety of abilities and resources necessary to attack multiple market segments.
- **Bypass Attack.** Rather than directly attacking the established competitor frontally or on its flanks, a company or business unit may choose to change the rules of the game. This tactic attempts to cut the market out from under the established defender by offering a new type of product that makes the competitor's product unnecessary. For example, instead of competing directly against Microsoft's Pocket PC and Palm Pilot for the handheld computer market, Apple introduced the iPod as a personal digital music player. By redefining the market, Apple successfully sidestepped both Intel and Microsoft, leaving them to play "catch-up."
- **Guerrilla Warfare.** Instead of a continual and extensive resource-expensive attack on a competitor, a firm or business unit may choose to "hit and run." Guerrilla warfare involves small, intermittent assaults on a competitor's different market segments. In this way, a new entrant or small firm can make some gains without seriously threatening a large, established competitor and evoking some form of retaliation. To be successful, the firm or unit conducting guerrilla warfare must be patient enough to accept small gains and to avoid pushing the established competitor to the point that it must make a response or else lose face. Microbreweries, which make beer for sale to local customers, use this tactic against national brewers.

Defensive Tactics. According to Porter, defensive tactics aim to lower the probability of attack, divert attacks to less-threatening avenues, or lessen the intensity of an attack. Instead of increasing competitive advantage per se, they make a company's or business unit's competitive advantage more sustainable by causing a challenger to conclude that an attack is unattractive. These tactics deliberately reduce short-term profitability to ensure long-term profitability.[7]

- **Raise Structural Barriers.** Entry barriers act to block a challenger's logical avenues of attack. According to Porter, some of the most important barriers are to (1) offer a full line of products in every profitable market segment to close off any entry points, (2) block channel access by signing exclusive agreements with distributors, (3) raise buyer switching costs by offering low-cost training to users, (4) raise the cost of gaining trial users by keeping prices low on items new users most likely will purchase, (5) increase economies of scale to reduce unit costs, (6) foreclose alternative technologies through patenting or licensing, (7) limit outside access to facilities and personnel, (8) tie up suppliers by obtaining exclusive contracts or purchasing key locations, (9) avoid suppliers that also serve competitors, and (10) encourage the government to raise barriers such as safety and pollution standards or favorable trade policies.
- **Increase Expected Retaliation.** This tactic is an action that increases the perceived threat of retaliation for an attack. For example, management may strongly defend

any erosion of market share by drastically cutting prices or matching a challenger's promotion through a policy of accepting any price-reduction coupons for a competitor's product. This counterattack is especially important in markets that are important to the defending company or business unit. For example, when Clorox challenged Procter & Gamble in the detergent market with Clorox Super Detergent, P&G retaliated by test-marketing its liquid bleach Lemon Fresh Comet in an attempt to scare Clorox into retreating from the detergent market.

- **Lower the Inducement for Attack.** This third tactic reduces a challenger's expectations of future profits in the industry. Like Southwest Airlines, a company can deliberately keep prices low and constantly invest in cost-reducing measures. Keeping prices very low gives a new entrant little profit incentive.

What Are Cooperative Strategies?

Cooperative strategies are those strategies that are used to gain competitive advantage within an industry by working with rather than against other firms. Other than collusion, which is illegal, the primary type of cooperative strategy is the strategic alliance.

A **strategic alliance** is a partnership of two or more corporations or business units formed to achieve strategically significant objectives that are mutually beneficial. Alliances between companies or business units have become a fact of life in modern business. Each of the top 500 global business firms now average 60 major alliances. Some alliances are very short term, only lasting long enough for one partner to establish a beachhead in a new market. Over time, conflicts over objectives and control often develop among the partners. For these and other reasons, around half of all alliances (including international alliances) perform unsatisfactorily. Others are more long lasting and may even be preludes to full mergers between companies.

Companies or business units may form a strategic alliance for a number of reasons, such as to obtain technology or manufacturing capabilities and access to specific markets, to reduce financial or political risk, and to achieve competitive advantage. A study by Cooper and Lybrand found that firms involved in strategic alliances had 11 percent higher revenue and 20 percent higher growth rate than did companies not involved in alliances.[8] It is likely that forming and managing strategic alliances is a capability that is learned over time. Research reveals that the more experience a firm has with strategic alliances, the more likely its alliances will be successful.

Cooperative arrangements between companies and business units fall along a continuum from weak and distant to strong and close (see **Figure 5.4**.). The types of strategic alliances range from mutual service consortia to joint ventures and licensing arrangements to value-chain partnerships.[9]

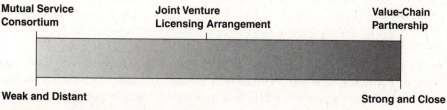

FIGURE 5.4   Continuum of Strategic Alliances

Source: Suggested by R. M. Kanter, "Collaborative Advantage: The Art of Alliances," *Harvard Business Review* (July–August 1994), pp. 96–108.

WHAT IS A MUTUAL SERVICE CONSORTIUM?

A *mutual service consortium* is a partnership of similar companies in similar industries who pool their resources to gain a benefit that is too expensive to develop alone, such as access to advanced technology. For example, IBM established a research alliance with Sony Electronics and Toshiba to build its next generation of computer chips. The result was the "cell" chip, a microprocessor running at 256 gigaflops—around ten times the performance of the fastest chips currently used in desktop computers. Referred to as a "supercomputer on a chip," cell chips were to be used by Sony in its PlayStation 3, by Toshiba in its high-definition televisions, and by IBM in its supercomputers. The mutual service consortium is a fairly weak and distant alliance; there is very little interaction or communication among the partners.

WHAT IS A JOINT VENTURE?

A *joint venture* is a cooperative business activity, formed by two or more separate organizations for strategic purposes, that creates an independent business entity and allocates ownership, operational responsibilities, and financial risks and rewards to each member, while preserving their separate identity and autonomy. Along with licensing arrangements, joint ventures lay at the midpoint of the continuum and are formed to pursue an opportunity that needs a capability from two companies or business units, such as the technology of one and the distribution channels of another.

Joint ventures are the most popular form of strategic alliance. They often occur because the companies involved do not want to or cannot legally merge permanently. Joint ventures provide a way to temporarily combine the different strengths of partners to achieve an outcome of value to all. For example, Procter & Gamble formed a joint venture with Clorox to produce food-storage wraps. P&G brought its cling-film technology and 20 full-time employees to the venture, while Clorox contributed its bags, containers, and wraps business.

Extremely popular in international undertakings because of financial and political-legal constraints, joint ventures are a convenient way for corporations to work together without losing their independence. Disadvantages of joint ventures include loss of control, lower profits, probability of conflicts with partners, and the likely transfer of technological advantage to the partner. Joint ventures are often meant to be temporary, especially by some companies who may view them as a way to rectify a competitive weakness until they can achieve long-term dominance in the partnership. Partially for this reason, joint ventures have a high failure rate. Research does indicate, however, that joint ventures tend to be more successful when both partners have equal ownership in the venture and are mutually dependent on each other for results.

WHAT IS A LICENSING ARRANGEMENT?

A *licensing arrangement* is an agreement in which the licensing firm grants rights to another firm in another country or market to produce or sell a product. The licensee pays compensation to the licensing firm in return for technical expertise. Licensing is an especially useful strategy if the trademark or brand name is well known, but a company does not have sufficient funds to finance entering another country directly. For example, Yum! Brands successfully used franchising and licensing to establish its KFC, Pizza Hut, Taco Bell, Long John Silvers, and A&W restaurants throughout the world. This strategy also becomes important if the country makes entry through investment either difficult or impossible. The danger always exists, however, that the licensee might develop its competence to the point that it becomes a competitor to the licensing firm. Therefore, a company should never license its distinctive competence, even for some short-run advantage.

WHAT IS A VALUE-CHAIN PARTNERSHIP?

The *value-chain partnership* is a strong and close alliance in which one company or unit forms a long-term arrangement with a key supplier or distributor for mutual advantage. Value-chain partnerships are becoming extremely popular as more companies and business units outsource activities that were previously done within the company or business unit. For example, TiVo, the digital video recorder service, entered into partnerships with manufacturers around the world to make its hardware and with cable television operators to provide TiVo hardware and program guide technology to viewers throughout North America.

To improve the quality of parts they purchase, companies in the auto industry have decided to work more closely with fewer suppliers and involve them more in product design decisions. Activities which had been previously done internally by an auto maker are being outsourced to suppliers specializing in those activities. The benefits of such relationships do not just accrue to the purchasing firm. Research suggests that suppliers who engage in long-term relationships are more profitable than suppliers with multiple short-term contracts.

Discussion Questions

1. What industry forces might cause a propitious niche to disappear?
2. Is it possible for a company or business unit to follow a cost leadership strategy and a differentiation strategy simultaneously? Why or why not?
3. Is it possible for a company to have a sustainable competitive advantage when its industry becomes hypercompetitive?
4. What are the advantages and disadvantages of being a first mover in an industry? Give some examples of first mover and late mover firms. Were they successful?
5. Why are most strategic alliances temporary?

Key Terms (listed in order of appearance)

strategy formulation 72
SWOT 73
SFAS Matrix 73
propitious niche 76
TOWS Matrix 77
business strategy 78

competitive strategy 78
cost leadership 79
differentiation 80
cost focus 80
differentiation focus 80

tactic 83
timing tactic 83
market location tactic 83
cooperative strategies 85
strategic alliance 85

Notes

1. T. Hill and R. Westbrook, "SWOT Analysis: It's Time for a Product Recall," *Long Range Planning* (February 1997), pp. 46–52.

2. M. E. Porter, *Competitive Strategy* (New York: The Free Press, 1980), pp. 34–41 as revised in M. E. Porter, *The Competitive Advantage of Nations* (New York: The Free Press, 1990), pp. 37–40.

3. Porter, *Competitive Strategy*, p. 35.

4. R. M. Hodgetts, "A Conversation with Michael E. Porter: A 'Significant Extension' Toward Operational Improvement and Positioning," *Organizational Dynamics* (Summer 1999), pp. 24–33.

5. R. A. D'Aveni, *Hypercompetition* (New York: The Free Press, 1994), pp. xiii–xiv.

6. Summarized from various articles by L. Fahey in *The Strategic Management Reader*, edited by L. Fahey (Englewood Cliffs, N.J.: Prentice Hall, 1989), pp. 178–205.

7. This information on defensive tactics is summarized from M. E. Porter, *Competitive Advantage* (New York: The Free Press, 1985), pp. 482–512.

8. L. Segil, "Strategic Alliances for the 21st Century," *Strategy & Leadership* (September/October 1998), pp. 12–16.

9. R. M. Kanter, "Collaborative Approach: The Art of Alliances," *Harvard Business Review* (July–August 1994), pp. 96–108.

6 | STRATEGY FORMULATION: CORPORATE STRATEGY

What is the best way for a company to grow if its primary business is maturing? A study of 1,850 companies by Zook and Allen revealed two conclusions: First, the most sustained profitable growth occurs when a corporation pushes out of the boundary around its core business into adjacent businesses and second, those corporations that consistently outgrow their rivals do so by developing a formula for expanding those boundaries in a predictable, repeatable manner.[1]

Nike is a classic example of this process. Despite its success in athletic shoes, no one expected Nike to be successful when it diversified in 1995 from shoes into golf apparel, balls, and equipment. Only a few years later, it was acknowledged to be a major player in the new business. According to researchers Zook and Allen, the key to Nike's success was a formula for growth that the company had applied and adapted successfully in a series of entries into sports markets, from jogging to volleyball to tennis to basketball to soccer and most recently, to golf. First, Nike established a leading position in athletic shoes in the target market, that is, golf shoes. Second, Nike launched a clothing line endorsed by the sports' top athletes—in this case Tiger Woods. Third, the company formed new distribution channels and contracts with key suppliers in the new business. Nike's reputation as a strong marketer of new products gave it credibility. Fourth, the company introduced higher-margin equipment into the new market. In the case of golf clubs, it started with irons and then moved to drivers. Once it had captured a significant share in the U.S. market, Nike's final step was global distribution.

Zook and Allen propose that this formula was the reason Nike moved past Reebok in the sporting goods industry. In 1987, Nike's operating profits were only $164 million compared to Reebok's much larger $309 million. Fifteen years later, Nike's profits had grown to $1.1 billion, while Reebok's had declined to $247 million. Reebok was subsequently acquired by Adidas in 2005, while Nike went on to generate operating profits of $2.4 billion in 2008.

6.1   CORPORATE STRATEGY

Corporate strategy deals with three key issues facing the corporation as a whole:

1. The firm's overall orientation toward growth, stability, or retrenchment (*directional strategy*)
2. The industries or markets in which the firm competes through its products and business units (*portfolio strategy*)
3. The manner in which management coordinates activities, transfers resources, and cultivates capabilities among product lines and business units (*parenting strategy*)

Corporate strategy is therefore concerned with the direction of the firm and the management of its product lines and business units. This is true whether the firm is a small, one-product company or a large, multinational corporation. Corporate headquarters must play the role of the banker, in that it must decide how much to fund each of its various products and business units. Even though each product line or business unit has its own competitive or cooperative strategy that it uses to obtain its own competitive advantage in the marketplace, the corporation must act as a "parent" to coordinate these different business strategies so that the corporation as a whole succeeds as a "family." Through a series of coordinating devices, a company transfers skills and capabilities developed in one unit to other units that need such resources. In this way, it attempts to obtain synergies among numerous product lines and business units so that the corporate whole is greater than the sum of its individual business unit parts. All corporations, from the smallest company offering one product in only one industry to the largest conglomerate operating in many industries with many products must, at one time or another, consider one or more of these issues.

To deal with each of the key issues, this chapter is organized into three parts that examine corporate strategy in terms of **directional strategy** (orientation toward growth), **portfolio analysis** (coordination of cash flow among units), and **corporate parenting** (building corporate synergies through resource sharing and development).

6.2   DIRECTIONAL STRATEGY

Just as every product or business unit must follow a business strategy to improve its competitive position, every corporation must decide its orientation toward growth by asking the following three questions:

1. Should we expand, cut back, or continue our operations unchanged?
2. Should we concentrate our activities within our current industry or should we diversify into other industries?
3. If we want to grow and expand, should we do so through internal development or through external acquisitions, mergers, or strategic alliances?

A corporation's directional strategy is composed of three general orientations toward growth (sometimes called grand strategies):

- **Growth strategies** expand the company's activities.
- **Stability strategies** make no change to the company's current activities.
- **Retrenchment strategies** reduce the company's level of activities.

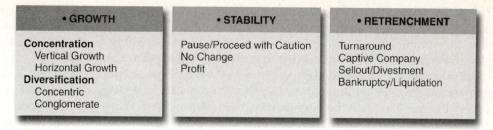

• GROWTH	• STABILITY	• RETRENCHMENT
Concentration Vertical Growth Horizontal Growth **Diversification** Concentric Conglomerate	Pause/Proceed with Caution No Change Profit	Turnaround Captive Company Sellout/Divestment Bankruptcy/Liquidation

FIGURE 6.1   Corporate Directional Strategies

Each of these orientations can be further categorized into more specific strategies as shown in **Figure 6.1**.

What Are Growth Strategies?

By far the most widely pursued corporate strategies of business firms are those designed to achieve growth in sales, assets, profits, or some combination of these. There are two basic corporate growth strategies: concentration within one product line or industry and diversification into other products or industries. These can be achieved either internally by investing in new product development or externally through mergers, acquisitions, or strategic alliances. Although firms growing through acquisitions do not typically perform financially as well as firms that grow through internal means, acquisitions enable firms to achieve growth objectives sooner. For example, Oracle purchased over 56 companies in order to quickly achieve the size needed to compete effectively with SAP and Microsoft.

WHY USE CONCENTRATION STRATEGIES?

If a company's current product lines have real growth potential, concentration of resources on those product lines makes sense as a strategy for growth. There are two basic concentration strategies: vertical and horizontal growth.

Vertical Growth can be achieved by taking over a function previously provided by a supplier or a distributor. This may be done to reduce costs, gain control over a scarce resource, guarantee quality of a key input, or obtain access to new customers. This is a logical strategy for a corporation or business unit with a strong competitive position in a highly attractive industry. Vertical growth results in **vertical integration**, the degree to which a firm operates vertically in multiple locations on an industry's value chain from extracting raw materials to manufacturing to retailing. More specifically, assuming a function previously provided by a supplier is called *backward integration*. Assuming a function previously provided by a distributor is labeled *forward integration*. The firm, in effect, builds on its distinctive competence in an industry to gain greater competitive advantage by expanding along the industry value chain. The amount of vertical integration for a company can range from *full integration*, in which a firm makes 100 percent of key supplies and distributors, to *taper integration*, in which a firm internally produces less than half of its key supplies, to *quasi-integration*, in which a firm makes nothing, but owns part of a key supplier, to *outsourcing*, in which a firm uses long-term contracts with other firms to provide key supplies and distribution.[2]

Although backward integration is usually more profitable than forward integration (because of typical low margins in retailing), it can reduce a corporation's strategic flexibility. By creating an encumbrance of expensive assets that might be hard to sell, it can thus create for the corporation an exit barrier to leaving that particular industry.

Transaction cost economics proposes that vertical integration is more efficient than contracting for goods and services in the marketplace when the transaction costs of buying goods on the open market become too great. When highly vertically integrated firms become excessively large and bureaucratic, however, the costs of managing the internal transactions may become greater than simply purchasing the needed goods externally—thus justifying outsourcing over vertical integration.

Horizontal Growth can be achieved by expanding the firm's products into other geographic locations and by increasing the range of products and services offered to current markets. Horizontal growth results in **horizontal integration**, the degree to which a firm operates in multiple locations at the same point in the industry's value chain. A company can acquire market share, production facilities, distribution outlets, or specialized technology through internal development or externally through acquisitions or joint ventures with another firm in the same industry. For example, Delta Airlines acquired Northwest Airlines in 2008 to obtain access to Northwest's Asian markets and those American markets that Delta was not then serving.

A popular method of horizontal growth is to expand internationally into other countries. Research indicates that going international is positively associated with firm profitability. A corporation can select from several strategic options the most appropriate method for it to use in entering a foreign market or establishing manufacturing facilities in another country. The options vary from simple exporting to acquisitions to management contracts. Some of the more popular options for international entry are:

- *Exporting.* Shipping goods produced in the company's home country to other countries for marketing is a good way to minimize risk and experiment with a specific product. The company could choose to handle all critical functions itself, or it could contract these functions to an export management company.
- *Licensing.* The licensing firm grants rights to another firm in the host country to produce and/or sell a product. The licensee pays compensation to the licensing firm in return for technical expertise. This is an especially useful strategy if the trademark or brand name is well known, but the company does not have sufficient funds to finance its entering the country directly. Anheuser-Busch uses this strategy to produce and market Budweiser beer in the United Kingdom, Japan, Israel, Australia, Korea, and the Philippines.
- *Franchising.* A franchiser grants rights to another company to open a retail store using the franchiser's name and operating system. In exchange, the franchisee pays the franchiser a percentage of its sales as a royalty. Franchising provides an opportunity for firms, such as Yum! Brands, to establish a presence in countries where the population or per capita spending is not sufficient for a major expansion effort.
- *Joint Ventures.* The most popular entry strategy, joint ventures are used to combine the resources and expertise needed to develop new products or technologies. It also enables a firm to enter a country that restricts foreign ownership. The corporation can enter another country with fewer assets at stake and thus lower risk.

- *Acquisitions*. A relatively quick way to move into another country is to purchase another firm already operating in that area. Synergistic benefits can result if the company acquires a firm with strong complementary product lines and a good distribution network. For example, Belgium's InBev purchased Anheuser-Busch in 2008 for $52 billion to obtain a solid position in the profitable North American beer market. In some countries, however, acquisitions can be difficult to arrange because of a lack of available information about potential candidates or government restrictions on ownership by foreigners.
- *Green-Field Development*. If a company doesn't want to purchase another company's problems along with its assets, it may choose to build its own manufacturing plant and distribution system. This is usually a far more complicated and expensive operation than acquisition, but it allows a company more freedom in designing the plant, choosing suppliers, and hiring a workforce. For example, BMW built an auto factory in Spartanburg, South Carolina, and then hired a young workforce with no experience in the industry.
- *Production Sharing (Outsourcing)*. When labor costs are high at home, the corporation can combine the higher labor skills and technology available in the developed countries with the lower-cost labor available in developing countries. For example, hiring tech services employees in India allowed IBM to eliminate 20,000 jobs in high-cost locations in the United States, Europe, and Japan.
- *Turnkey Operations*. These are typically contracts for the construction of operating facilities in exchange for a fee. The facilities are transferred to the host country or firm when they are complete. The customer is usually a government agency of country that has decreed that a particular product must be produced locally and under its control. For example, Fiat built an auto plant in Russia to produce an older model of Fiat under the Lada brand.
- *Management Contracts*. Once a turnkey operation is completed, the corporation assists local management in the operation for a specified fee and period of time. Management contracts are common when a host government expropriates part or all of a foreign-owned company's holdings in its country. The contracts allow the firm to continue to earn some income from its investment and keep the operations going until local management is trained.
- *BOT (build, operate, transfer) Concept*. Instead of turning the facility (usually a power plant or toll road) over to the host country when completed (as is with the turnkey operation), the company operates the facility for a fixed period of time during which it earns back its investment, plus a profit. It then turns the facility over to the government at little or no cost to the host country.

WHY USE DIVERSIFICATION STRATEGIES?

If a company's current product lines do not have much growth potential, management may choose to diversify. There are two basic diversification strategies: concentric and conglomerate.

Concentric (Related) Diversification. Growth through concentric diversification is expansion into a related industry. This may be an appropriate corporate strategy when a firm has a strong competitive position but industry attractiveness is low. By focusing on the characteristics that have given the company its distinctive competence, the company uses those very strengths as its means of diversification. The firm attempts to secure a strategic fit in a new industry where it can apply its product knowledge, manufacturing capabilities, and the marketing skills it used so effectively in the original industry. The corporation's products are related in some way; they possess some common thread. The search is for **synergy**, the concept that two businesses will generate more profits together than they could separately. The point of commonality may be similar technology, customer usage, distribution, managerial skills, or product similarity. For example, Quebec-based Bombardier expanded beyond snowmobiles into making light rail equipment and aviation. Defining itself as a transportation company, it entered the aircraft business with its purchases of Canadair and Learjet.

Conglomerate (Unrelated) Diversification.   When management realizes that the current industry is unattractive and that the firm lacks outstanding abilities or skills it could easily transfer to related products or services in other industries, the most likely strategy is conglomerate diversification—diversifying into an industry unrelated to its current one. Rather than maintaining a common thread throughout their organization, managers who adopt this strategy are concerned primarily with financial considerations of cash flow or risk reduction. It is also a good strategy for a firm that is able to transfer its own excellent management system into less well-managed acquired firms. General Electric and Berkshire Hathaway are examples of companies that have used conglomerate diversification to grow successfully.

What Are Stability Strategies?

A corporation may choose stability over growth by continuing its current activities without any significant change in direction. The stability family of corporate strategies can be appropriate for a successful corporation operating in a reasonably predictable environment. Stability strategies can be very useful in the short run but can be dangerous if followed for too long. Some of the more popular of these strategies are the pause/proceed-with-caution, no-change, and profit strategies.

WHY USE A PAUSE/PROCEED-WITH-CAUTION STRATEGY?

A **pause/proceed-with-caution strategy** is, in effect, a time-out—an opportunity to rest before continuing a growth or retrenchment strategy. It is typically a temporary strategy to be used until the environment becomes more hospitable or to enable a company to consolidate its resources after prolonged rapid growth. This was the strategy followed by many companies during the recession of 2008 and 2009 when credit was tight and sales were slim.

WHY USE A NO-CHANGE STRATEGY?

A **no-change strategy** is a decision to do nothing new—a choice to continue current operations and policies for the foreseeable future. Rarely articulated as a definite strategy, a no-change strategy's success depends on a lack of significant change in a corporation's situation. The corporation has probably found a reasonably profitable and stable niche for its products. Unless the industry is undergoing consolidation, the relative comfort that a company in this situation experiences is likely to cause management to follow a no-change strategy in which the future is expected to continue as an extension of the present. Most small-town businesses probably follow this strategy before a Wal-Mart enters their areas.

WHY USE A PROFIT STRATEGY?

A **profit strategy** is a decision to do nothing new in a worsening situation, but instead to act as though the company's problems are only temporary. The profit strategy is an attempt to *artificially support* profits when a company's sales are declining by reducing investment and short-term discretionary expenditures. Rather than announcing the company's poor position to stockholders and the investment community at large, top management may be tempted to follow this seductive strategy. Blaming the company's problems on a hostile environment (such as antibusiness government policies, unethical competitors, finicky customers, or greedy lenders), management defers investments or cuts expenses, such as R&D, maintenance, and advertising, to keep profits at a stable level during this period. The profit strategy is useful to help a company get through a temporary difficulty or when it is making itself more attractive for a potential buyer.

What Are Retrenchment Strategies?

Management may pursue retrenchment strategies when the company has a weak competitive position in some or all of its product lines resulting in poor performance—when sales are down and profits are becoming losses. These strategies generate a great deal of pressure to improve performance. In an attempt to eliminate the weaknesses that are dragging the company down, management may follow one of several retrenchment strategies ranging from turnaround or becoming a captive company to selling out, bankruptcy, or liquidation.

WHY USE A TURNAROUND STRATEGY?

The **turnaround strategy** emphasizes the improvement of operational efficiency and is probably most appropriate when a corporation's problems are pervasive but not yet critical. Analogous to a diet, the two basic phases of a turnaround strategy include contraction and consolidation.

Contraction is the initial effort to quickly "stop the bleeding" with a general, across-the-board cutback in size and costs. For example, when Howard Stringer was selected to be CEO of Sony Corporation, he immediately implemented the first stage of a turnaround plan by eliminating 10,000 jobs, closing 11 of 65 plants, and divesting many unprofitable electronics businesses. The second phase, *consolidation*, is the implementation of a program to stabilize the now leaner corporation. To streamline the company, management develops plans to reduce unnecessary overhead and justify the costs of functional activities. This is a crucial time for the organization. If the consolidation phase is not conducted in a positive manner, many of the company's best people will leave. If, however, all employees are encouraged to get involved in productivity improvements, the firm is likely to emerge from this strategic retrenchment period as a much stronger and better organized company.

WHY USE A CAPTIVE COMPANY STRATEGY?

A **captive company strategy** is becoming another company's sole supplier or distributor in exchange for a long-term commitment from that company. The firm, in effect, gives up independence in exchange for security. A company with a weak competitive position may offer to be a captive company to one of its larger customers in order to guarantee the company's continued existence with a long-term contract. In this way, the corporation may be able to reduce the scope of some of its functional activities, such as marketing, thus reducing costs significantly. For example, in order to become the sole supplier of an auto part to General Motors, Simpson Industries of Birmingham, Michigan, agreed to have its engine parts facilities and books inspected and its employees interviewed by a special team from GM. In return, nearly 80 percent of the company's production was sold to GM through long-term contracts.

WHY USE A SELL-OUT OR DIVESTMENT STRATEGY?

If a corporation with a weak competitive position in this industry is unable either to pull itself up by its bootstraps or to find a customer to which it can become a captive company, it may have no choice but to sell out and leave the industry completely. In a **sell-out strategy**, the entire company is sold. This makes sense if management can still obtain a good price for its shareholders by selling the entire company to another firm.

If the corporation has multiple business lines, it may choose **divestment**, that is, the selling of a business unit. This was the strategy Ford used when it sold its struggling Jaguar and Land Rover units to Tata Motors in 2008 for $2 billion.

WHY USE A BANKRUPTCY OR LIQUIDATION STRATEGY?

When a company finds itself in the worst possible situation with a poor competitive position in an industry with few prospects, management has only a limited number of alternatives, all of them distasteful. Because no one is interested in buying a weak company in an unattractive industry, the firm must pursue a bankruptcy or liquidation strategy. **Bankruptcy** involves giving up management of the firm to the courts in return for some settlement of the corporation's obligations. Faced with a recessionary economy and falling market demand for casual dining, restaurants like Bennigan's Grill & Tavern and Steak & Ale, that once thrived by offering mid-priced menus with potato skins and thick hamburgers, filed for bankruptcy in July 2008.

In contrast to bankruptcy, which seeks to perpetuate the corporation, **liquidation** is piecemeal sale of all of the firm's assets. Because the industry is unattractive and the company is too weak to be sold as a going concern, management may choose to convert as many salable assets as possible to cash, which is then distributed to the stockholders after all obligations are paid. This is what happened in 2009 to the electronics retailer, Circuit City. The benefit of liquidation over bankruptcy is that the board of directors, as a representative of the stockholders, together with top management, makes the decisions instead of turning them over to the court, which may choose to ignore stockholders completely.

6.3 PORTFOLIO ANALYSIS

Chapter 5 dealt with how individual product lines and business units can gain competitive advantage in the marketplace by using competitive and cooperative strategies. Companies with multiple product lines or business units must also ask themselves how these various products and business units should be managed to boost overall corporate performance:

- How much of our time and money should we spend on our best products and business units to ensure that they continue to be successful?
- How much of our time and money should we spend developing new costly products, most of which will never be successful?

One of the most popular aids to developing corporate strategy in a multibusiness corporation is portfolio analysis. Although its popularity has dropped since the 1970s and 1980s when over half of the largest business corporations used portfolio analysis, it is still used by many firms in corporate strategy formulation. In **portfolio analysis**, top management views its product lines and business units as a series of investments from which it expects a profitable return. Corporate headquarters, in effect, acts as an internal banker. The product lines/business units form a portfolio of investments that top management must constantly juggle to ensure the best return on the corporation's invested money. A study of the performance of the 200 largest U.S. corporations by McKinsey & Company found that those companies that actively managed their business portfolios through acquisitions and divestitures created substantially more shareholder value than those companies that passively held their businesses.[3] Two of the most popular portfolio approaches are the BCG Growth-Share Matrix and the GE Business Screen.

Why Use the Boston Consulting Group Growth-Share Matrix?

The **Boston Consulting Group (BCG) Growth-Share Matrix** as depicted in **Figure 6.2** is the simplest way to portray a corporation's portfolio of investments. Each of the corporation's product lines or business units is plotted on the matrix according to (1) the growth rate of the industry in which it competes, and (2) its relative market share. A unit's relative competitive position is defined as its market share in the industry divided by that of the largest other competitor. By this calculation, a relative market share above 1.0 belongs to the market leader. The business growth rate is the percentage of market growth, that is, the percentage by which sales of a particular business unit classification of products have increased. The matrix assumes that, other things being equal, a growing market is an attractive one.

The line separating areas of high and low relative competitive position is set at 1.5 times. A product line or business unit must have relative strengths of this magnitude to ensure that it will have the dominant position needed to be a "star" or "cash cow." On the other hand, a product line or unit in a low growth industry having a relative competitive position less than 1.0 has "dog" status. Each product or unit is represented in Figure 6.2 by a circle, the area which represents the relative significance of each business unit or product line to the corporation in terms of assets used or sales generated.

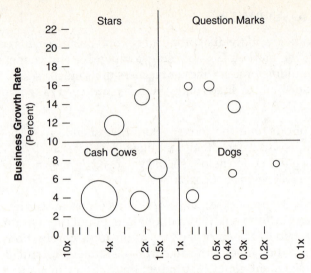

FIGURE 6.2 BCG Growth-Share Matrix

Source: Reprinted from *Long Range Planning*, February 1977,
B. Hedley, "Strategy and the Business Portfolio," p. 12.
Copyright © 1977, with kind permission from Elsevier Science
Ltd.,The Boulevard, Langford Lane, Kidlington 0X5 1GB, U.K.

The growth-share matrix has a lot in common with the product life cycle. As a product moves through its life cycle, it is categorized into one of four types for the purpose of funding decisions:

- *Question marks* are new products with the potential for success but that need a lot of cash for development. If one of these products is to gain enough market share to become a market leader and thus a star, money must be taken from more mature products and spent on a question mark.
- *Stars* are market leaders typically at the peak of their product life cycle and are usually able to generate enough cash to maintain their high share of the market. When their market growth rate slows, stars become cash cow products.
- *Cash cows* typically bring in far more money than is needed to maintain their market share. As these products move along the decline stage of their life cycle, they are "milked" for cash that will be invested in new question mark products. Question mark products that fail to obtain a dominant market share (and thus become a star) by the time the industry growth rate inevitably slows become "dogs."
- *Dogs* are those products with low market share that do not have the potential (because they are in an unattractive industry) to bring in much cash. According to the BCG Growth-Share Matrix, dogs should be either sold off or managed carefully for the small amount of cash they can generate.

Underlying the BCG Growth-Share Matrix is the concept of the experience curve (discussed in Chapter 4). The key to success is assumed to be market share. Firms with the highest market share tend to have a cost leadership position based on economies of scale, among other things. If a company uses the experience curve to its advantage, it should be able to manufacture and sell new products at a price low enough to garner early market share leadership. When a product becomes a star, it is destined to be very profitable, considering its inevitable future as a cash cow.

After the current positions of a company's product lines or business units have been plotted on a matrix, a projection can be made of their future positions, assuming no change in strategy. Management can then use the present and projected matrixes to identify major strategic issues facing the organization. The goal of any company is to maintain a balanced portfolio so that the firm can be self-sufficient in cash and always work to harvest mature products in declining industries to support new ones in growing industries.

Research into the growth-share matrix generally supports its assumptions and recommendations except for the advice that dogs should be promptly harvested or liquidated. A product with a low share in a declining industry can be very profitable if the product has a niche in which market demand remains stable and predictable. Some firms may also keep a dog because its presence creates an entry barrier for potential competitors. All in all, the BCG Growth-Share Matrix is a popular technique because it is quantifiable and easy to use.

Nevertheless, the growth-share matrix has been criticized because it is too simplistic. For example, growth rate is only one aspect of an industry's attractiveness. Four cells of the growth-share matrix are too few. It put too much emphasis on market share and on being the market leader; this is a problem given that the link between market share and profitability is not necessarily strong.

Why Use the General Electric Business Screen?

General Electric (GE) developed a more complicated matrix with the assistance of the McKinsey & Company consulting firm. As depicted in **Figure 6.3**, the **GE Business Screen** includes nine cells based on (1) industry attractiveness, and (2) business strength and competitive position. The GE Business Screen, in contrast to the BCG Growth-Share Matrix, includes much more data in its two key factors than just business growth rate and comparable market share. For example, at GE, industry attractiveness includes market growth rate, industry profitability, size, and pricing practices, among other possible opportunities and threats. Business strength/competitive position includes market share as well as technological position, profitability, and size, among other possible strengths and weaknesses.

The individual product lines or business units are identified by a letter and are plotted as circles on the GE Business Screen. The area of each circle is in proportion to the size of the industry in terms of sales. The pie slices within the circles depict the market share of each product line or business unit.

To plot product lines or business units on the GE Business Screen, the following four steps are recommended:

Step 1 Select criteria to rate the industry for each product line or business unit. Assess overall industry attractiveness for each product line or business unit on a scale from 1 (very unattractive) to 5 (very attractive).

Step 2 Select the key factors needed for success in each product line or business unit. Assess business strength/competitive position for each product line or business unit on a scale of 1 (very weak) to 5 (very strong).

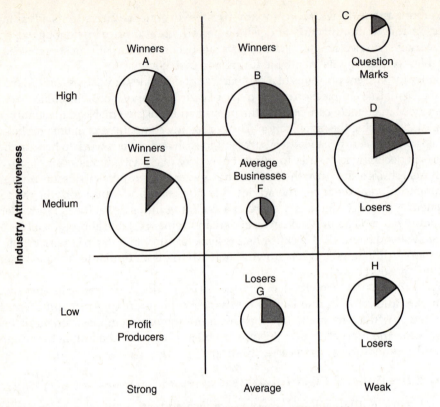

FIGURE 6.3 General Electric's Business Screen

Source: Adapted from *Strategic Management in GE,* Corporate Planning and Development, General Electric Corporation. Reprinted with permission of General Electric Company.

Step 3 Plot each product line's or business unit's current position on a matrix like that depicted in Figure 6.3.

Step 4 Plot the firm's future portfolio, assuming that present corporate and business strategies remain unchanged. If there is a performance gap between projected and desired portfolios, this gap should serve as a stimulus for management to seriously review the corporation's current mission, objectives, strategies, and policies.

Overall, the nine-cell GE Business Screen is an improvement over the BCG Growth-Share Matrix. The GE Business Screen considers many more variables and does not lead to such simplistic conclusions. It recognizes, for example, that the attractiveness of an industry can be assessed in many different ways (other than simply using growth rate), and thus it allows users to select whatever criteria they feel are most appropriate to their situation. Nevertheless, it can get quite complicated and cumbersome. The numerical estimates of industry attractiveness or business strength/competitive position give the appearance of objectivity but are in reality subjective judgments that may vary from one person to another. Another shortcoming of this portfolio matrix is that it cannot effectively depict the positions of new products or business units in developing industries.

How Can Portfolio Analysis be Used with Strategic Alliances?

Just as product lines/business units form a portfolio of investments that top management must constantly juggle to ensure the best return on the corporation's invested money, strategic alliances can also be viewed as a portfolio of investments—investments of money, time, and energy. The way a company manages these intertwined relationships can significantly influence corporate competitiveness. Alliances are thus recognized as an important source of competitive advantage and superior performance.

A study of 25 leading European corporations found four tasks of multialliance management that are necessary for successful alliance portfolio management:

1. *Developing and implementing a portfolio strategy for each business unit and a corporate policy for managing all the alliances of the entire company*. Alliances are primarily determined by business units. The corporate level develops general rules concerning when, how, and with whom to cooperate. The task of alliance policy is to strategically align all of the corporation's alliance activities with corporate strategy and values. Every new alliance is thus checked against corporate policy before it is approved.

2. *Monitoring the alliance portfolio in terms of implementing business unit strategies and corporate strategy and policies*. Each alliance is measured in terms of achievement of objectives (e.g., market share), financial measures (e.g., profits and cash flow), contributed resource quality and quantity, and the overall relationship. The more a firm is diversified, the less the need for motoring at the corporate level.

3. *Coordinating the portfolio to obtain synergies and avoid conflicts among alliances*. Because the interdependencies among alliances within a business unit are usually greater than among different businesses, the need for coordination is greater at the business level than at the corporate level. The need for coordination increases as the number of alliances in one business unit and the company as a whole increases, the average number of partners per alliance increases, and/or the overlap of the alliances increases.

4. *Establishing an alliance management system to support other tasks of multialliance management*. This infrastructure consists of formalized processes, standardized tools, and specialized organizational units. All but two of the 25 companies studied established centers of competence for alliance management. The centers were often part of a department for corporate development or a department of alliance management at the corporate level. In other corporations, specialized positions for alliance management were created at both the corporate and business unit levels or only at the business unit level. Most corporations prefer a system in which the corporate level provides the methods and tools to support alliances centrally, but decentralizes day-to-day alliance management to the business units.[4]

6.4   CORPORATE PARENTING

Campbell, Goold, and Alexander contend that corporate strategists must address two crucial questions:

1. Which businesses should this company own and why?
2. Which organizational structure, management processes, and philosophy will foster superior performance from the company's business units?

Portfolio analysis tends to primarily view matters financially, regarding business units and product lines as separate and independent investments. **Corporate parenting**, in contrast, views the corporation in terms of resources and capabilities that can be used to build business unit value as well as generate synergies across business units. According to Campbell, Goold, and Alexander,

> Multibusiness companies create value by influencing—or parenting—the businesses they own. The best parent companies create more value than any of their rivals would if they owned the same businesses. Those companies have what we call parenting advantage.[5]

Corporate parenting generates corporate strategy by focusing on the core competencies of the parent corporation and the value created from the relationship between the parent and its businesses. If there is a good fit between the parent's skills and resources and the needs and opportunities of the business units, the corporation is likely to create value. If, however, there is not a good fit, the corporation is likely to destroy value. This approach to corporate strategy is useful not only in deciding what new businesses to acquire, but also in choosing how each existing business unit should be best managed. The primary job of corporate headquarters is, therefore, to obtain synergy among the business units by providing needed resources to units, transferring skills and capabilities among the units, and coordinating the activities of shared unit functions to attain economies of scope (as in centralized purchasing).

How Is a Corporate Parenting Strategy Developed?

Campbell, Goold, and Alexander recommend that the search for appropriate corporate strategy involves three analytical steps:

1. *Examine each business unit (or target firm in the case of acquisition) in terms of its strategic factors.* Strategic factors will likely vary from company to company and from one business unit to another. People in the business units probably identified the strategic factors when they were generating business strategies for their units.
2. *Examine each business unit (or target firm) in terms of areas in which performance can be improved.* These are considered to be parenting opportunities. For example, two business units might be able to gain economies of scope by combining their sales forces. In another instance, a unit may have good, but not great, manufacturing and logistics skills. A parent company having world-class expertise in these areas can improve that unit's performance. The corporate parent could also transfer some people from one business unit having the desired skills to another in need of those skills. People at corporate headquarters may, because of their experience in

many industries, spot areas where improvements are possible that even people in the business unit may not have noticed. Unless specific areas are significantly weaker in regard to the competition, people in the business units may not even be aware that these areas could be improved, especially if each business unit only monitors its own particular industry.

3. *Analyze how well the parent corporation fits with the business unit (or target firm).* Corporate headquarters must be aware of its own strengths and weaknesses in terms of resources, skills, and capabilities. To do this, the corporate parent must ask if it has the characteristics that fit the parenting opportunities in each business unit. It must also ask if there is a misfit between the parent's characteristics and the strategic factors of each business unit.

Can a Parenting Strategy also be a Competitive Strategy?

Although competitive strategy was discussed in Chapter 5 in terms of a company or a business unit operating only in one industry, it can also be used *across* business units. A **horizontal strategy** is a corporate parenting strategy that cuts across boundaries of business units to build synergy across them and improve the competitive position of one or more business units. When used to build synergy, it acts like a parenting strategy; when used to improve the competitive position of one or more business units, it can be thought of as a corporate competitive strategy.

Large multibusiness corporations often compete against other large multibusiness firms in a number of markets. These **multipoint competitors** are firms that compete with each other not only in one business unit, but also in a number of business units. At one time or another, a cash-rich competitor may choose to build its own market share in a particular market to the disadvantage of another corporation's business unit. Although each business unit has primary responsibility for its own business strategy, it may sometimes need some help from its corporate parent, especially if the competitor business unit is getting heavy financial support from its corporate parent. In this instance, corporate headquarters develops a horizontal strategy to coordinate the various goals and strategies of related business units.[6]

For example, Procter & Gamble, Kimberly-Clark, Scott Paper, and Johnson and Johnson compete with one another in varying combinations of consumer paper products, from disposable diapers to facial tissue. If (purely hypothetically) Johnson and Johnson had just developed a toilet tissue with which it chose to challenge Procter & Gamble's high-share Charmin brand in a particular district, it might charge a low price for its new brand to build sales quickly. Procter & Gamble might not choose to respond to this attack on its share by cutting prices on Charmin. Because of Charmin's high market share, Procter & Gamble would lose significantly more sales dollars in a price war than Johnson and Johnson would with its initially low-share brand. To retaliate, Procter & Gamble might thus challenge Johnson and Johnson's high-share baby shampoo with its own low-share brand of the same product in a different district. Once Johnson and Johnson had perceived Procter & Gamble's response, it might choose to stop challenging Charmin so that Procter & Gamble would stop challenging Johnson and Johnson's baby shampoo.

Multipoint competition and the resulting use of horizontal strategy may actually slow the development of hypercompetition in an industry. The realization that an attack on a market leader's position could result in a response in another market leads to mutual forbearance in which managers behave more conservatively toward multimarket rivals, and competitive rivalry is reduced. Multipoint competition is likely to become even more prevalent in the future, as corporations become global competitors and expand into more markets through strategic alliances.

Discussion Questions

1. How does horizontal growth differ from vertical growth as a corporate strategy? How does it differ from concentric diversification?
2. What are the trade-offs between an internal and an external growth strategy? Which approach is best as an international entry strategy?
3. Is stability really a strategy or is it just a term for no strategy?
4. Compare and contrast SWOT analysis with portfolio analysis.
5. How is corporate parenting different from portfolio analysis and how is it similar to it? Is it a useful concept in a global industry?

Key Terms (listed in order of appearance)

corporate strategy 90
directional strategy 90
portfolio strategy 90
parenting strategy 90
growth strategies 90
stability strategies 90
retrenchment strategies 90
concentration strategies 91
vertical growth strategy 91
vertical integration 91
transaction cost economics 92
horizontal growth strategy 92

horizontal integration 92
diversification strategies 93
concentric diversification 93
synergy 94
conglomerate diversification 94
pause/proceed-with-caution strategy 94
no-change strategy 94
profit strategy 95
turnaround strategy 95
captive company strategy 96

sellout/divestment strategy 96
bankruptcy 96
liquidation 96
portfolio analysis 97
BCG Growth-Share Matrix 97
GE Business Screen 99
corporate parenting 102
horizontal strategy 103
multipoint competitors 103

Notes

1. C. Zook and J. Allen, "Growth Outside the Core," *Harvard Business Review* (December 2003), pp. 66–73.
2. K. R. Harrigan, *Strategies for Vertical Integration* (Lexington, Mass.: Lexington Books, 1983), pp. 16–21.
3. L. Dranikoff, T. Koller, and A. Schneider, "Divestiture: Strategy's Missing Link," *Harvard Business Review* (May 2002), pp. 74–83.
4. W. H. Hoffmann, "How to Manage a Portfolio of Alliances," *Long Range Planning* (April 2005), pp. 121–143.
5. A. Campbell, M. Goold, and M. Alexander, "Corporate Strategy: The Quest for Parenting Advantage," *Harvard Business Review* (March–April 1995), p. 121.
6. M. E. Porter, *Competitive Advantage* (New York: The Free Press, 1985), pp. 317–382.

7

STRATEGY FORMULATION: FUNCTIONAL STRATEGY AND STRATEGIC CHOICE

For almost 150 years, the Church & Dwight Company has been building market share on a brand name whose products are in 95 percent of all U.S. households. Yet if you asked the average person what products this company makes, few would know. Although Church & Dwight may not be a household name, the company's ubiquitous orange box of Arm & Hammer brand baking soda is common throughout North America. Church & Dwight provides a classic example of a marketing functional strategy called *market development*—finding new uses and/or new markets for an existing product. Shortly after its introduction in 1878, Arm & Hammer baking soda became a fundamental item on the pantry shelf as people found many uses for sodium bicarbonate other than baking, such as cleaning, deodorizing, and tooth brushing. Hearing of the many uses people were finding for its product, the company advertised that its baking soda was good not only for baking, but also for deodorizing refrigerators—simply by leaving an open box in the refrigerator. In a brilliant marketing move, the firm then suggested that consumers buy the product and throw it away—deodorize a kitchen sink by dumping Arm & Hammer baking soda down the drain!

The company did not stop here. It initiated a *product development* strategy by looking for other uses of its sodium bicarbonate in new products. Church & Dwight has achieved consistent growth in sales and earnings through the use of *brand extensions*, putting the Arm & Hammer brand first on baking soda, then on laundry detergents, toothpaste, and deodorants. By the beginning of the twenty-first century, Church & Dwight had become a significant competitor in markets previously dominated only by giants such as Procter & Gamble, Unilever, and Colgate—using only one brand name. Was there a limit to this growth? Was there a point at which these continuous brand extensions would begin to eat away at the integrity of the Arm & Hammer name?

7.1 FUNCTIONAL STRATEGY

Functional strategy is the approach a functional area takes to achieve corporate and business unit objectives and strategies by maximizing resource productivity. It is concerned with developing and nurturing a capability to provide a company or business unit with a competitive advantage. Just as a multidivisional corporation has several business units, each with its own business strategy, each business unit has its own set of departments, each with its own functional strategy. The Church & Dwight example shows how a company's marketing functional strategy took advantage of its well-marketed brand name and distinctive competency in sodium bicarbonate technology to increase corporate sales and profits.

What Marketing Strategies Can be Employed?

Marketing strategy deals with pricing, selling, and distributing a product. Using a **market development strategy**, a company or business unit can (1) capture a larger share of an existing market for current products through market saturation and market penetration or (2) develop new uses and/or markets for current products. Consumer product giants such as P&G, Colgate-Palmolive, and Unilever are experts at using advertising and promotion to implement a market saturation/penetration strategy to gain dominant market share in a product category. As seeming masters of the product life cycle, these companies are able to extend product life almost indefinitely through "new and improved" variations of product and packaging that appeal to most market niches. A company, such as Church & Dwight, follows the second market development strategy by finding new uses for its successful current product, baking soda.

Using the **product development strategy**, a company or unit can (1) develop new products for *existing markets* or (2) develop new products for *new markets*. Church & Dwight has had great success by following the first product development strategy by developing new products to sell to its current customers in its existing markets. Acknowledging the widespread appeal of its Arm & Hammer brand baking soda, the company has generated new uses for its sodium bicarbonate by reformulating it as toothpaste, deodorant, and detergent. Using a successful brand name to market other products is called *brand extension*, and it is a good way to appeal to a company's current customers.[1] Church & Dwight has successfully followed the second product development strategy (new products for new markets) by developing pollution-reduction products (using sodium bicarbonate compounds) for sale to coal-fired electric utility plants—a very different market from grocery stores.

There are numerous other marketing strategies. In advertising and promotion, for example, a company or business unit can choose between "push" or "pull" marketing strategy. Many large food and consumer product companies in North America have followed a **push strategy** by spending a large amount of money on trade promotion in order to gain or hold shelf space in retail outlets. Trade promotion includes discounts, in-store special offers, and advertising allowances designed to "push" products through the distribution system. The Kellogg Company changed its emphasis a few years ago from a push to a **pull strategy**, in which advertising "pulls" the products through the distribution channels. The company now spends more money on consumer advertising designed to build brand awareness so that shoppers will ask for the products.

Other marketing strategies deal with distribution and pricing. Should a firm use distributors to sell its products or should it sell directly to mass merchandisers or through the Internet? When pricing a new product, a company or business unit can follow one of two strategies. For new-product pioneers, *skim pricing* offers the opportunity to "skim the cream" from the top of the demand curve with a high price while the product is novel and competitors are few. *Penetration pricing*, in contrast, attempts to hasten market development and offers the pioneer the opportunity to use the experience curve to gain market share with a low price and then dominate the industry. Depending on corporate and business unit objectives and strategies, either of these choices may be desirable to a particular company or unit. Penetration pricing is, however, more likely than skim pricing to raise a unit's operating profit in the long run.

What Financial Strategies Can be Employed?

Financial strategy examines the financial implications of corporate and business-level strategic options and identifies the best financial course of action. It can also provide competitive advantage through a lower cost of funds and a flexible ability to raise capital to support a business strategy. A firm's financial strategy is influenced by its corporate diversification strategy. Equity financing, for example, is preferred for related diversification, while debt financing is preferred for unrelated diversification.[2]

The trade-off between achieving the desired debt-to-equity ratio and relying on internal long-term financing by way of cash flow is a key issue in financial strategy. Higher debt levels not only deter takeover by other firms (by making the company less attractive), but also lead to improved productivity and cash flows by forcing management to focus on core businesses. Conversely, other firms, such as Apple, have little to no long-term debt and instead keep a large amount of money in cash and short-term investments in order to preserve their flexibility and autonomy.

A popular financial strategy is the leveraged buyout (LBO). In a **leveraged buyout**, a company is acquired in a transaction financed largely by debt, which is usually obtained from a third party such as an insurance company. Ultimately the debt is paid with money generated from the acquired company's operations or by sales of its assets. The acquired company, in effect, pays for its own acquisition. Management of the LBO is then under tremendous pressure to keep the highly leveraged company profitable. Unfortunately, the huge amount of debt on the acquired company's books may actually cause its eventual decline unless it goes public once again. For example, one year after the buyout, the cash flow of eight of the largest LBOs made during 2006–2007 was barely enough to cover interest payments.[3]

The management of dividends to stockholders is an important part of a corporation's financial strategy. Corporations in fast-growing industries, such as computers and computer software, often do not declare dividends. They use the money they might have spent on dividends to finance rapid growth. If the company is successful, its growth in sales and profits is reflected in a higher stock price—eventually resulting in a hefty capital gain when stockholders sell their common stock.

What Research and Development (R&D) Strategies Are Available?

Research and Development (R&D) strategy deals with product and process innovation and improvement. One of the R&D choices is to be either a **technological leader** that pioneers an innovation or a **technological follower** that imitates the products of competitors. Porter suggests that making the decision to become a technological leader or follower can be a way of achieving either overall low cost or differentiation (see **Table 7.1**).

One example of an effective use of the leader R&D functional strategy to achieve a differentiation competitive advantage is Nike, Inc. Nike spends more than most companies in the industry on R&D in order to differentiate its athletic shoes from its competitors in terms of performance. As a result, its products have become the favorite of serious athletes.

A new approach to R&D is *open innovation*, in which a firm uses alliances and connections with corporate, government, academic labs, and even consumers to develop new products and processes. P&G pioneered that practice when it decided that half of the company's ideas must come from outside, up from 10 percent in 2000. The use of "technology scouts" to search beyond the company for promising innovations enabled the company to achieve its 50 percent objective by 2007.[4]

What Operations Strategies May be Used?

Operations strategy determines how and where a product or service is to be manufactured, the level of vertical integration, the deployment of physical resources, and relationships with suppliers. A firm's manufacturing strategy is often affected by a product's life cycle. This concept describes the increase in production volume ranging from lot sizes as low as that in a *job shop* (one-of-a-kind production using skilled labor) through *connected line batch flow* (components are standardized; each machine functions like a job shop but is positioned in the same order as the parts are

Table 7.1 R&D Strategy and Competitive Advantage

	Technological Leader	Technological Follower
Cost Advantage	Pioneer the lowest-cost product design. Be the first firm down the learning curve. Create low-cost ways of performing value activities.	Lower the cost of the product or value activities by learning from the leader's experience. Avoid R&D costs through imitation.
Differentiation	Pioneer a unique product that increases buyer value. Innovate in other activities to increase buyer value.	Adapt the product or delivery system more closely to buyer needs by learning from the leader's experience.

Source: Reprinted with the permission of The Free Press, a division of Simon & Schuster, from *Competitive Advantage: Creating and Sustaining Superior Performance* by Michael E. Porter. Copyright © 1985 by Michael E. Porter.

processed) to *flexible manufacturing systems* (parts are grouped into manufacturing families to produce a wide variety of mass-produced items) in which lot sizes as high as 10,000 or more per year are produced) and *dedicated transfer lines* (highly automated assembly lines making one mass-produced product using little human labor). According to this concept, the product becomes standardized into a commodity over time in conjunction with increasing demand, as flexibility gives way to efficiency.

Increasing competitive intensity in many industries has forced companies to switch from traditional mass production using dedicated transfer lines to a **continuous improvement** production strategy, in which cross-functional work teams strive constantly to improve production processes. Because continuous improvement enables firms to use the same lower-cost competitive strategy as mass-production firms but at a significantly higher level of quality, it is rapidly replacing mass production as an operations strategy. To further this strategy, firms in the automobile industry use *modular manufacturing* in which preassembled subassemblies are delivered as they are needed (*just-in-time*) to a company's assembly-line workers, who quickly piece the modules together into a finished product.

Mass customization is being increasingly used as an operations strategy. In contrast to continuous improvement, mass customization requires flexibility and quick responsiveness. Appropriate for an ever-changing environment, mass customization requires that people, processes, units, and technology reconfigure themselves to give customers exactly what they want, and when they want it; the result is low-cost, high-quality, customized goods and services.

To be successful, an operations strategy needs to be integrated with well-conceived purchasing and logistics strategies. **Purchasing strategy** deals with obtaining the raw materials, parts, and supplies needed to perform the operations function. The basic purchasing choices are multiple, sole, and parallel sourcing.[5] **Logistics strategy** deals with the flow of products into and out of the manufacturing process.

What Human Resource Strategies Can be Used?

Human resource management (HRM) strategy attempts to find the best fit between people and the organization. It addresses the issue of whether a company or business unit should hire a large number of low-skilled employees who receive low pay, perform repetitive jobs, and most likely quit after a short time (e.g., the McDonald's restaurant strategy) or hire skilled employees who receive relatively high pay and are cross-trained to participate in self-managed work teams (appropriate in continuous improvement). To reduce costs and obtain increased flexibility, many companies are not only using increasing numbers of part-time and temporary employees, but also experimenting with leasing employees from employee-leasing companies. Companies are also finding that hiring a more diverse workforce (in terms of race, age, and nationality) can provide a competitive advantage. Avon Company, for example, was able to turn around its unprofitable inner-city markets by putting African Americans and Hispanic managers in charge of marketing to these markets.

Companies following a differentiation through high-quality competitive strategy use input from subordinates and peers in performance appraisals to a greater extent than do firms following other business strategies.[6] Complete **360-degree appraisals**, in which input is gathered from multiple sources, are now being used by more than 10 percent of U.S. corporations and has become one of the most popular tools in developing new managers.

The higher the complexity of work, the more suited it is for teams. An increasing number of corporations are using autonomous work teams. The use of work teams leads to increased quality and productivity as well as to higher employee satisfaction and commitment.

What Information Technology Strategies Are Available?

Corporations are increasingly adopting **information technology strategies** to provide business units with competitive advantage. When Federal Express first provided its customers with PowerShip computer software to store addresses, print shipping labels, and track package location, its sales jumped significantly. UPS soon followed with its own MaxiShips software. Viewing its information system as a distinctive competency, Federal Express continued to push for further advantage against UPS by using its Web site to enable customers to track their packages.

Many companies, such as Lockheed Martin, General Electric, and Whirlpool, use information technology to form closer relationships with both their customers and suppliers through sophisticated extranets. For example, General Electric's Trading Process Network reduces processing time by one-third by allowing suppliers to electronically download GE's requests for proposals, view diagrams of parts specifications, and communicate with GE purchasing managers.

7.2   THE SOURCING DECISION: LOCATION OF FUNCTIONS AND CAPABILITIES

For a functional strategy to have the best chance of success, it should be built on a strong capability residing within that functional area. If a corporation does not have a strong capability in a particular functional area, even if it is still part of a core competency, that functional area could be a candidate for outsourcing.

Outsourcing is purchasing from someone else a product or service that had been previously provided internally. Thus, it is the opposite of vertical integration. Outsourcing is becoming an increasingly important part of strategic decision making and an important way to increase efficiency and often quality. One study found that outsourcing resulted in a 9 percent average reduction in costs and a 15 percent increase in capacity and quality.[7] According to an American Management Association survey of member companies, 94 percent of the firms outsource at least one activity.[8]

Offshoring is the outsourcing of an activity or a function to a wholly owned company or an independent provider in another country. Offshoring is a global phenomenon which has been supported by advances in information and communication technologies; the development of stable, secure, and high-speed data transmission systems; and logistical advances like containerized shipping. According to Bain & Company, 51 percent of large firms in North America, Europe, and Asia outsource offshore.[9]

The key to outsourcing is to purchase from outside only those activities that are not key to the company's distinctive competence. Otherwise, the company may give up the very core technologies or capabilities that made it successful in the first place—thus putting itself on the road to eventual decline. Therefore, in deciding on functional strategy, a strategic manager must (1) identify the company's or business unit's core competencies, (2) ensure that the competencies are continually being strengthened, and (3) manage the competencies in such a way that best preserves the competitive advantage they create. An outsourcing decision depends on the fraction of total value added by the activity under consideration and by the amount of competitive advantage in that activity for the company or business unit. Only when the fraction of total value is small and the competitive advantage in the activity is low, should a company or business unit outsource.

7.3   STRATEGIES TO AVOID

Several strategies, which could be considered corporate, business, or functional, are very dangerous. Managers who have made a poor analysis or lack creativity may be trapped into considering them.

- *Follow the Leader*. Imitating the strategy of a leading competitor might seem a good idea, but it ignores a firm's particular strengths and weaknesses and the possibility that the leader may be wrong.
- *Hit Another Home Run*. If a company is successful because it pioneered an extremely successful product, it has a tendency to search for another super product that will ensure growth and prosperity. Like betting on long shots at the horse races, the probability of finding a second winner is slight.
- *Arms Race*. Entering into a spirited battle with another firm for an increase in market share might increase sales revenue, but that increase will probably be more than offset by increases in advertising, promotion, R&D, and manufacturing costs.
- *Do Everything*. When faced with several interesting opportunities, management might tend to leap at all of them. At first, a corporation might have enough resources to develop each idea into a project, but money, time, and energy are soon exhausted as each of the many projects demands large infusions of resources.
- *Losing Hand*. A corporation might have invested so much in a particular strategy that top management is unwilling to accept the fact that the strategy is not successful. Believing that it has too much invested to quit, the corporation continues to throw "good money after bad."

7.4   STRATEGIC CHOICE: SELECTION OF THE BEST STRATEGY

After the pros and cons of the potential strategic alternatives have been identified and evaluated, one must be selected for implementation. By now, many feasible alternatives probably will have emerged. How is the best strategy determined?

Perhaps the most important criterion is the ability of the proposed strategy to deal with the specific strategic factors developed earlier in the SWOT analysis. If the alternative doesn't take advantage of environmental opportunities and corporate strengths and lead away from environmental threats and corporate weaknesses, it will probably fail.

Another important consideration in the selection of a strategy is the ability of each alternative to satisfy agreed-on objectives with the least use of resources and with the fewest negative side effects. It is therefore important to develop a tentative implementation plan so that the difficulties that management is likely to face are addressed. This should be done in light of societal trends, the industry, and the company's situation based on the construction of alternative scenarios.

How Are Corporate Scenarios Constructed?

Corporate scenarios are *pro forma* balance sheets and income statements that forecast the effect that each alternative strategy and its various programs will likely have on division and corporate return on investment. Strategists in most large corporations use spreadsheet-based scenarios and various computer simulation models in strategic planning.

Corporate scenarios are simply extensions of the industry scenarios (discussed in Chapter 3 of this book). If, for example, industry scenarios suggest that a strong market demand is likely to emerge for certain products, a series of alternative strategy scenarios can be developed for a specific firm. The alternative of acquiring another company having these products can be compared with the alternative of developing the products internally. Using three sets of estimated sales figures (optimistic, pessimistic, and most likely) for the new products over the next five years, the two alternatives can be evaluated in terms of their effect on future company performance as reflected in its probable future financial statements. Pro forma balance sheets and income statements can be generated with spreadsheet software on a personal computer.

To construct a corporate scenario, follow these steps:

1. *Use the industry scenarios discussed earlier in Chapter 3 and develop a set of assumptions about the task environment. Optimistic, pessimistic,* and *most likely assumptions should* be listed for key economic factors such as the gross domestic product (GDP), consumer price index (CPI), prime interest rate, and for other key external strategic factors such as governmental regulation and industry trends. These underlying assumptions should be listed for each of the alternative scenarios to be developed.

2. *Develop common-size financial statements (discussed in Chapter 11 of this book) for the company's or business unit's previous years.* These common-size financial statements are the basis for the projections of pro forma financial statements. Use the historical common-size percentages to estimate the level of revenues, expenses, and other categories in estimated pro forma statements for future years. For each strategic alternative, develop a set of *optimistic, pessimistic,* and *most likely* assumptions about the impact of key variables on the company's future financial statements. Forecast three sets of sales and cost of goods sold figures for at least five years into the future. Look at historical data and make adjustments based on the environmental assumptions made. Do the same for other figures that can vary significantly. For the rest, assume that they will continue in their historical relationship to sales or some other key determining factor. Plug in expected inventory levels, accounts receivable, accounts payable, R&D expenses, advertising and promotion expenses, capital expenditures, and debt payments (assuming that debt is used to finance the strategy), among others. Consider not only historical trends, but also programs that might be needed to implement each alternative strategy (such as building a new manufacturing facility or expanding the sales force). **Table 7.2** presents a form to use in developing pro forma financial statements using historical averages from common-size financial statements.

Table 7.2 Scenario Box for Use in Generating Financial Pro Forma Statements

Factor	Last Year	Historical Average	Trend Analysis	Projections*									Comments
				20–			20–			20–			
				O	P	ML	O	P	ML	O	P	ML	
GDP													
CPI													
Other													
Sales—units													
Sales—dollars													
COGS													
Advertising and marketing													
Interest expense													
Plant expansion													
Dividends													
Net profits													
EPS													
ROI													
ROE													
Other													

*O = Optimistic; P = Pessimistic; ML = Most Likely.

Source: T. L. Wheelen and J. D. Hunger, "Scenario Box for Use in Generating Financial Pro Forma Statements." Copyright © 1987, 1988, 1989, 1990, 1992, and 2005 by T. L. Wheelen. Copyright © 1993 and 2005 by Wheelen and Hunger Associates. Reprinted by permission.

3. *Construct detailed pro forma financial statements for each strategic alternative.* Using a spreadsheet program, list the actual figures from last year's financial statements in the left column. To the right of this column, list the optimistic figures for year one, year two, year three, year four, and year five. Repeat this same process with the same strategic alternative but now list the pessimistic figures for the next five years. Do the same with the most likely figures. Then develop a similar set of *optimistic* (O), *pessimistic* (P), and *most likely* (ML) pro forma statements for the second strategic alternative. This process generates six different pro forma scenarios reflecting three different situations (O, P, and ML) for two strategic alternatives. Next, calculate financial ratios and common-size income statements, and balance sheets to accompany the pro forma statements. To determine the feasibility of the scenarios, compare the assumptions underlying the scenarios with these financial statements and ratios. For example, if cost of goods sold drops from 70 percent to 50 percent of total sales revenue in the pro forma income statements, this drop should result from a change in the production process or a shift to cheaper raw materials or labor costs, rather than from a failure to keep the cost of goods sold in its usual percentage relationship to sales revenue when the predicted statement was developed.

The result of this detailed scenario construction should be anticipated net profits, cash flow, and net working capital for each of three versions of the two alternatives for five years into the future. Corporate scenarios can quickly become very complicated, especially if three sets of acquisition prices and development costs are calculated. Nevertheless, this sort of detailed "what if" analysis is needed in order to realistically compare the projected outcome of each reasonable alternative strategy and its attendant programs, budgets, and procedures. Regardless of the quantifiable pros and cons of each alternative, the actual decision probably will be influenced by several subjective factors like the ones described in the following sections.

Why Consider Management's Attitude Toward Risk?

The attractiveness of a particular strategic alternative is partially a function of the amount of risk it entails. **Risk** is composed not only of the *probability* that the strategy will be effective, but also of the *amount of assets* the corporation must allocate to that strategy, and the *length of time* the assets will be unavailable for other uses. The greater the assets involved and the longer they are committed, the more likely top management is to demand a high probability of success. Do not expect managers with no ownership position in a company to have much interest in putting his/her job in danger with a risky decision. Managers who own a significant amount of stock in their firms are more likely to engage in risk-taking actions than are managers with no stock.

A new approach to evaluating alternatives under conditions of high environmental uncertainty (and thus high risk) is to use real options theory. According to the **real options** approach, when the future is highly uncertain, it pays to have a broad range of options open. This is in contrast to using *net present value* (NPV) to calculate the value of a project by predicting its payouts, adjusting them for risk, and subtracting the amount invested. By boiling everything down to one scenario, NPV doesn't provide any flexibility in case circumstances change. NPV is also difficult to apply to projects in which the potential payoffs are currently unknown. The real options approach, however, deals with these issues by breaking the investment into stages. Management allocates a small amount of funding to initiate multiple projects, monitors their development, and then cancels the projects that aren't successful and funds those that are doing well.[10] This approach is very similar to the way venture capitalists fund an entrepreneurial venture in stages of funding based on the venture's performance.

What Pressures from Stakeholders affect Decisions?

The attractiveness of a strategic alternative is affected by its perceived compatibility with the key stakeholders in a corporation's task environment. Creditors want to be paid on time. Unions exert pressure for comparable wage and employment security. Governments and interest groups demand social responsibility. Shareholders want dividends. Management must consider all of these pressures in selecting the best alternative.

To assess the importance of stakeholder concerns in a particular decision, strategic managers should ask four questions: (1) How will this decision affect each stakeholder? (2) How much of what each stakeholder wants is it likely to get under this alternative? (3) What is each stakeholder likely to do if it doesn't get what it wants? (4) What is the probability that stakeholders will take action?

With answers to these questions, strategy makers should be better able to choose strategic alternatives that minimize external pressures and maximize stakeholder support. In addition, top management can propose a **political strategy** aimed at influencing key stakeholders. Some of the most commonly used political strategies are constituency building, political action committee (PAC) contributions, advocacy advertising, lobbying, and coalition building.

What Pressures from the Corporate Culture affect Strategic Decisions?

If a strategy is incompatible with the corporate culture, it probably will not succeed. Foot-dragging and even sabotage could result, as employees fight to resist a radical change in corporate philosophy. Precedents tend to restrict the kinds of objectives and strategies that management can seriously consider. The "aura" of the founders of a corporation can linger long past their lifetimes because they have imprinted their values on a corporation's members.

In considering a strategic alternative, strategy makers must assess its compatibility with the corporate culture. If the fit is questionable, management must decide whether it should (1) take a chance on ignoring the culture, (2) manage around the culture and change the implementation plan, (3) try to change the culture to fit the strategy, or (4) change the strategy to fit the culture. Further, a decision to proceed with a particular strategy without a commitment to change the culture or manage around the culture (endeavors that are tricky and time consuming) is dangerous. Nevertheless, restricting a corporation to only those strategies that are completely compatible with its culture might eliminate the most profitable alternatives from consideration. (See Chapter 9 for more information on managing corporate culture.)

How do the Needs and Desires of Key Managers affect Decisions?

Even the most attractive alternative might not be selected if it is contrary to the needs and desires of important managers. People's egos may be tied to a particular proposal to the extent that they strongly lobby against all other alternatives. Key executives in operating divisions, for example, might be able to influence other people in top management to favor a particular alternative and ignore objections to it. For example, a study by McKinsey & Company found that 36 percent of responding managers admitted hiding, restricting, or misrepresenting information when submitting capital-investment proposals.[11]

People tend to maintain the status quo, which means that decision makers continue with existing goals and plans beyond the point when an objective observer would recommend a change in course. People may ignore negative information about a particular course of action to which they are committed because they want to appear competent and consistent. It may take a crisis or an unlikely event to cause strategic decision makers to seriously consider an alternative they had previously ignored or discounted. For example, it wasn't until the CEO of ConAgra, a multinational food products company, had a heart attack that ConAgra started producing the Healthy Choice line of low-fat, low-cholesterol, low-sodium frozen-food entrées.

What Is the Process of Strategic Choice?

Strategic choice is the evaluation of alternative strategies and the selection of the best alternative. Mounting evidence shows that when an organization faces a dynamic environment, the best strategic decisions are not arrived at through consensus—they actually involve a certain amount of heated disagreement and even conflict. Because unmanaged conflict often carries a high emotional cost, authorities in decision making propose that strategic managers use programmed conflict to raise different opinions, regardless of the personal feelings of the people involved. One approach is to appoint someone as **devil's advocate**, a person or group assigned to identify potential pitfalls and problems with a proposed alternative. Another approach, called **dialectical inquiry**, requires that two proposals using different assumptions be generated for each alternative strategy under consideration. After advocates of each position present and debate the merits of their arguments before key decision makers, either one of the alternatives or a new compromise alternative is selected as the strategy to be implemented.

Regardless of the process used to generate strategic alternatives, each resulting alternative must be rigorously evaluated in terms of its ability to meet four criteria:

1. *Mutual Exclusivity*: Doing any one alternative would preclude doing any other.
2. *Success*: It must be feasible and have a good probability of success.
3. *Completeness*: It must take into account all the strategic factors.
4. *Internal Consistency*: It must make sense on its own as a strategic decision for the entire firm and not contradict key goals, policies, and strategies currently being pursued by the firm or its units.[12]

7.5   DEVELOPMENT OF POLICIES

The selection of the best strategic alternative is not the end of strategy formulation. Management must establish policies that define the ground rules for implementation. Flowing from the selected strategy, policies provide guidance for decision making and actions throughout the organization. At General Electric, for example, Chairman Welch insisted that GE be number one or number two in market share wherever it competed. This policy gave clear guidance to managers throughout the organization.

When crafted correctly, an effective policy accomplishes three things:

- It forces trade-offs between competing resource demands.
- It tests the strategic soundness of a particular action.
- It sets clear boundaries within which employees must operate while granting them freedom to experiment within those constraints.[13]

Policies tend to be rather long lived and can even outlast the particular strategy that created them. Interestingly, these general policies, such as "The customer is always right" (Nordstrom) or "Low prices every day" (Wal-Mart), can become, in time, part of a corporation's culture. Such policies can make the implementation of specific strategies easier, but they can also restrict top management's strategic options in the future. For this reason, a change in policies should quickly follow any change in strategy. Managing policy is one way to manage the corporate culture.

Discussion Questions

1. Are functional strategies interdependent or can they be formulated independently of other functions?

2. Why is penetration pricing more likely than skim pricing to raise a company's or a business unit's operating profit in the long run?

3. How does mass customization support a business unit's competitive strategy?

4. When should a corporation or business unit outsource a function or activity?

5. What is the relationship of policies to strategies?

Key Terms (listed in order of appearance)

functional strategy *106*
marketing strategy *106*
market development
   strategy *106*
product development
   strategy *106*
push strategy *106*
pull strategy *106*
financial strategy *107*
leveraged buyout *107*
R&D strategy *108*

technological leader *108*
technological follower *108*
operations strategy *108*
continuous improvement *109*
mass customization *109*
purchasing strategy *109*
logistics strategy *109*
HRM strategy *109*
360-degree appraisals *109*
information technology
   strategy *110*

outsourcing *110*
offshoring *110*
corporate scenarios *112*
risk *114*
real options *114*
political strategy *115*
strategic choice *116*
devil's advocate *116*
dialectical inquiry *116*

Notes

1. A *line extension*, in contrast, is the introduction of additional items in the same product category under the same brand name, such as new flavors, added ingredients, or package sizes.

2. R. Kochhar and M. A. Hitt, "Linking Corporate Strategy to Capital Structure: Diversification Strategy, Type and Source of Financing," *Strategic Management Journal* (June 1998), pp. 601–610.

3. "Private Investigations," *The Economist* (July 5, 2008), pp. 84–85.

4. J. Greene, J. Carey, M. Arndt, and O. Port, "Reinventing Corporate R&D," *Business Week* (September 22, 2003), pp. 74–76; J. Birkinshaw, S. Crainer, and M. Mol, "From R&D to Connect + Develop at P&G," *Business Strategy Review* (Spring 2007), pp. 66–69; L. Huston and N. Sakkab, "Connect and Develop: Inside Procter & Gamble's New Model for Innovation," *Harvard Business Review* (March 2006), pp. 58–66.

5. See T. L. Wheelen and J. D. Hunger, *Strategic Management and Business Policy*, 12th ed. (Upper Saddle River, N.J.: Prentice Hall, 2010), pp. 244–246, for an explanation of these purchasing strategies.

6. V. Y. Haines III, S. St-Onge, and A. Marcoux, "Performance Management Design and Effectiveness in Quality-Driven Organizations," *Canadian Journal of Administrative Sciences* (June 2004), pp. 146–160.

7. B. Kelley, "Outsourcing Marches On," *Journal of Business Strategy* (July/August 1995), p. 40.

8. J. Greco, "Outsourcing: The New Partnership," *Journal of Business Strategy* (July/August 1997), pp. 48–54.

9. "Outsourcing: Time to Bring It Back Home?" *The Economist* (March 5, 2005), p. 63.

10. J. J. Janney and G. G. Dess, "Can Real-Options Analysis Improve Decision-Making? Promises and Pitfalls," *Academy of Management Executive* (November 2004), pp. 60–75; S. Maklan, S. Knox, and L. Ryals, "Using Real Options to Help Build the Business Case for CRM Investment," *Long Range Planning* (August 2005), pp. 393–410.

11. M. Garbuio, D. Lovallo, and P. Viguerie, "How Companies Spend Their Money: A McKinsey Global Survey," *McKinsey Quarterly Online* (June 2007).

12. S. C. Abraham, "Using Bundles to Find the Best Strategy," *Strategy & Leadership* (July/August/September 1999), pp. 53–55.

13. O. Gadiesh and J. L. Gilbert, "Transforming Corner-Office Strategy into Frontline Action," *Harvard Business Review* (May 2001), pp. 73–79.

8

STRATEGY IMPLEMENTATION: ORGANIZING FOR ACTION

Cisco Systems is one of the most successful computer companies in the world. The company's domination of the networking market allows it to earn high gross margins. It not only makes hardware, such as routers and switches, to direct traffic through a computer network, but also provides operating system software to support Internet-type corporate networks and services to help customers maintain those networks. Following a growth strategy of concentric diversification, the firm has acquired dozens of other networking firms in order to build its portfolio of products and services—all related to networking.

As its portfolio grew, Cisco organized its many activities into the three market-based divisions of telecom operators, large enterprises, and small businesses. This structure soon became inefficient. The divisions wasted effort by each building its own routers, even though the routers were very similar. Having to reduce costs, Cisco centralized the functions of each division so that employees were now organized around functions rather than customer segments. Realizing that a functional structure often leads to standardized products which ignored different market needs, Cisco's management decided to implement a matrix structure. It developed an elaborate system of groups made up of managers from different functions. The primary goal of these cross-functional teams was to develop products for new markets. "Councils" were in charge of markets that had the potential to reach $10 billion in sales. "Boards" were in charge of markets with the potential to reach $1 billion. Both types of teams were supported by "working groups" that dealt with a specific issue for a limited period of time. By 2009, approximately 750 people were part of 50 boards and councils. Since many managers had leading roles in both a function and a board or council, cooperation was enhanced. Virtual meetings enabled the firm to cut its travel budget in half. The matrix structure made it easier for Cisco to develop entire solutions rather than stand-alone products and to respond quickly to new opportunities. Thus far, the only disadvantage of the new structure was the large number of meetings demanded by the system.[1]

8.1   WHAT IS STRATEGY IMPLEMENTATION?

Strategy implementation is the sum total of the activities and choices required for the execution of a strategic plan. It is the process by which strategies and policies are put into action through the development of programs, budgets, and procedures. Although implementation is usually considered after strategy has been formulated, it is a key part of strategic management. Strategy formulation and strategy implementation should thus be considered as two sides of the same coin.

To begin the implementation process, strategy makers must consider three questions:

- *Who* are the people who will carry out the strategic plan?
- *What* must be done?
- *How* are they going to do what is needed?

Management should have addressed these questions and similar ones initially when they analyzed the pros and cons of strategic alternatives, but the questions must be addressed again before management can make appropriate implementation plans. Unless top management can answer these basic questions satisfactorily, even the best-planned strategy is unlikely to provide the desired outcome.

8.2   WHO IMPLEMENTS STRATEGY?

Depending on how the corporation is organized, those who implement strategy will probably be a much more diverse group of people than those who formulate it. In most large, multi-industry corporations, the implementers will be everyone in the organization. Vice presidents of functional areas and directors of divisions or SBUs will work with their subordinates to put together large-scale implementation plans. Plant managers, project managers, and unit heads will put together plans for their specific plants, departments, and units. Therefore, every operational manager down to the first-line supervisor and every employee will be involved in some way in implementing corporate, business, and functional strategies.

Most of the people in the organization who are crucial to successful strategy implementation probably had little, if anything, to do with the development of the corporate and even business strategy. Therefore, they might be entirely ignorant of the vast amount of data and work that went into the formulation process. Unless changes in mission, objectives, strategies, and policies and their importance to the company are communicated clearly to all operational managers, resistance and foot-dragging can result. Managers might hope to convince top management to abandon its new plans and return to its old ways. This is one reason why involving middle managers in the formulation as well as in the implementation of strategy tends to result in better organizational performance.

8.3   WHAT MUST BE DONE?

The managers of divisions and functional areas work with their fellow managers to develop programs, budgets, and procedures for the implementation of strategy. They also work to achieve synergy among the divisions and functional areas in order to establish and maintain a company's distinctive competence.

How Are Programs, Budgets, and Procedures Developed?

WHAT PROGRAMS MUST BE DEVELOPED?

A **program** is a statement of the activities or steps needed to accomplish a single-use plan. The purpose of a program is to make the strategy action-oriented. At Cisco Systems, for example, it involved developing a new corporate structure to support the firm's growth strategy. In contrast, when Xerox Corporation chose a turnaround strategy, management introduced a program called *Lean Six Sigma* to identify and improve a poorly performing process. Xerox first trained its top executives in the program and then launched around 250 individual Six Sigma projects throughout the corporation. The result was $6 million in savings one year later with even more expected in the following year.[2] (Six Sigma is explained later in this chapter.)

WHAT BUDGETS MUST BE DEVELOPED?

A **budget** is a statement of a corporation's programs in dollar terms. After programs are developed, the budget process begins. Planning a budget is the last real check a corporation has on the feasibility of its selected strategy. An ideal strategy might be found to be completely impractical only after specific implementation programs are costed in detail.

WHAT NEW PROCEDURES MUST BE DEVELOPED?

Procedures, sometimes termed *standard operating procedures (SOPs)*, are a system of sequential steps or techniques that describe in detail how a particular task or job is to be done. After program, divisional, and corporate budgets are approved, SOPs must be developed or revised. They typically detail the various activities that must be carried out to complete a corporation's programs. For example, a company following a differentiation competitive strategy manages its sales force more closely than does a firm following a low-cost strategy. Differentiation requires long-term customer relationships created out of close interaction with the sales force.

How Does a Company Achieve Synergy?

One of the goals to be achieved in strategy implementation is synergy between and among functions and business units, which is why corporations commonly reorganize after an acquisition. The acquisition or development of additional product lines is often justified on the basis of achieving some advantages of scale in one or more of a company's functional areas. Synergy can take place in one of six ways: shared know-how, coordinated strategies, shared tangible resources, economies of scale or scope, pooled negotiating power, and new business creation.[3]

Cisco Systems is an example of a company using a matrix structure to obtain all six forms of synergy, but especially the last one, new business creation.

8.4 HOW IS STRATEGY TO BE IMPLEMENTED? ORGANIZING FOR ACTION

Before plans can lead to actual performance, top management must ensure that the corporation is appropriately organized, programs are adequately staffed, and activities are being directed toward the achievement of desired objectives. Organizing activities are discussed in this chapter. (Staffing, directing, and control activities are discussed in Chapters 9 and 10.)

A change in corporate strategy will likely require some sort of change in organizational structure and in the skills needed in particular positions. Strategic managers must therefore closely examine how their company is structured to decide what, if any, changes should be made in the way work is accomplished. For example, in order to implement its corporate growth strategy, the management of Cisco Systems decided to introduce a matrix structure to enable collaboration across markets.

Does Structure Follow Strategy?

In a classic study of large U.S. corporations such as DuPont, General Motors, Sears, and Standard Oil, Alfred Chandler concluded that *structure follows strategy*—that is, changes in corporate strategy lead to changes in organizational structure.[4] He also concluded that organizations follow a pattern of development from one kind of structural arrangement to another as they expand. According to him, these structural changes occur because inefficiencies caused by the old structure have, by being pushed too far, become too obviously detrimental to live with. Chandler therefore proposed the following sequence of what occurs:

1. New strategy is created.
2. New administrative problems emerge.
3. Economic performance declines.
4. New appropriate structure is invented.
5. Profit returns to its previous level.

Chandler found that in their early years, corporations such as DuPont tend to have a centralized functional organizational structure that is well suited to producing and selling a limited range of products. As they add new product lines, purchase their own sources of supply, and create their own distribution networks, they become too complex for highly centralized structures. To remain successful, this type of organization needs to shift to a decentralized structure with several semiautonomous divisions (referred to in Chapter 4 as the divisional structure).

Research generally supports Chandler's proposition that structure follows strategy (as well as the reverse proposition that structure influences strategy). As mentioned earlier, changes in the environment tend to be reflected in changes in a corporation's strategy, thus leading to changes in a corporation's structure. Strategy, structure, and the environment need to be closely aligned; otherwise, organizational performance will likely suffer. For example, a business unit following a differentiation strategy needs more freedom from headquarters to be successful than does another unit following a low-cost strategy.

Although it is agreed that organizational structure must vary with different environmental conditions, which, in turn, affect an organization's strategy, there is no agreement about an optimal organizational design. What was appropriate for DuPont in the 1920s might not be appropriate today. Firms in the same industry do, however, tend to organize themselves in a similar manner. For example, automobile manufacturers tend to emulate DuPont's divisional concept, whereas consumer goods producers tend to emulate the brand management concept (a type of matrix structure) pioneered by Procter & Gamble. The general conclusion seems to be that firms following similar strategies in similar industries tend to adopt similar structures.

What Are the Stages of Corporate Development?

Successful firms tend to follow a pattern of structural development, called **stages of corporate development**, as they grow and expand. Beginning with the simple structure of the entrepreneurial firm (in which everybody does everything), they usually (if they are successful) get larger and organize along functional lines with marketing, production, and finance departments. With continuing success, the company adds new product lines in different industries and organizes itself into interconnected divisions.

WHAT IS STAGE I? SIMPLE STRUCTURE

Stage I is completely centralized in the entrepreneur, who founds the company to promote an idea (product or service). The entrepreneur tends to make all the important decisions personally and is involved in every detail and phase of the organization. The Stage I company has little formal structure, which allows the entrepreneur to directly supervise the activities of every employee. (See Figure 4.3 for an illustration of the simple, functional, and divisional structures.) Planning is usually short range or reactive. The typical managerial functions of planning, organizing, directing, staffing, and controlling are usually performed to a very limited degree, if at all. The greatest strengths of a Stage I corporation are its flexibility and dynamism. The drive of the entrepreneur energizes the organization in its struggle for growth. Its greatest weakness is its extreme reliance on the entrepreneur to decide general strategies as well as detailed procedures. If the entrepreneur falters, the company usually flounders.

Stage I describes Oracle Corporation, the computer software firm, under the management of its co-founder and CEO Lawrence Ellison. Unfortunately Ellison's technical wizardry was not sufficient to manage the company. Often working at home, he lost sight of details outside his technical interests. Although the company's sales were rapidly increasing, its financial controls were so weak that management had to restate an entire year's results to rectify irregularities. After the company recorded its first loss, Ellison hired a set of functional managers to run the company while he retreated to focus on new product development.

WHAT IS STAGE II? FUNCTIONAL STRUCTURE

Stage II is the point when the entrepreneur is replaced by a team of managers who have functional specializations. The transition to this stage requires a substantial managerial style change for the chief officer of the company, especially if he or she was the Stage I entrepreneur. Otherwise, having additional staff members yields no benefits to the organization. Lawrence Ellison's retreat from top management at Oracle Corporation to new product development manager is one way that technically brilliant founders are able to get out of the way of the newly empowered functional managers. Once into Stage II, the corporate strategy favors protectionism through dominance of the industry, often through vertical or horizontal integration. The great strength of a Stage II corporation lies in its concentration and specialization in one industry. Its great weakness is that all of its eggs are in one basket.

By concentrating on one industry while that industry remains attractive, a Stage II company, like Oracle Corporation in computer software, can be very successful. Once a functionally structured firm diversifies into other products in different industries, however, the advantages of the functional structure break down. A crisis can now develop in which people managing diversified product lines need more decision-making freedom than top management is willing to delegate to them. The company needs to move to a different structure.

WHAT IS STAGE III? DIVISIONAL STRUCTURE

Stage III is typified by the corporation's managing diverse product lines in numerous industries; it decentralizes the decision-making authority. These organizations grow by diversifying their product lines and expanding to cover wider geographic areas. They move to a divisional or strategic business unit structure with a central headquarters and decentralized operating divisions; each division or business unit is a functionally organized Stage II company. They may also use a conglomerate structure if top management chooses to keep its collection of Stage II subsidiaries operating autonomously. A crisis can now develop in which the various units act to optimize their own sales and profits without regard to the overall corporation, whose headquarters seems so far away and almost irrelevant.

Headquarters attempts to coordinate the activities of its operating divisions through performance- and results-oriented control and reporting systems, and by stressing corporate planning techniques. The divisions are not tightly controlled but are held responsible for their own performance results. Therefore, to be effective, the company has to have a decentralized decision process. The greatest strength of a Stage III corporation is its almost unlimited resources. Its most significant weakness is that it is usually so large and complex that it tends to become relatively inflexible. General Electric, DuPont, and General Motors are examples of Stage III corporations.

STAGE IV: BEYOND SBUs

Even with its evolution into strategic business units (SBUs) during the 1970s and 1980s, the divisional form is not the last word in organization structure. The use of SBUs may result in a crisis in which the corporation has grown too large and complex to be managed through formal programs and rigid systems and procedures take precedence over problem solving. The matrix and the network are two possible candidates for a fourth stage in corporate development—a stage that not only emphasizes horizontal over vertical connections between people and groups, but also organizes work around temporary projects in which sophisticated information systems support collaborative activities. According to Greiner, it is likely that this stage of development will have its own crisis as well. He predicts that employees in these collaborative organizations will eventually grow emotionally and physically exhausted from the intensity of teamwork and the heavy pressure for innovative solutions.[5]

WHAT ARE THE BLOCKS TO CHANGING STAGES?

Corporations often experience difficulty because they are blocked from moving into the next logical stage of development. Blocks to development may be internal, such as lack of resources, lack of ability, or a refusal of top management to delegate decision making to others, or they may be external, such as economic conditions, labor shortages, and lack of market growth. For example, Chandler noted in his study that the successful founder/CEO in one stage was rarely the person who created the new structure to fit the new strategy, and that, as a result, the transition from one stage to another was often painful. This was true of General Motors Corporation under the management of William Durant, Ford Motor Company under Henry Ford I, Polaroid Corporation under Edwin Land, Apple Computer under Steve Jobs, and Sun Microsystems under Scott McNealy.

Is there an Organizational Life Cycle?

Instead of considering stages of development in terms of structure, the organizational life cycle approach places the primary emphasis on the dominant issue facing the corporation. Organizational structure is only a secondary concern. The **organizational life cycle** describes how organizations grow, develop, and eventually decline. It is the organizational equivalent of the product life cycle in marketing. The stages of the organizational life cycle are Birth (Stage I), Growth (Stage II), Maturity (Stage III), Decline (Stage IV), and Death (Stage V). The impact of these stages on corporate strategy and structure is summarized in **Table 8.1**. Note that the first three stages are similar to the three commonly accepted stages of corporate development. The only significant difference is the addition of Decline and Death stages to complete the cycle. Even though a company's strategy may still be sound, its aging structure, culture, and processes may be such that they prevent the strategy from being executed properly. Its core competencies become *core rigidities* that are no longer able to adapt to changing conditions—thus the company moves into Decline.[6]

Movement from Growth to Maturity to Decline and finally to Death is not, however, inevitable. A Revival phase may occur sometime during the Maturity or Decline stages. Managerial and product innovations can extend the corporation's life cycle. This often occurs during the implementation of a turnaround strategy.

Unless a company is able to resolve the critical issues facing it in the Decline stage, it is likely to move into Stage V: Death, also known as bankruptcy. This is what happened to Montgomery Ward, Kmart, Macy's, Polaroid, Baldwin-United, Eastern

Table 8.1 Organizational Life Cycle

	Stage I	Stage II	Stage III*	Stage IV	Stage V
Dominant Issue	Birth	Growth	Maturity	Decline	Death
Popular Strategies	Concentration in a niche	Horizontal and vertical growth	Concentric and conglomerate diversification	Profit strategy followed by retrenchment	Liquidation or bankruptcy
Likely Structure	Entrepreneur-dominated	Functional management emphasized	Decentralization into profit or investment centers	Structural surgery	Dismemberment of structure

*An organization may enter a Revival phase during either the Maturity or the Decline stage and thus extend the organization's life.

Airlines, Colt's Manufacturing, Orion Pictures, and Wheeling-Pittsburgh Steel, as well as to many other firms. As in the cases of Johns Manville, International Harvester, Macy's, and Kmart—all of whom went bankrupt—a corporation might nevertheless rise like a phoenix from its own ashes and live again under the same or a different name. The company may be reorganized or liquidated, depending on individual circumstances.

Few corporations move through these five stages in sequence. Some corporations, for example, might never move past Stage II. Others might go directly from Stage I to Stage III. Many entrepreneurial ventures jump from Stage I into Stages IV and V. The key is to be able to identify indications that a firm is in the process of changing stages and to make the appropriate strategic and structural adjustments to ensure that corporate performance is maintained or even improved.

What are Advanced Types of Organizational Structures?

The basic structures (simple, functional, and divisional) were discussed earlier in Chapter 4 and summarized under the first three stages of corporate development. A new strategy may require more flexible characteristics than the traditional functional or divisional structure can offer. Today's business organizations are becoming less centralized with a greater use of cross-functional work teams. Although many variations and hybrid structures contain these characteristics, two forms stand out: the matrix structure and the network structure.

WHAT IS A MATRIX STRUCTURE?

Most organizations find that organizing either around functions (in the functional structure) or around products and geography (in the divisional structure) provides an appropriate organizational structure. The matrix structure, in contrast, may be very appropriate when organizations conclude that neither functional nor divisional forms are right for their situations. In the **matrix structure**, functional and product forms are typically combined simultaneously at the same level of the organization (see **Figure 8.1**). Employees have two superiors: a product or project manager and a functional manager. The "home" department—engineering, manufacturing, or sales—is usually functional and is reasonably permanent. People from these functional units are often assigned on a temporary basis to one or more product units or projects. The product units or projects are usually temporary and act like divisions in that they are differentiated on a product-market basis.

The matrix structure is likely to be used in an organization or within an SBU when the following three conditions exist:

- Cross-fertilization of ideas across projects or products is needed.
- Resources are scarce.
- The abilities to process information and to make decisions need improvement.[7]

Although a corporation may not organize itself as a full-blown matrix organization, it is becoming common to use some of the horizontal connections common to a matrix structure. It may use cross-functional work teams (e.g., Cisco Systems) or brand management (e.g., Procter & Gamble).

<u>Matrix Structure</u>

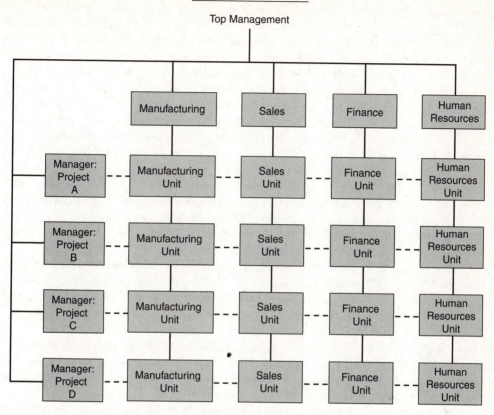

<u>Network Structure</u>

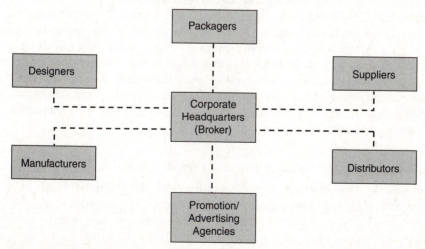

FIGURE 8.1   **Matrix and Network Structures**

WHAT IS A NETWORK STRUCTURE?

A newer and somewhat more radical organizational design, the **network structure** (see Figure 8.1) is an example of what could be termed a nonstructure because it virtually eliminates in-house business functions; most activities are outsourced. Sometimes called a *virtual organization*, the network structure becomes most useful when the firm's environment is unstable and is expected to remain so. Under such conditions, the need for innovation and quick response is usually strong. The company draws up long-term contracts with suppliers and distributors to replace services that it could provide for itself through vertical integration. Electronic markets and sophisticated information systems reduce the transaction costs of the marketplace, thus justifying a buy over a make decision. Rather than being located in a single building or area, an organization's business functions are scattered worldwide. The organization is, in effect, only a shell, with a small headquarters acting as a "broker," electronically connected to some completely owned divisions, partially owned subsidiaries, and other independent companies. In its ultimate form, the network organization is a series of independent firms or business units linked by computers in an information system that designs, produces, and markets a product or service.

Entrepreneurial ventures often start out as network organizations. For example, Randy and Nicole Wilburn of Dorchester, Massachusetts, run real estate, consulting, design, and baby food companies out of their home. Nicole, a stay-at-home mom and graphic designer, farms out design work to freelancers and cooks her own line of organic baby food—for $300, an Indian artist designed the logo for Nicole's "Baby Fresh Organic Baby Foods" and a London-based freelancer wrote promotional materials. Instead of hiring a secretary, Randy hired "virtual assistants" in Jerusalem to transcribe voice mail, update his Web site, and design PowerPoint graphics. Retired brokers in Virginia and Michigan deal with his real-estate paperwork.[8]

Larger companies like Nike, Reebok, and Benetton use the network structure in their operations function by subcontracting (outsourcing) manufacturing to other companies in low-cost locations around the world. The network organization structure gives a company the increased flexibility and adaptability it needs to cope with rapidly changing technology and shifting patterns of international trade and competition. It allows a company to concentrate on its distinctive competencies, while the other functions can be delegated to firms that specialize in those functions. The network structure does, however, have disadvantages. The availability of numerous potential partners can be a source of trouble. Contracting out functions to separate suppliers/distributors may keep the firm from discovering any synergies by combining activities. If a particular firm overspecializes on only a few functions, it runs the risk of choosing the wrong functions and thus becoming noncompetitive.

CELLULAR/MODULAR ORGANIZATION: A NEW TYPE OF STRUCTURE?

The evolution of organizational forms is leading from the matrix and the network to a new form called the **cellular/modular structure**. According to Miles et al., this type of structure "is composed of cells (self-managing teams, autonomous business units, etc.) that can operate alone but that can interact with other cells to produce a more potent and competent business mechanism."[9] It is this combination of independence and interdependence that allows the cellular/modular form to generate and share the knowledge and expertise to facilitate continuous innovation.

The cellular/modular form includes the dispersed entrepreneurship of the divisional structure, customer responsiveness of the matrix, self-organizing knowledge, and asset sharing of the network. Bombardier, for example, broke up the design of its Continental business jet into 12 parts provided by internal divisions and external contractors. The cockpit, center, and forward fuselage were produced in-house, but other major parts were supplied by manufacturers spread worldwide. The cellular/modular structure is used when it is possible to break up a company's products into self-contained modules or cells and where interfaces can be specified such that the cells/modules work when they are joined together.

The impetus for such a new structure is the pressure for a continuous process of innovation in all industries. Each cell has an entrepreneurial responsibility to the larger organization. Beyond knowledge creation and sharing, the cellular/modular form adds value by keeping the firm's total knowledge assets more fully in use than any other type of structure. It is beginning to appear in those firms focused on rapid product and service innovation and those providing unique or state-of-the-art offerings.

Why Is Reengineering Important to Strategy Implementation?

Reengineering is the radical redesign of business processes to achieve major gains in cost, service, or time. It is not a type of structure in itself, but an effective program to implement a turnaround strategy. Reengineering strives to break away from the old rules and procedures that developed and became ingrained in every organization over the years. These may be a combination of policies, rules, and procedures that have never been seriously questioned since they were established years earlier and may range from "Credit decisions are made by the credit department" to "Local inventory is needed for good customer service." These rules of organization and work design were based on assumptions about technology, people, and organizational goals that may no longer be relevant. Rather than attempting to fix existing problems through minor adjustments and fine-tuning existing processes, the key to reengineering is to ask, "If this were a new company, how would we run this place?"

Michael Hammer, who popularized the concept, suggests the following principles for reengineering:

- *Organize around outcomes, not tasks.* Design a person's or a department's job around an objective or outcome instead of a single task or series of tasks.
- *Have those who use the output of the process perform the process.* With computer-based information systems, processes can now be reengineered so that the people who need the result of the process can do it themselves.
- *Subsume information-processing work into the real work that produces the information.* People or departments that produce information can also process it for use instead of just sending raw data to others in the organization to interpret.
- *Treat geographically dispersed resources as though they were centralized.* With modern information systems, companies can provide flexible service locally while keeping the actual resources in a centralized location for coordination purposes.

- *Link parallel activities instead of integrating their results.* Instead of having separate units perform different activities that must eventually come together, have them communicate while they work so that they can do the integrating.
- *Put the decision point where the work is performed and build control into the process.* The people who do the work should make the decisions and be self-controlling.
- *Capture information once and at the source.* Instead of each unit developing its own database and information-processing activities, the information can be put on a network so all can have access to the data.[10]

Studies of the performance of reengineering programs show mixed results. One study of North American financial firms found that the average reengineering project took 15 months, consumed 66 person-months of effort, and delivered cost savings of 24 percent.[11] Other studies report, however, that anywhere from 50 to 70 percent of reengineering programs fail to achieve their objectives.[12]

What Is Six Sigma?

Originally conceived by Motorola as a quality improvement program in the mid-1980s, Six Sigma has become a cost-saving program for all types of manufacturers. Briefly, **Six Sigma** is an analytical method for achieving near-perfect results on a production line. Although the emphasis is on reducing product variance in order to boost quality and efficiency, it is increasingly being applied to accounts receivable, sales, and R&D. In statistics, the Greek letter *sigma* denotes variation in the standard bell-shaped curve. One sigma equals 690,000 defects per 1 million. Most companies are only able to achieve three sigma, or 66,000 errors per million. Six Sigma reduces the defects to only 3.4 per million—thus saving money by preventing waste. The process of Six Sigma encompasses five steps:

1. *Define* a process where results are poorer than average.
2. *Measure* the process to determine exact current performance.
3. *Analyze* the information to pinpoint where things are going wrong.
4. *Improve* the process and eliminate the error.
5. *Control* the process to prevent future defects from occurring.[13]

Savings attributed to Six Sigma programs have ranged from 1.2 to 4.5 percent of annual revenue for a number of *Fortune 500* firms. Firms which have successfully employed Six Sigma are General Electric, Allied Signal, ABB, Pfizer, Target, and Ford Motor Company. Some of these firms went one step further by developing a new program called *Lean Six Sigma*. It incorporates the statistical approach of Six Sigma with the lean manufacturing program originally developed by Toyota. About 35 percent of U.S. companies now have a Six Sigma program in place.[14] Pfizer, for example, initiated 85 Six Sigma programs in 2009 to reduce the cost of delivering medicines. A disadvantage of the Six Sigma program is that training costs in the beginning may outweigh any savings. The expense of compiling and analyzing data, especially in areas where a process cannot be easily standardized, may exceed whatever is saved. In addition, the heavy focus on measurement can inhibit creativity and slow innovation.

How Are Jobs Designed to Implement Strategy?

Organizing a company's activities and people to implement strategy involves more than simply redesigning a corporation's overall structure; it also involves redesigning the way jobs are done. With the increasing emphasis on reengineering, many companies are beginning to rethink their work processes with an eye toward phasing unnecessary people and activities out of the process. Process steps that had traditionally been performed sequentially can be improved by performing them concurrently using cross-functional work teams. Harley-Davidson, for example, reduced total plant employment by 25 percent while reducing by 50 percent the time needed to build a motorcycle. Restructuring through fewer people requires broadening the scope of jobs and encouraging teamwork. The design of jobs and subsequent job performance are therefore increasingly being considered as sources of competitive advantage.

Job design is the rethinking of individual tasks in order to make them more relevant to the company and to the employee(s). In an effort to minimize some of the adverse consequences of task specialization, corporations have turned to new job design techniques: *job enlargement* (combining tasks to give a worker more of the same type of duties to perform), *job rotation* (moving workers through several jobs to increase variety), and *job enrichment* (altering jobs by giving the worker more autonomy and control over activities). Although each of these methods has its adherents, none of them seems to work in all situations.

The *job characteristics model* is an advanced approach to job enrichment based on the belief that tasks can be described in terms of certain objective characteristics and that these characteristics affect employee motivation. For the job to be motivating, (1) the worker needs to feel a sense of responsibility, feel the task to be meaningful, and receive useful feedback on performance, and (2) the job has to satisfy needs that are important to the worker. The model proposes that managers follow five principles for redesigning work:

1. Combine tasks to increase task variety and enable workers to identify with what they are doing.
2. Form natural work units to make a worker more responsible and accountable for the performance of the job.
3. Establish client relationships so the worker will know what performance is required and why.
4. Load the job vertically by giving workers increased authority and responsibility over their activities.
5. Open feedback channels by providing workers information on how they are performing.[15]

8.5 INTERNATIONAL ISSUES IN STRATEGY IMPLEMENTATION

Strategic alliances, such as joint ventures and licensing agreements, between an MNC and a local partner in a host country are becoming an increasingly popular means for an MNC to gain entry into other countries, especially less-developed countries. The key to the successful implementation of these strategies is the selection of the local partner. Each party needs to assess not only the strategic fit of each company's project strategy, but also the fit of each company's respective resources. A successful joint venture may require as many as two years of prior contacts between both parties.

A basic dilemma facing an MNC is how to organize authority centrally so that it operates as a vast interlocking system that achieves synergy and at the same time decentralize authority so that local managers can make the decisions necessary to meet the demands of the local market or host government. To deal with this problem, MNCs tend to structure themselves either along product groups or geographic areas. They may even combine both in a matrix structure, the design chosen by 3M Corporation. One side of 3M's matrix represents the company's product divisions; the other side includes the company's international country and regional subsidiaries.

Simultaneous pressures for decentralization to be locally responsive and centralization to be maximally efficient are causing interesting structural adjustments in most large corporations. This situation is summed up by the phrase, "Think globally, act locally." Companies decentralize those operations closest to the customers: manufacturing and marketing. At the same time, the companies consolidate centrally less visible internal functions, such as R&D, finance, and information systems, to achieve significant economies of scale.

Discussion Questions

1. How should a corporation attempt to achieve synergy among functions and business units?
2. How should an owner-manager prepare a company for its movement from Stage I to Stage II?
3. How can a corporation keep from sliding into the Decline stage of the organizational life cycle?
4. Is reengineering just another management fad or does it offer something of lasting value?
5. How is the cellular/modular organization different from the network structure?

Key Terms (listed in order of appearance)

strategy implementation *120*
program *121*
budget *121*
procedures *121*
stages of corporate
    development *123*

organizational life cycle *125*
matrix structure *126*
network structure *128*
cellular/modular structure *128*

reengineering *129*
Six Sigma *130*
job design *131*

Notes

1. "The World According to Chambers," *Economist* (August 29, 2009), pp. 59–62; J. McGregor, "There Is No More Normal," *Business Week* (March 23 and 30, 2009), pp. 30–34.
2. F. Arner and A. Aston, "How Xerox Got Up to Speed," *Business Week* (May 3, 2004), pp. 103–104.
3. M. Goold and A. Campbell, "Desperately Seeking Synergy," *Harvard Business Review* (September–October 1998), pp. 131–143.
4. A. D. Chandler, *Strategy and Structure* (Cambridge, Mass.: MIT Press, 1962).
5. L. E. Greiner, "Evolution and Revolution as Organizations Grow," *Harvard Business Review* (May–June 1998), pp. 55–67.

6. W. P. Barnett, "The Dynamics of Competitive Intensity," *Administrative Science Quarterly* (March 1997), pp. 128–160; D. Miller, *The Icarus Paradox: How Exceptional Companies Bring About Their Own Downfall* (New York: Harper Business, 1990).

7. L. G. Hrebiniak and W. F. Joyce, *Implementing Strategy* (New York: Macmillan, 1984), pp. 85–86.

8. P. Engardio, "Mom-and-Pop Multinationals," *Business Week* (July 14 and 21, 2008), pp. 77–78.

9. R. E. Miles, C. C. Snow, J. A. Mathews, G. Miles, and H. J. Coleman, Jr., "Organizing in the Knowledge Age: Anticipating the Cellular Form," *Academy of Management Executive* (November 1997), pp. 7–24.

10. M. Hammer, "Reengineering Work: Don't Automate, Obliterate," *Harvard Business Review* (July–August 1990), pp. 104–112.

11. S. Drew, "BPR in Financial Services: Factors for Success," *Long Range Planning* (October 1994), pp. 25–41.

12. K. Grint, "Reengineering History: Social Resonances and Business Process Reengineering," *Organization* (July 1994), pp. 179–201; A. Kleiner, "Revisiting Reengineering," *Strategy + Business* (3rd Quarter 2000), pp. 27–31.

13. M. Arndt, "Quality Isn't Just for Widgets," *Business Week* (July 22, 2002), pp. 72–73.

14. R. O. Crockett, "Six Sigma Still Pays Off at Motorola," *Business Week* (December 4, 2006), p. 50.

15. J. R. Hackman and G. R. Oldham, *Work Redesign* (Reading, Mass.: Addison-Wesley, 1980), pp. 135–141.

9 STRATEGY IMPLEMENTATION: STAFFING AND LEADING

Have you heard of Enterprise Rent-A-Car? Hertz, Avis, and National car rental operations are much more visible at airports. Yet Enterprise owns more cars and operates in more locations than Hertz or Avis. Enterprise began operations in St. Louis in 1957, but didn't locate at an airport until 1995. It is the largest rental car company in North America, but only 230 out of its 7,000 worldwide offices are at airports. In virtually ignoring the highly competitive airport market, Enterprise has chosen a cost leadership competitive strategy by marketing to people in need of a spare car at neighborhood locations. Its offices are within 15 miles of 90 percent of the U.S. population. Instead of locating many cars at a few high-priced locations at airports, Enterprise sets up inexpensive offices throughout metropolitan areas. As a result, cars are rented for 30 percent less than they cost at airports. Why is this competitive strategy so successful for Enterprise even though its locations are now being imitated by Hertz and Avis?

The secret to Enterprise's success is its well-executed strategy implementation. Clearly laid out programs, budgets, and procedures support the company's competitive strategy by making Enterprise stand out in the mind of the consumer. It was ranked on *Business Week's* list of "Customer Service Champs" in 2007, 2008, and 2009. When a new rental office opens, employees spend time developing relationships with the service managers of every auto dealership and body shop in the area. Enterprise employees bring pizza and doughnuts to workers at the auto garages across the country. Enterprise forms agreements with dealers to provide replacements for cars brought in for service. At major accounts, the company actually staffs an office at the dealership and has cars parked outside so customers don't have to go to an Enterprise office to complete paperwork.

One key to implementation at Enterprise is *staffing*—hiring and promoting a certain kind of person. Virtually every Enterprise employee is a college graduate, usually from the bottom half of the class. According to COO Donald Ross, "We hire from the half of the college class that makes the upper half possible. We want athletes, fraternity types—especially fraternity presidents and social directors. People people." These new employees begin as management trainees. Instead of regular raises, their pay is tied to branch office profits.

Another key to implementation at Enterprise is *leading*—specifying clear performance objectives and promoting a team-oriented corporate culture. The company stresses promotion from within and advancement based on performance. Every Enterprise employee, including top executives, starts at the bottom. As a result, a bond of shared experience connects all employees and managers. Enterprise was included in *Business Week's* "50 Best Places to Launch a Career" four years in a row. To reinforce a cohesive culture of camaraderie, senior executives routinely do "grunt work" at branch offices. Even Andy Taylor, the CEO, joins the work. "We were visiting an office in Berkeley and it was mobbed, so I started cleaning cars," says Taylor. "As it was happening, I wondered if it was a good use of my time, but the effect on morale was tremendous."[1]

This example from Enterprise Rent-A-Car illustrates how a strategy must be implemented with carefully considered programs in order to succeed. This chapter discusses strategy implementation in terms of staffing and leading.

9.1 STAFFING

Staffing focuses on the selection and utilization of employees. The implementation of new strategies and policies often calls for new human resource management priorities and a different utilization of personnel. This may mean hiring new people with new skills, firing people with inappropriate or substandard skills, and/or training existing employees to learn new skills.

If growth strategies are to be implemented, new people may need to be hired and trained. Experienced people with the necessary skills need to be promoted to newly created managerial positions. It is also imperative that programs be developed to retain outstanding employees.

If the corporation adopts a retrenchment strategy, however, a large number of people may need to be laid off or fired, and top management and divisional managers need to specify the criteria to be used in making these personnel decisions. Should employees be fired on the basis of low seniority or poor performance? Sometimes corporations find it easier to close an entire division than choose which individuals to fire.

Does Staffing Follow Strategy?

As in the case of structure, staffing requirements are also likely to follow a change in strategy.

HOW DO HIRING AND TRAINING REQUIREMENTS CHANGE?

Training and development is one way to implement a company's corporate or business strategy. A study of 155 U.S. manufacturing firms revealed that those with training programs had 19 percent higher productivity than did those without such a program.[2] Training is especially important for a differentiation strategy emphasizing quality or customer service.

Training is also important when implementing a retrenchment strategy. As suggested earlier, successful downsizing means that the company has to invest in its remaining employees. General Electric's Aircraft Engine Group used training to maintain its share of the market even though it had cut its workforce from 42,000 to 33,000 in the 1990s.

HOW DOES A COMPANY MATCH THE MANAGER TO THE STRATEGY?

The most appropriate type of general manager needed to effectively implement a new corporate or business strategy depends on the strategic direction of the particular firm or business unit. An **executive type** is a classification of managers with particular mixes of skills and experiences. A certain type may be paired with a specific corporate strategy for best results. For example, a corporation following a concentration strategy that emphasizes vertical or horizontal growth would probably want an aggressive new chief executive with a great deal of experience in that particular industry—a *dynamic industry expert*. A diversification strategy, in contrast, might call for someone with an analytical mind who is highly knowledgeable in other industries and can manage diverse product lines—an *analytical portfolio manager*. A corporation choosing to follow a stability strategy would probably want as its CEO a person with a conservative style, a production or engineering background, and experience in controlling budgets, capital expenditures, inventories, and standardization procedures—a *cautious profit planner*. Weak companies in a relatively attractive industry tend to turn to a challenge-oriented executive to save the company—a *turnaround specialist*. If a company cannot be saved, a *professional liquidator* might be called on by a bankruptcy court to close the firm and liquidate its assets. Research supports the conclusion that as a firm's environment changes, it tends to change the type of top executive to implement a new strategy.

This approach is in agreement with Chandler who proposed (discussed in Chapter 8) that the most appropriate CEO of a company changes as a firm moves from one stage of development to another. Because priorities change over an organization's life, successful corporations need to select managers who have skills and characteristics appropriate to the organization's particular stage of development and position in its life cycle.

Nevertheless, one study of 173 firms over a 25-year period revealed that CEOs in these companies tended to have the same functional specialization as the former CEO, especially when the past CEO's strategy was successful. This may be a pattern for successful corporations.[3] In particular, this success explains why so many prosperous companies tend to recruit their top executives from one particular background. At Procter & Gamble, for example, the route to the CEO's position has always been through brand management. In other firms, the route may be through manufacturing, marketing, accounting, or finance, depending on what the corporation has always considered its principal area of expertise.

How Important Are Selection and Management Development?

Selection and development are important not only to ensure that people with the right mix of skills and experiences are hired initially, but also to help them grow on the job and be prepared for future promotions.

EXECUTIVE SUCCESSION: SHOULD A CEO COME FROM INSIDE THE COMPANY?

Executive succession is the process of replacing a key top manager. Given that two-thirds of all major corporations worldwide replace their CEO at least once in a five-year period, it is important that the firm plan for this eventuality. It is especially important for a company that usually promotes from within to prepare its current managers for promotion. Unfortunately, only 42.4 percent of U.S. firms have any sort of succession plan in place.[4] Prosperous firms tend to look outside for CEO candidates only if they have no obvious internal candidates. For example, 85 percent of the CEOs selected to run S&P 500 companies in 2006 were insiders, according to executive search firm Spencer Stuart.[5] Firms in trouble, however, tend to choose outsiders to lead them. Boards realize that the best way to force a change in strategy is to hire a new CEO with no connections to the current strategy. Nevertheless, hiring an outsider to be CEO can be a risky gamble. According to RHR International, 40–60 percent of high-level executives brought in from outside a company failed within two years.[6]

HOW CAN ABILITIES BE IDENTIFIED AND POTENTIAL DEVELOPED?

A company can identify and prepare its people for important positions in several ways. One approach is to establish a sound **performance appraisal system**, which not only evaluates a person's performance, but also identifies promotion potential. Approximately 80 percent of large U.S. firms make some attempt to identify managers' talents and behavioral tendencies so that they could place a manager with a likely fit to a given competitive strategy.

Many large organizations are using **assessment centers**, a method of evaluating a person's suitability for an advanced position. Corporations such as IBM, Sears, and GE have successfully used assessment centers. Because each is specifically tailored to its corporation, these assessment centers are unique. They use special interviews, management games, in-basket exercises, leaderless group discussions, case analyses, decision-making exercises, and oral presentations to assess the potential of employees for specific positions. Promotions into these positions are based on performance levels in the assessment center. Many assessment centers have proved to be highly predictive of subsequent job performance.

Job rotation is also used in many large corporations to ensure that employees are gaining the appropriate mix of experiences to prepare them for future responsibilities. Rotating people among divisions is one way that the corporation can improve the level of organizational learning. For example, companies that pursue related diversification strategies through internal development make greater use of interdivisional transfers of people than do companies that grow through unrelated acquisitions. Following a parenting corporate strategy, the companies that grow internally attempt to transfer important knowledge and skills throughout the corporation in order to achieve synergy.

Does Retrenchment Create Problems?

Downsizing refers to the planned elimination of positions or jobs. Companies commonly use this program to implement retrenchment strategies. Because the financial community is likely to react favorably to announcements of downsizing from a company in difficulty, such a program may provide some short-term benefits, such as supporting the company's stock price.

If not done properly, however, downsizing may result in less rather than more productivity. One study found that a 10 percent reduction in people resulted in only a 1.5 percent reduction in costs; profits increased in only half the firms downsizing; and that the stock price of downsized firms increased over three years, but not as much as firms that did not downsize.[7] The problem with downsizing is that those still employed often don't know how to do the work of those who have left—resulting in a drop in both morale and productivity. In addition, cost-conscious executives tend to defer maintenance, skimp on training, delay new product introductions, and avoid risky new businesses—all of which decrease sales and eventually profits. A situation can thus develop in which retrenchment feeds on itself and acts to further weaken the company instead of strengthening it.

Following are some proposed guidelines for successful downsizing:

- *Eliminate Unnecessary Work Instead of Making Across-the-Board Cuts*. Spend the time to research where money is going and eliminate the task, not the workers, if it doesn't add value to what the firm is producing.
- *Contract Out Work That Others Can Do Cheaper*. For example, Bankers Trust of New York contracted out to a division of Xerox its mail room and printing services and some of its payroll and accounts payable activities.
- *Plan for Long-Run Efficiencies*. Don't simply eliminate all postponable expenses, such as maintenance, R&D, and advertising, in the unjustifiable hope that the environment will become more supportive.
- *Communicate the Reasons for Actions*. Tell employees not only why the company is downsizing, but also what the company is trying to achieve.
- *Invest in the Remaining Employees*. Because most "survivors" in a corporate downsizing probably will be doing different tasks after the change, firms need to draft new job specifications, performance standards, appraisal techniques, compensation packages, and additional training.
- *Develop Value-Added Jobs to Balance Out Job Elimination*.When no other jobs are currently available within the organization to transfer employees, management should consider some other alternatives, such as taking on work that was previously done by suppliers or distributors.

What Are International Issues in Staffing?

Because of cultural differences, managerial style and human resource practices must be tailored in other countries to fit particular situations. Most MNCs attempt to fill managerial positions in their subsidiaries with well-qualified citizens of the host countries. Unilever and IBM adopt this approach. This policy serves to placate nationalistic governments and better attune management practices to the host country's culture. The danger in using primarily host country nationals to staff managerial positions in foreign subsidiaries is the increased likelihood of suboptimization (the local subsidiary ignores the needs of the larger parent corporation). This makes it difficult for an MNC to meet its long-term, worldwide objectives. Communication and coordination across subsidiaries become more difficult. As it becomes harder to coordinate the activities of several international subsidiaries, an MNC will have serious problems operating in a global industry.

Another approach to staffing the managerial positions of MNCs is to use people with an international orientation, regardless of their country of origin or host country assignment. This is a widespread practice among European firms. For example, A.B. Electrolux, a Swedish firm, had a French director in its Singapore factory. This approach to using third-country nationals allows for more opportunities for promotion than does Unilever's policy of hiring local people, but it can result in a greater number of misunderstandings and conflicts with the local employees and with the host country's government.

Companies that do a good job of managing foreign assignments follow three general practices:

- When making international assignments, they focus on transferring knowledge and developing global leadership.
- They make foreign assignments to people whose technical skills are matched or exceeded by their cross-cultural abilities.
- They end foreign assignments with a deliberate repatriation process with career guidance and jobs where the employees can apply what they learned in their assignments.[8]

9.2   LEADING

Implementation also involves **leading**: motivating people to use their abilities and skills most effectively and efficiently to achieve organizational objectives. Without direction, people tend to do their work according to their personal view of what tasks should be done, how, and in what order. They may approach their work as they have in the past or emphasize those tasks that they most enjoy, regardless of the corporation's priorities. Leading may take the form of management leadership, communicated norms of behavior from the corporate culture, or agreements among workers in autonomous work groups. It may also be accomplished more formally through action planning or through programs such as Management by Objectives (MBO) and Total Quality Management (TQM).

How Can a Company Manage Corporate Culture?

Because an organization's culture can exert a powerful influence on the behavior of all employees, it can strongly affect a company's ability to shift its strategic direction. A problem for a strong culture is that a change in mission, objectives, strategies, or policies is not likely to be successful if it is in opposition to the accepted culture of the company. Corporate culture has a strong tendency to resist change because its very reason for existence often rests on preserving stable relationships and patterns of behavior. For example, when Robert Nardelli tried unsuccessfully to replace Home Depot's informal, collegial culture with one of military efficiency, customer satisfaction fell and he was replaced as CEO.

There is no best corporate culture. An optimal culture is one that best supports the mission and strategy of the company of which it is a part. This means that, like structure and staffing, *corporate culture should follow strategy*. Thus, a significant change in strategy should be followed by a modification of the organization's culture (unless, of course, the current culture is in complete agreement with the new strategy). Although corporate culture can be changed, it may often take a long time and require much effort. A key job of management is therefore to evaluate (1) what a particular strategy change will mean to the corporate culture, (2) whether or not a change in culture will be needed, and (3) whether an attempt to change the culture will be worth the likely costs.

HOW CAN ONE ASSESS STRATEGY–CULTURE COMPATIBILITY?

When implementing a new strategy, management should consider the following questions regarding the corporation's *strategy–culture compatibility*—the fit between the new strategy and the existing culture:

1. *Is the planned strategy compatible with the company's current culture?* If *yes*, full steam ahead. Tie organizational changes into the company's culture by identifying how the new strategy will achieve the mission better than does the current strategy. *If not...*
2. *Can the culture be easily modified to make it more compatible with the new strategy?* If *yes*, move forward carefully by introducing a set of culture-changing activities, such as minor structural modifications, training and development activities, and/or hiring new managers who are more compatible with the new strategy. When Procter & Gamble's top management decided to implement a strategy aimed at reducing costs, for example, it changed how some things were done but did not eliminate its brand management system. The culture was able to adapt to these modifications over a couple of years and productivity increased. *If not...*
3. *Is management willing and able to make major organizational changes and accept probable delays and a likely increase in costs?* If *yes*, manage around the culture by establishing a new structural unit to implement the new strategy. At General Motors, for example, top management realized that in order to be more competitive, the company had to make some radical changes. Because the structure, culture, and procedures existing at the time were very inflexible, management decided to establish a completely new division (GM's first new division since 1918), Saturn, to build its new auto. In cooperation with the United Auto Workers, an entirely new labor agreement was developed based on decisions reached by consensus. Carefully selected employees received from 100 to 750 hours of training, and a whole new culture was built piece by piece. *If not...*
4. *Is management still committed to implementing the strategy?* If *yes*, find a joint-venture partner or contract with another company to carry out the strategy. If *not*, formulate a different strategy.

HOW CAN COMMUNICATION BE USED TO MANAGE CULTURE?

Communication is crucial to effectively managing change. The rationale for strategic changes should be communicated to workers not only in newsletters and speeches but also in training and development programs. Companies in which major cultural changes have successfully taken place had the following characteristics in common:

- The CEO and other top managers had a strategic vision of what the company could become and communicated this vision to employees at all levels. The current performance of the company was compared to that of its competition and constantly updated.
- The vision was translated into the key elements necessary to accomplish that vision. For example, if the vision called for the company to become a leader in quality or service, aspects of quality and service were pinpointed for improvement and appropriate measurement systems were developed to monitor them. These measures were communicated widely through contests, formal and informal recognition, and monetary rewards, among other devices.[9]

HOW CAN DIVERSE CULTURES BE MANAGED IN AN ACQUISITION GROWTH STRATEGY?

When merging with or acquiring another company, top management must consider a potential clash of cultures. To assume that the firms can simply be integrated into the same reporting structure is dangerous. The greater the gap between the cultures of acquired and acquiring firms, the faster executives in the acquired firms quit their jobs and valuable talent is lost. Studies reveal that 61 percent of an acquired company's top management team either quit or was asked to leave within five years.[10] To deal with staffing issues such as these, companies are appointing *integration managers* to shepherd companies through the implementation process. The job of the integrator is to prepare a competitive profile of the combined company in terms of its strengths and weaknesses, draft an ideal profile of what the combined company should look like, develop action plans to close the gap between the actuality and the ideal, and establish training programs to unite the combined company and make it more competitive.[11]

The four general methods of managing two different cultures are integration, assimilation, separation, and deculturation (see **Figure 9.1**). The choice of which method to use should be based on the degree to which members of the acquired firm (1) value the preservation of their own culture and (2) value the attractiveness of the acquirer.[12]

1. *Integration* involves a relatively balanced give-and-take of cultural and managerial practices between the merger partners and no strong imposition of cultural change on either company. It allows the two cultures to merge while preserving the

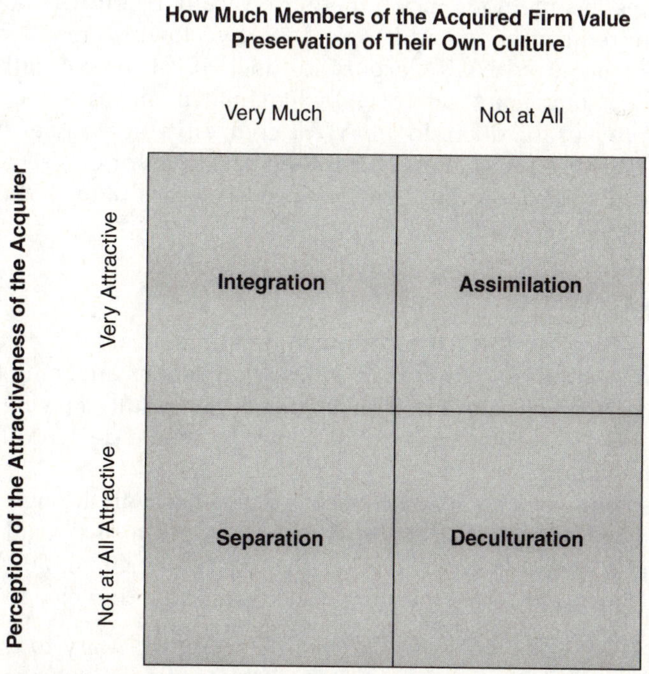

FIGURE 9.1   Methods of Managing the Culture of an Acquired Firm
Source: A. Nahavandi and A. R. Malekzadeh, "Acculturation in Mergers and Acquisitions," *Academy of Management Review* (January 1988), p. 83. Copyright © 1988 by the Academy of Management. Reprinted by permission.

separate cultures of both firms in the resulting culture. This is what occurred when France's Renault purchased a controlling interest in Japan's Nissan Motor Company and installed Carlos Ghosn as Nissan's new CEO to turn around the company. Ghosn was very sensitive to Nissan's culture and allowed the company room to develop a new corporate culture based on the best elements of Japan's national culture.

2. *Assimilation* involves the domination of one organization by another. The domination is not forced but is welcomed by members of the acquired firm, who may feel for many reasons that their culture and managerial practices have not produced success. The acquired firm surrenders its culture and adopts the culture of the acquiring company. This was the case when Maytag (now a part of Whirlpool) acquired Admiral. Admiral employees were willing to accept the quality-oriented culture of Maytag because they respected it and knew that without significant changes at Admiral, they would soon be out of work.

3. *Separation* is characterized by a separation of the two companies' cultures. For example, when Boeing acquired McDonnell-Douglas, known for its expertise in military aircraft and missiles, Boeing created a separate unit to house both McDonnell's operations and Boeing's own military business. All commercial operations were combined in a separate unit.

4. *Deculturation* involves the disintegration of one company's culture resulting from unwanted and extreme pressure from the other to impose its culture and practices. A great deal of confusion, conflict, resentment, and stress often accompanies this method. Such a merger typically results in poor performance by the acquired company and its eventual divestment. This is what happened when AT&T acquired NCR Corporation in 1990 for its computer business. It replaced NCR managers with an AT&T management team, reorganized sales, forced employees to adhere to the AT&T code of values, and even dropped the proud NCR name (for National Cash Register) in favor of a sterile GIS (Global Information Solutions) nonidentity. After six years (and a $1.2 billion loss), AT&T sold the NCR unit.

WHAT IS ACTION PLANNING?

Activities can be directed toward accomplishing strategic objectives through action planning. At a minimum, an **action plan** states what actions are going to be taken, by whom, during what time frame, and with what expected results. Having selected a program to implement a particular strategy, the company should develop an action plan to put the program in place.

Take the example of a company choosing vertical growth through the acquisition of a retailing chain as its growth strategy. Now that it owns its own retail outlets, it must integrate them into the company. One of the many programs it would have to develop is a new advertising program for the stores. The resulting action plan to develop a new advertising program should include the following elements:

1. *Specific actions to be taken to make the program operational.* One action might be to contact three reputable advertising agencies and ask them to prepare a proposal for a new radio and newspaper ad campaign based on the theme "Jones Surplus is now a part of Ajax Continental. Prices are lower. Selection is better."

2. *Dates to begin and end each action.* Time must be allotted not only to select and contact three agencies, but to allow them sufficient time to prepare a detailed proposal. For example, allow one week to select and contact the agencies and three months for them to prepare detailed proposals to present to the company's marketing director. Also allow some time to make a decision on which proposal to accept.
3. *Person (identified by name and title) responsible for carrying out each action.* List someone, such as the advertising manager, who can be put in charge of the program.
4. *Person responsible for monitoring the timeliness and effectiveness of each action.* Indicate that the advertising manager is responsible for ensuring that the proposals are of good quality and are priced within the planned program budget. He or she is the primary company contact for the ad agencies and is expected to report on the progress of the program once a week to the company's marketing director.
5. *Expected financial and physical consequences of each action.* Estimate when a completed ad campaign will be ready to show top management and how long it will take after approval to begin to air the ads. Estimate also the expected increase in store sales over the six-month period after the ads are first aired. Indicate if "recall" measures will be used to help assess the ad campaign's effectiveness and how, when, and by whom the recall data will be collected and analyzed.
6. *Contingency plans.* Indicate how long it will take to get another acceptable ad campaign ready to show top management if none of the initial proposals is acceptable.

Action plans are important for several reasons. *First*, they serve as a link between strategy formulation and evaluation and control. *Second*, the action plan specifies what needs to be done differently from the way operations are currently carried out. *Third*, during the evaluation and control process that comes later, an action plan helps appraise performance and identify any remedial actions, as needed. *Fourth*, the explicit assignment of responsibilities for implementing and monitoring the programs may improve motivation.

What Is Management by Objectives?

Management by Objectives (MBO) is an organization-wide approach to help assure purposeful action toward desired objectives by linking organizational objectives with individual behavior. Because it is a system that links plans with performance, MBO is a powerful implementation technique.

The MBO process involves the following:

1. Establishing and communicating organizational and unit objectives
2. Setting individual objectives (through superior–subordinate interaction) that help implement organizational and unit objectives
3. Developing an action plan of activities needed to achieve the objectives
4. Periodically (at least quarterly) reviewing performance as it relates to the objectives and including the results in the annual performance appraisal

Management by Objectives provides an opportunity for the corporation to connect the objectives of people at each level to those at the next higher level. Therefore,

MBO ties together corporate, business, and functional objectives and the strategies developed to achieve them.

One of the real benefits of MBO is that it can reduce the amount of internal politics operating within a large corporation. Political actions can cause conflict and divide the very people and groups who should be working together to implement strategy. People are less likely to jockey for position if the company's mission and objectives are clear and they know that the reward system is based not on game playing, but on achieving clearly communicated, measurable objectives.

What Is Total Quality Management?

Total Quality Management (TQM) is an operational philosophy that stresses commitment to customer satisfaction and continuous improvement. TQM is committed to quality and excellence and to being the best in all functions. TQM has four objectives:

1. Better, less-variable quality of the product and service.
2. Quicker, less-variable response in processes to customer needs.
3. Greater flexibility in adjusting to customers' shifting requirements.
4. Lower cost through quality improvement and elimination of non-value-adding work.[13]

Because TQM aims to reduce costs as well as improve quality, it can be used as a program to implement both an overall low cost or a differentiation business strategy. About 92 percent of manufacturing companies and 69 percent of service firms have implemented some form of quality management practices.[14]

According to TQM, faulty processes, not poorly motivated employees, cause defects in quality. To succeed in a company, the program usually involves a significant change in corporate culture, requiring strong leadership from top management, employee training, empowerment of lower-level employees (giving people more control over their work), and teamwork. The emphasis in TQM is on prevention, not correction. Inspection for quality still takes place, but the emphasis is on improving the process to prevent errors and deficiencies. Thus *quality circles* or quality improvement teams are formed to identify problems and suggest how to improve the processes that may be causing the problems.

The essential ingredients of TQM are:

- *An intense focus on customer satisfaction.* Everyone (not just people in the sales and marketing departments) understands that his or her job exists only because of customer needs. Thus all employees must approach their jobs in terms of how their work will affect customer satisfaction.
- *Customers are internal as well as external.* An employee in the shipping department may be the internal customer of another employee who completes the assembly of a product, just as a person who buys the product is a customer of the entire company. An employee must be just as concerned with pleasing the internal customer as with pleasing the external customer.
- *Accurate measurement of every critical variable in a company's operations.* Employees have to be trained in what to measure, how to measure, and how to interpret the data. A rule of TQM is, "you only improve what you measure."

- *Continuous improvement of products and services.* Everyone realizes that operations need to be continuously monitored to find ways to improve products and services.
- *New work relationships based on trust and teamwork.* A key is the idea of *empowerment*: giving employees wide latitude in how they go about in achieving the company's goals.

What Are International Considerations in Leading?

In a study of 53 different national cultures, Hofstede found that each nation's unique culture could be identified using five dimensions. The **dimensions of national culture** are *power distance* (the extent to which a society accepts an unequal distribution of power in organizations), *uncertainty avoidance* (the extent to which a society feels threatened by uncertain and ambiguous situations), *individualism–collectivism* (the extent to which a society values individual freedom and independence of action compared with a tight social framework and loyalty to the group), *masculinity–femininity* (the extent to which a society is oriented toward money and things or toward people), and *long-term orientation* (the extent to which a society is oriented toward the long versus the short term).

Hofstede found that national culture is so influential that it tends to overwhelm even a strong corporate culture. In measuring the differences among these dimensions of national culture from country to country, he was able to explain why a certain management practice might be successful in one nation, but not in another.[15]

These dimensions of national culture may help to explain why some management practices work well in some countries but not in others. For example, MBO, which originated in the United States, has succeeded in Germany, according to Hofstede, because the idea of replacing the arbitrary authority of the boss with the impersonal authority of mutually agreed-upon objectives fits the small power distance and strong uncertainty avoidance that are dimensions of the German culture. It has failed in France, however, because the French are used to large power distances and to accepting orders from a highly personalized authority. Some of the difficulties experienced by U.S. companies in using Japanese-style quality circles may stem from the extremely high value U.S. culture places on individualism.

When one successful company in one country merges with another successful company in another country, the clash of corporate cultures is compounded by the clash of national cultures. Given the growing number of cross-border mergers and acquisitions, the management of cultures is becoming a key issue in strategy implementation.

Discussion Questions

1. What skills should a person have for managing a business unit following a differentiation strategy? Why? What should a company do if no one is available internally and the company has a policy of promotion from within?
2. When should someone from outside the company be hired to manage the company or one of its business units?
3. What are some ways to implement a retrenchment strategy without creating a lot of resentment and conflict with labor unions?
4. How can corporate culture be changed?
5. Why is an understanding of national cultures important in strategic management?

Key Terms (listed in order of appearance)

staffing *135*
executive type *136*
executive succession *136*
performance appraisal
  system *137*
assessment centers *137*

downsizing *137*
leading *139*
action plan *142*
Management by Objectives
  (MBO) *143*

Total Quality Management
  (TQM) *144*
dimensions of national
  culture *145*

Notes

1. B. O'Reilly, "The Rent-A-Car Jocks Who Made Enterprise #1," *Fortune* (October 28, 1996), pp. 125–128; J. Schlereth, "Putting People First," an interview with Andrew Taylor, *BizEd* (July/August 2003), pp. 16–20; P. Lehman, "A Clear Road to the Top," *Business Week* (September 18, 2006), p. 72; *Business Week* Web site at www.businessweek.com. Company Web site at www.enterprise.com

2. *High Performance Work Practices and Firm Performance* (Washington, D.C.: U.S. Department of Labor, Office of the American Workplace, 1993), pp. i, 4.

3. M. Smith and M. C. White, "Strategy, CEO Specialization, and Succession," *Administrative Science Quarterly* (June 1987), pp. 263–280.

4. M. Boyle, "Art of Succession," *Business Week* (May 11, 2009), pp. 31–32.

5. J. Weber, "The Accidental CEO," *Business Week* (April 23, 2007), pp. 64–72.

6. N. Byrnes and D. Kiley, "Hello, You Must Be Going," *Business Week* (February 12, 2007), pp. 30–32.

7. K. E. Mishra, G. M. Spreitzer, and A. K. Mishra, "Preserving Employee Morale During Downsizing," *Sloan Management Review* (Winter 1998), pp. 83–95.

8. J. S. Black and H. B. Gregersen, "The Right Way to Manage Expats," *Harvard Business Review* (March–April 1999), pp. 52–61.

9. G. G. Gordon, "The Relationship of Corporate Culture to Industry Sector and Corporate Performance," in *Gaining Control of the Corporate Culture*, edited by R. H. Kilmann,

M. J. Saxton, R. Serpa, and Associates (San Francisco: Jossey-Bass, 1985), p. 123.

10. See M. Lubatkin, D. Schweiger, and Y. Weber, "Top Management Turnover in Related M&Ss: An Additional Test of the Theory of Relative Standing," *Journal of Management*, Vol. 25, No. 1 (1999), pp. 55–73.

11. A. Hinterhuber, "Making M&A Work," *Business Strategy Review* (September 2002), pp. 7–9.

12. A. R. Malekzadeh, and A. Nahavandi, "Making Mergers Work by Managing Cultures," *Journal of Business Strategy* (May–June 1990), pp. 53–57; A. Nahavandi, and A. R. Malekzadeh, "Acculturation in Mergers and Acquisitions," *Academy of Management Review* (January 1988), pp. 79–90.

13. R. J. Schonberger, "Total Quality Management Cuts a Broad Swath—Through Manufacturing and Beyond," *Organizational Dynamics* (Spring 1992), pp. 16–28.

14. S. S. Masterson and M. S. Taylor, "Total Quality Management and Performance Appraisal: An Integrative Perspective," *Journal of Quality Management*, Vol. 1, No. 1 (1996), pp. 67–89.

15. G. Hofstede, *Cultures and Organizations: Software of the Mind* (London: McGraw-Hill, 1991); G. Hofstede, and M. H. Bond, "The Confucius Connection: From Cultural Roots to Economic Growth," *Organizational Dynamics* (Spring 1988), pp. 5–21; R. Hodgetts, "A Conversation with Geert Hofstede," *Organizational Dynamics* (Spring 1993), pp. 53–61.

10 | EVALUATION **AND CONTROL**

Nucor Corporation, one of the most successful steel firms operating in the United States, keeps its evaluation and control process simple and easy to manage. According to Kenneth Iverson, Chairman of the Board,

> We try to keep our focus on what really matters—bottom-line performance and long-term survival. That's what we want our people to be thinking about. Management takes care not to distract the company with a lot of talk about other issues. We don't clutter the picture with lofty vision statements or ask employees to pursue vague, intermediate objectives like "excellence" or burden them with complex business strategies. Our competitive strategy is to build manufacturing facilities economically and to operate them efficiently. Period. Basically, we ask our employees to produce more product for less money. Then we reward them for doing that well.[1]

Evaluation and control is the process by which corporate activities and performance results are monitored so that actual performance can be compared with desired performance. The process provides the feedback necessary for management to evaluate the results and take corrective action, as needed. This process can be viewed as a five-step feedback model, as depicted in **Figure 10.1**:

1. *Determine what to measure.* Top managers and operational managers must specify implementation processes and results to be monitored and evaluated. The processes and results must be measurable in a reasonably objective and consistent manner. The focus should be on the most significant elements in a process—the ones that account for the highest proportion of expense or the greatest number of problems. Measurements must be found for all important areas regardless of difficulty.
2. *Establish standards of performance.* Standards used to measure performance are detailed expressions of strategic objectives. They are measures of acceptable performance results. Each standard usually includes a tolerance range, which defines any acceptable deviations. Standards can be set not only for final output but also for intermediate stages of production.

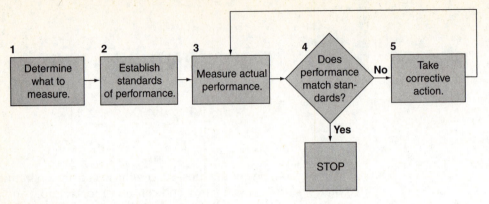

FIGURE 10.1 Evaluation and Control Process

3. *Measure actual performance.* Measurements must be made at predetermined times.
4. *Compare actual performance with the standard.* If the actual performance results are within the desired tolerance range, the measurement process stops here. Reward good performance.
5. *Take corrective action.* If the actual results fall outside the desired tolerance range, action must be taken to correct the deviation. The action must not only correct the deviation, but also prevent its recurrence. The following issues must be resolved:
   a. Is the deviation only a chance fluctuation?
   b. Are the processes being carried out incorrectly?
   c. Are the processes appropriate for achieving the desired standard?
   d. Who is the best person to take corrective action?

Top management is often better at the first two steps of the control model than they are in the last three follow-through steps. The tendency to establish a control system and then delegate the implementation to others can have unfortunate results. Nucor is unusual in its ability to deal with the entire evaluation and control process.

10.1 EVALUATION AND CONTROL IN STRATEGIC MANAGEMENT

Evaluation and control information consists of performance data and activity reports (gathered in Step 3 of Figure 10.1). Operational managers must identify any inappropriate use of strategic management processes that causes undesired performance so that they can correct the employee activity. Top management need not be involved in this process. If, however, the processes themselves cause the undesired performance, both top managers and operational managers must know about it so that they can develop new implementation programs or procedures.

Evaluation and control information must be relevant to what is being monitored. Evaluation and control is not an easy process. One of the obstacles to effective control is the difficulty in developing appropriate measures of important activities and outputs.

10.2 MEASURING PERFORMANCE

Performance is the end result of activity. Which measures to select to assess performance depends on the organizational unit to be appraised and the objectives to be achieved. The objectives that were established earlier in the strategy formulation part of the strategic management process (dealing with profitability, market share, and cost reduction, among others) should certainly be used to measure corporate performance once the strategies have been implemented.

When should Measures be Used?

Some measures, such as return on investment (ROI) and earnings per share (EPS), are appropriate for evaluating the corporation's or division's ability to achieve a profitability objective. These measures, however, are inadequate for evaluating additional corporate objectives such as social responsibility or employee development. Even though profitability is a corporation's major objective, ROI and EPS can be computed only *after* profits are totaled for a period. It tells what happened after the fact, not what is happening or what will happen. A firm, therefore, needs to develop measures that predict likely profitability. These are referred to as *steering controls* because they measure variables that influence future profitability. Every industry has its own set of key metrics which tends to predict profits. Airlines, for example, closely monitor cost per passenger mile. In the 1990s, Southwest Airline's cost per passenger mile was 6.43¢, the lowest in the industry, contrasted with American Airline's 12.95¢, the highest in the industry. Its low costs gave Southwest a significant competitive advantage.

How do Behavior and Output Controls Differ?

Controls can be established to focus on actual performance results (output), on the activities that generate the performance (behavior), or on the inputs that go into the performance (inputs). **Behavior controls** specify *how* something is to be done through policies, rules, standard operating procedures, and orders from a superior. **Output controls** specify *what* is to be accomplished by focusing on the end result of the behaviors through the use of objectives and performance targets or milestones. **Input controls** focus on resources, such as knowledge, skills, abilities, values, and motives of employees.

Behavior, output, and input controls are not interchangeable. Behavior controls (e.g., following company procedures, making sales calls to potential customers, and getting to work on time) are most appropriate when performance results are hard to measure and a clear cause–effect connection exists between activities and results. Output controls (e.g., sales quotas, specific cost reduction or profit objectives, and surveys of customer satisfaction) are most appropriate when specific output measures are agreed upon and no clear cause–effect connection exists between activities and results. Input controls (e.g., number of years of education and experience) are most appropriate when output is difficult to measure and there is no clear cause–effect relationship between behavior and performance (as in college teaching). Corporations following the strategy of conglomerate diversification tend to emphasize output controls with their divisions and subsidiaries (presumably because they are managed independently of each other), whereas, corporations following concentric diversification use all three types of controls (presumably because synergy is desired). Even if all three types of control are used, one or two of them may be emphasized more than another depending on the circumstances.

Examples of increasingly popular behavior controls are the ISO 9000 and 14000 Standards Series on quality and environmental assurance developed by the International Standards Association of Geneva, Switzerland. The *ISO 9000 Series* (composed of five sections from 9000 to 9004) is a way of objectively documenting a company's high level of quality operations. A company wanting ISO 9000 certification would document its process for product introductions, among other things. The *ISO 14000 Series* is a way to document the company's impact on the environment. ISO 14001 specifies how companies should establish, maintain, and continually improve an environmental management system.

What is the Value of Activity-Based Costing?

Activity-based costing (ABC) is a new accounting method for allocating indirect and fixed costs to individual products or product lines based on the value-added activities going into that product. This accounting method is thus very useful in doing a value-chain analysis of a firm's activities for making outsourcing decisions. Traditional cost accounting, in contrast, focuses on valuing a company's inventory for financial reporting purposes. To obtain a unit's cost, cost accountants typically add direct labor to the cost of materials. Then they compute overhead from rent to R&D expenses, based on the number of direct labor hours it takes to make a product. To obtain unit cost, they divide the total by the number of items made during the period under consideration.

ABC accounting allows accountants to charge costs more accurately than the traditional method because it allocates overhead far more precisely. ABC can be used in many types of industries. For example, a bakery may use standard costs to allocate costs to products and to price customers' orders. Under the traditional standard cost system, overhead costs such as selling, advertising, warehousing, shipping, and administration are allocated to products and spread over the entire customer base. Under this system, a bakery would allocate order-handling charges on a percentage of sales basis. When this is done, profitable accounts tend to subsidize unprofitable ones—without anyone's knowledge. What is ignored is that the amount of time and expense spent processing an order is usually the same, regardless of whether the order is for 200 or 2,000 donuts. The cost driver is not the number of cases ordered but the number of separate sales orders that must be processed. By assigning costs based on the number of orders to be processed, instead of by the dollar value of the order, the bakery can calculate a much more accurate cost for processing each customer's order. This information is crucial if management is to assess the profitability of different customers and make strategic decisions regarding growth or retrenchment.[2]

What Are the Primary Measures of Corporate Performance?

The most commonly used measure of corporate performance (in terms of profits) is **return on investment**. ROI is simply the result of dividing net income before taxes by total assets. ROI has several *advantages*. It is a single comprehensive figure that is influenced by everything that happens. It measures how well a division manager uses the division's assets to generate profits. It is a common measure that can be compared with other companies and business units. It provides an incentive to use existing assets efficiently and buy new ones only when it would increase profits. Nevertheless, ROI has several distinct *limitations*. Although ROI gives the impression of objectivity and precision, it can be easily manipulated. For example, ROI is very sensitive to depreciation policy and book value of assets—both of which can be manipulated by self-serving managers. A given amount of profits provides a greater ROI figure if the book value of the assets is low than if it is high. Further, it is difficult to set a *transfer price*, the price at which one division sells its product to another. A more powerful division could force a less powerful one to sell its product at a lower price than it would get on the open market, thus reducing the selling division's ROI and increasing that of the purchasing division. Since ROI can be calculated for the short run as well as for the long run, there is a tendency to use it primarily for short-run purposes, such as quarterly or annual bonuses, thus driving out long-term strategic planning in favor of short-run tactical maneuvers.

Earnings per share, which involves dividing net earnings by the number of common stock shares, also has the advantage of being used as one overall measure of corporate performance. Nevertheless, it has several deficiencies as an evaluation of past and future performance. First, because alternative accounting principles are available, EPS can have several different but equally acceptable values, depending on the principle selected for its computation. Second, because EPS is based on accrual income, the conversion of income to cash can be near term or delayed. Therefore, EPS does not consider the present value of money. **Return on equity (ROE)**, obtained by dividing net income by total equity (the shareholders' total investment in the corporation), is another popular performance measure, but has its share of limitations because it is also derived from accounting-based data. In addition, EPS and ROE are often unrelated to a company's stock price. **Operating cash flow**, the amount of money generated by a company before the cost of financing and taxes, is a broad measure of a company's funds. Although cash flow may be harder to manipulate than earnings, the number can be increased by selling accounts receivable, classifying outstanding checks as accounts payable, trading securities, and capitalizing certain expenses, such as direct-response advertising. Because of these and other limitations, ROI, EPS, ROE, and operating cash flow by themselves are not adequate measures of corporate performance.

WHAT ARE STAKEHOLDER MEASURES?

Each stakeholder has its own set of criteria to determine how well the corporation is performing. These criteria typically deal with the direct and indirect impact of corporate activities on stakeholder interests. Top management should establish one or more simple measures for each stakeholder category so that it can keep track of stakeholder concerns. For example, sales and sales growth are good measures to use with customers; costs and delivery time with suppliers; stock price and number of "buy lists" with the financial community; turnover and grievances with employees; number of pieces of negative legislation and amount of financial incentives with government; and hostile encounters and legal actions with consumer and environmental advocates.

WHAT IS SHAREHOLDER VALUE?

Because of the belief that accounting-based numbers such as ROI, ROE, and EPS are not reliable indicators of a corporation's economic value, many corporations are using shareholder value as a better measure of corporate performance and strategic management effectiveness. **Shareholder value** is defined as the present value of the anticipated future stream of cash flows from the business plus the value of the company if liquidated. Arguing that the purpose of a company is to increase shareholder wealth, shareholder value analysis concentrates on cash flow as the key measure of performance. The value of a corporation is thus the value of its cash flows discounted back to their present value, using the business's cost of capital as the discount rate. As long as the returns from a business exceed its cost of capital, the business will create value and be worth more than the capital invested in it.

Economic value added (EVA) is after-tax operating profit minus the total annual cost of capital. It measures the difference between the pre- and poststrategy value of the business. If the difference, discounted by the cost of capital, is positive, the strategy is generating value for the shareholders. Among the many companies using the new measure are Coca-Cola, AT&T, Quaker Oats, Briggs & Stratton, and CSX. , When he was CEO of Coca-Cola, Roberto Goizueta explained it as follows: "We raise capital to make concentrate, and sell it at an operating profit. Then we pay the cost of that capital. Shareholders pocket the difference."[3] Unlike ROI, one of EVA's most powerful properties is its strong relationship to stock price. Managers can improve their company's or business unit's EVA by (1) earning more profit without using more capital, (2) using less capital, and (3) investing capital in high-return projects. The EVA approach can be further extended to an additional measure, *market value added (MVA)*, which measures the stock market's estimate of the net present value of a firm's past and expected capital investment projects.[4]

WHAT IS THE BALANCED SCORECARD APPROACH?

The **balanced scorecard** combines financial measures that tell the results of actions already taken with operational measures on customer satisfaction, internal processes, and the corporation's innovation and improvement activities: the drivers of future financial performance. This approach is especially useful given that research indicates that nonfinancial assets explain 50–80 percent of a firm's value.[5] Management should develop goals or objectives in each of four areas:

1. **Financial:** How do we appear to shareholders?
2. **Customer:** How do customers view us?
3. **Internal Business Perspective:** What must we excel at?
4. **Innovation and Learning:** Can we continue to improve and create value?[6]

Each goal in each area (e.g., increased sales) is then assigned one or more measures, as well as a target. These measures can be considered as **key performance measures**—measures that are essential for achieving a desired strategic option. For example, a company could include cash flow, quarterly sales growth, and ROE as measures for success in the financial area; market share (competitive position goal) and percentage of new sales coming from new products (customer acceptance goal) as measures under the customer perspective; cycle time and unit cost (manufacturing excellence goal) as measures under the internal business perspective; and time to develop next-generation products (technology leadership objective) under the innovation and learning perspective. The balanced scorecard is used by over half of the *Fortune Global 1000* companies.[7]

HOW IS TOP MANAGEMENT EVALUATED?

Through its strategy, audit, and compensation committees, a board of directors closely evaluates the job performance of the CEO and the top management team. The vast majority of American, European, and Asian boards review the CEO's performance using a formalized process. The board is concerned primarily with overall profitability as measured quantitatively by ROI, ROE, EPS, and shareholder value. The absence of short-run profitability is certainly a factor contributing to the firing of any CEO, but the board is also concerned with other factors.

Members of the compensation committees of today's boards of directors generally agree that measuring a CEO's ability to establish strategic direction, build a management team, and provide leadership is more critical in the long run than are a few quantitative measures. The board should evaluate top management not only on the typical output-oriented quantitative measures, but also on behavioral measures—factors relating to its strategic management practices. Performance evaluations of the overall board's performance are also standard practice;[8] evaluations of individual directors are less common.

What Are the Primary Measures of Divisional and Functional Performance?

Companies use a variety of techniques to evaluate and control performance in divisions, strategic business units (SBUs), and functional areas. If a corporation is composed of SBUs or divisions, it will use many of the same performance measures (ROI or EVA, for instance) that it uses to assess overall corporation performance. To the extent that it can isolate specific functional units, such as R&D, the corporation may develop responsibility centers. It will also use typical functional measures such as market share and sales per employee (marketing), unit costs and percentage of defects (operations), percentage of sales from new products and number of patents (R&D), and turnover and job satisfaction (HRM).

During strategy formulation and implementation, top management approves a series of programs and supporting operating budgets from its business units. *Operating budgets* list the costs and expenses for each proposed program in dollar terms. During evaluation and control, management contrasts actual expenses with planned expenditures and assesses the degree of variance, typically on a monthly basis. In addition, top management probably will require *periodic statistical reports*, which summarize data on key factors, such as the number of new customer contracts, volume of received orders, and productivity figures.

WHAT ARE RESPONSIBILITY CENTERS?

Control systems can be established to monitor specific functions, projects, or divisions. For example, budgets are typically used to control the financial indicators of performance. Responsibility centers are used to isolate a unit so that it can be evaluated separately from the rest of the corporation. A **responsibility center** has its own budget, is evaluated on its use of budgeted resources, and is headed by a manager who is responsible for its performance. The center uses resources (measured in terms of costs or expenses) to produce a service or a product (measured in terms of volume or revenues). The way in which the corporation's control system measures these resources and services or products determines which of the five major types of responsibility centers is used.

- *Standard cost centers.* Primarily used in manufacturing facilities, standard (or expected) costs are computed for each operation on the basis of historical data. In evaluating the center's performance, its total standard costs are multiplied by the units produced; the result is the expected cost of production, which is then compared to the actual cost of production.
- *Revenue centers.* Production, usually in terms of unit or dollar sales, is measured without considering resource costs (e.g., salaries). The center is thus judged in terms of effectiveness rather than efficiency. The effectiveness of a sales region, for example, is determined by comparing its actual sales to its projected or previous year's sales. Profits are not considered because sales departments have limited influence over the cost of the products they sell.
- *Expense centers.* Resources are measured in dollars without considering service or product costs. Thus budgets are prepared for engineered expenses (costs that can be calculated) and for discretionary expenses (costs that can be only estimated). Typical expense centers are administrative, service, and research departments. They cost money, but contribute only indirectly to revenues.
- *Profit centers.* Performance is measured in terms of the difference between revenues (which measure production) and expenditures (which measure resources). A profit center is typically established whenever an organizational unit controls both its resources and its products or services. By having such centers, a company can be organized into divisions of separate product lines.
- *Investment centers.* Because many divisions in large manufacturing corporations use significant assets to make their products, their asset base should be factored into their performance evaluation. Thus to focus only on profits, as in the case of profit centers, is insufficient. An investment center's performance is measured in terms of the difference between its resources and its services or products. The most widely used measure of investment center performance is ROI.

Most single-business corporations, such as Apple, tend to use a combination of cost, expense, and revenue centers. In these corporations, most managers are functional specialists who manage against a budget. Total profitability is integrated at the corporate level. Multidivisional corporations with one dominating product line, such as Anheuser-Busch, which have diversified into a few small businesses but which still depend on a single product line (e.g., beer) for most of their revenue and income, generally use a combination of cost, expense, revenue, and profit centers. Multidivisional corporations, such as General Electric, tend to emphasize investment centers, although various units throughout the corporation use other types of responsibility centers. One problem with using responsibility centers, however, is that the separation needed to measure and evaluate a division's performance can make it difficult to achieve the level of cooperation among divisions needed to attain synergy for the corporation as a whole.

HOW IS BENCHMARKING USED TO EVALUATE PERFORMANCE?

According to Xerox Corporation, the company that pioneered this concept in the United States, benchmarking is the continual process of measuring products, services, and practices against the toughest competitors or those companies recognized as industry leaders. **Benchmarking** involves openly learning how other companies do something better and not only imitating, but perhaps even improving on their techniques. The benchmarking process usually involves the following steps:

1. Identify the area or process to be examined: It should be an activity which has the potential to determine a business unit's competitive advantage.
2. Find behavioral and output measures of the area or process and obtain measurements.
3. Select an accessible set of competitors and best-in-class companies against which to benchmark: These may very often be companies that are in completely different industries but perform similar activities. For example, when Xerox wanted to improve its order fulfillment, it went to L. L. Bean, the successful mail order firm, to learn how it achieved excellence in this area.
4. Calculate the differences among the company's performance measurements and those of the best-in-class: Determine why the differences exist.
5. Develop programs for closing performance gaps.
6. Implement the programs and then compare the resulting new measurements with those of the best-in-class companies.

A recent survey of 1,430 international executives indicated that benchmarking was used by 76 percent of the companies—the most widely used management tool.[9] Cost reductions range from 15 to 45 percent.[10] Benchmarking can also increase sales, improve goal setting, and boost employee motivation.[11] APQC (American Productivity & Quality Center), a Houston research group, established the Open Standards Benchmarking Collaborative database, composed of more than 1,200 commonly used measures and individual benchmarks (see http://www.apqc.org).

What Are International Measurement Issues?

The three most widely used techniques for international performance evaluation are ROI, budget analysis, and historical comparisons. Even though ROI is the single most used measure of international operations, it has serious limitations. Because of foreign currencies, different rates of inflation, different tax laws, and the use of transfer pricing, both the net income figure and the investment base may be seriously distorted. Transfer pricing is used heavily in MNCs not only to calculate the ROI for responsibility centers in various countries, but also to minimize taxes. For example, parts made in a subsidiary of an MNC in a low-tax country like Singapore can be shipped to its subsidiary in a high-tax country like the United States at such a high price that the U.S. subsidiary reports very little profit (and thus pays few taxes), while the Singapore subsidiary reports a very high profit (but also pays few taxes because of the lower tax rate). The MNC can, therefore, earn more profit worldwide by reporting less profit in high-tax countries and more profit in low-tax ones (assuming governments in high-tax countries do not retaliate with tariff barriers and lawsuits).

The control and reward systems used by a global MNC are usually different from those used by a multidomestic MNC. The *multidomestic MNC* uses loose controls on its foreign units. The management of each geographic unit is given considerable operational latitude, but is expected to meet some performance targets. Multiple measures are used to differentiate between the worth of the subsidiary and the performance of its management. The *global MNC*, in contrast, needs tight controls over its many units. To reduce costs and gain competitive advantage, it spreads the manufacturing and marketing operations of a few fairly uniform products around the world. Therefore, its key operational decisions are centralized. Foreign units are thus evaluated more as cost, revenue, or expense centers than as investment or profit centers because MNCs operating in a global industry do not often make the entire product in the country in which it is sold.

10.3   STRATEGIC INFORMATION SYSTEMS

Before performance measures can have any impact on strategic management, they must first be communicated to the people responsible for formulating and implementing strategic plans. Strategic information systems, whether computer based or manual, formal or informal, can perform this function. One of the key reasons for the success of Wal-Mart has been management's use of the company's sophisticated information system to control purchasing decisions. Cash registers in Wal-Mart retail stores transmit information hourly to computers at company headquarters. Consequently managers know every morning exactly how many of each item have been sold the day before, how many have been sold so far in the year, and how this year's sales compare to last year's. The information system allows all reordering to be done automatically by computers without any managerial input. It also allows the company to experiment with new toys without committing to big orders in advance. In effect, the system allows the customers to decide through their purchases what gets reordered.

Many corporations around the world are adopting *enterprise resource planning (ERP)* software. ERP unites all of a company's major business activities from order processing to production within a single family of software modules. The system provides instant access to critical information to everyone in the organization from the CEO to the factory floor worker. Because of the ability of ERP software to use a common information system throughout a company's many operations around the world, it is becoming the business information systems' global standard. Nevertheless, the system is extremely complicated and demands a high level of standardization throughout a corporation. The major providers of this software are SAP, Oracle, J. D. Edwards, Baan, and SSA.

At the divisional or SBU level of a corporation, the information system should be used to support, reinforce, or enlarge its business-level strategy through its decision support system. An SBU pursuing a strategy of overall cost leadership could use its information system to reduce costs either by improving labor productivity or by improving the use of other resources such as inventory or machinery. For example, *Radio frequency identification (RFID)* is an electronic tagging technology used in a number of companies to improve supply-chain efficiency. By tagging containers and items with tiny chips, companies use the tags as wireless bar codes to track inventory more efficiently.

10.4   GUIDELINES FOR PROPER CONTROL

Measuring performance is a crucial part of evaluation and control. The lack of quantifiable objectives or performance standards and the inability of the information system to provide timely, valid information are two obvious control problems. Without objective and timely measurements, making operational, let alone strategic, decisions would be extremely difficult. Nevertheless, the use of timely, quantifiable standards does not guarantee good performance. The very act of monitoring and measuring performance can cause side effects that interfere with overall corporate performance. Inappropriate controls can result in managers manipulating the measures for personal advantage to the detriment of the company.

In designing a control system, top management should remember that *controls should follow strategy*. Unless controls ensure the use of the proper strategy to achieve objectives, dysfunctional side effects are likely to completely undermine the implementation of the objectives. The following guidelines are recommended:

1. *Controls should involve only the minimum amount of information needed to give a reliable picture of events*. Too many controls create confusion. Focus on the strategic factors by following the **80/20 rule**: *Monitor those 20 percent of the factors that determine 80 percent of the results.*

2. *Controls should monitor only meaningful activities and results*. Regardless of measurement difficulty, if cooperation between divisions is important to corporate performance, some form of qualitative or quantitative measure should be established to monitor cooperation.

3. *Controls should be timely*. Corrective action must be taken before it is too late. Steering controls, that is, controls that monitor or measure the factors influencing performance, should be stressed so that advance notice of problems is given.

4. *Controls should be long term and short term*. If only short-term measures are emphasized, a short-term managerial orientation is likely.

5. *Controls should pinpoint exceptions*. Only those activities or results that fall outside a predetermined tolerance range should call for action.

6. *Controls should be used to reward meeting or exceeding standards rather than to punish failure to meet standards*. Heavy punishment of failure typically results in goal displacement. Managers will "fudge" reports and lobby for lower standards.

To the extent that the corporate culture complements and reinforces the strategic orientation of the firm, there is less need for an extensive formal control system.

10.5   STRATEGIC INCENTIVE MANAGEMENT

To ensure congruence between the needs of the corporation as a whole and the needs of the employees as individuals, management and the board of directors should develop an incentive program that rewards desired performance. Incentive plans should be linked in some way to corporate and divisional strategy. Research does reveal that firm performance is affected by its compensation policies. Companies using different business strategies tend to adopt different pay policies. For example, a survey of 600 business units indicates that the pay mix associated with a growth strategy emphasizes bonuses and other incentives over salary and benefits, whereas the pay mix associated with a stability strategy has the reverse emphasis.[12]

The following three approaches are tailored to help match measurements and rewards with explicit strategic objectives and time frames:[13]

- **Weighted-factor method.** This method is particularly appropriate for measuring and rewarding the performance of top SBU managers and group-level executives when performance factors and their importance vary from one SBU to another. The measurements that one corporation uses might contain the following variations: The performance of high-growth SBUs is measured in terms of market share, sales growth, designated future payoff, and progress on several future-oriented strategic projects; the performance of low-growth SBUs, in contrast, is measured in terms of ROI and cash generation; and the performance of medium-growth SBUs is measured with a combination of these factors (see **Table 10.1**).
- **Long-term evaluation method.** This method compensates managers for achieving objectives set over a multiyear period. An executive is promised some company stock or "performance units" (convertible into money) in amounts to be based on long-term performance. An executive committee, for example, might set a particular objective in terms of growth in EPS during a

Table 10.1 Weighted-Factor Approach to Strategic Incentive Management

Strategic Business Unit Category	Factor	Weight
High Growth	Return on assets	10%
	Cash flow	0%
	Strategic-funds programs (developmental expenses)	45%
	Market-share increase	45%
		100%
Medium Growth	Return on assets	25%
	Cash flow	25%
	Strategic-funds programs (developmental expenses)	25%
	Market-share increase	25%
		100%
Low Growth	Return on assets	50%
	Cash flow	50%
	Strategic-funds programs (developmental expenses)	0%
	Market-share increase	0%
		100%

Source: Reprinted by permission of Elsevier Science from Paul J. Stonich, "The Performance Measurement and Reward System: Critical to Strategic Management," *Organizational Dynamics* (Winter 1984), p. 51. Copyright © 1984 by American Management Association, New York. All rights reserved.

Table 10.2 Strategic-Funds Approach to an SBU's Profit and Loss Statement

Sales	$12,300,000
Cost of sales	−6,900,000
Gross margin	$ 5,400,000
General and administrative expenses	−3,700,000
Operating profit (return on sales)	$ 1,700,000
Strategic funds (development expenses)	−1,000,000
Pretax profit	$ 700,000

Source: Reprinted by permission of Elsevier Science from Paul J. Stonich, "The Performance Measurement and Reward System: Critical to Strategic Management," Organizational Dynamics (Winter 1984), p. 52. Copyright © 1984 by American Management Association, New York. All rights reserved.

five-year period. Awards would be contingent on the corporation's meeting that objective within the designated time. Any executive who leaves the corporation before the objective is met receives nothing. The typical emphasis on stock price makes this approach more applicable to top management than to business unit managers.

- **Strategic-funds method.** This method encourages executives to look at developmental expenses as being different from those expenses required for current operations. The accounting statement for a corporate unit enters strategic funds as a separate entry below the current ROI. It is therefore possible to distinguish between those expense dollars consumed in the generation of current revenues and those invested in the future of the business. Therefore, the manager can be evaluated on both a short- and a long-term basis and has an incentive to invest strategic funds in the future (see **Table 10.2**).

An effective way to achieve the desired strategic results through a reward system is to combine the three approaches in the following manner:

1. Segregate strategic funds from short-term funds, as is done in the strategic-funds method.
2. Develop a weighted-factor chart for each SBU.
3. Measure performance on three bases: the pretax profit indicated by the strategic-funds approach, the weighted factors, and the long-term evaluation of SBU and corporate performance.

Discussion Questions

1. Is Figure 10.1 a realistic model of the evaluation and control process?
2. What are some examples of behavior, output, and input controls?
3. Is EVA really an improvement over ROI, ROE, or EPS?
4. How much faith can a manager place in a transfer price as a substitute for a market price in measuring a profit center's performance?
5. Is the evaluation and control process appropriate for a corporation that emphasizes creativity? Are control and creativity compatible?

Key Terms (listed in order of appearance)

behavior controls *149*
output controls *149*
input controls *149*
activity-based costing *150*
return on investment *150*
earnings per share *151*
return on equity *151*

operating cash flow *151*
shareholder value *152*
economic value added *152*
balanced scorecard *152*
key performance measures *152*
responsibility center *154*

benchmarking *155*
80/20 rule *157*
weighted-factor method *158*
long-term evaluation
   method *158*
strategic-funds method *159*

Notes

1. K. F. Iverson with T. Varian, "Plain Talk," *Inc.* (October 1997), p. 81. Excerpted from Iverson's book, *Plain Talk: Lessons from a Business Maverick*, published by John Wiley, 1997.

2. T. R. V. Davis and B. L. Darling, "ABC in a Virtual Corporation," *Management Accounting* (October 1996), pp. 18–26.

3. S. Tully, "The Real Key to Creating Wealth," *Fortune* (September 20, 1993), p. 38.

4. A. B. Fisher, "Creating Stockholder Wealth: Market Value Added," *Fortune* (December 11, 1995), pp. 105–116.

5. D. I. Goldenberg, "Shareholder Value Debunked," *Strategy & Leadership* (January/February 2000), p. 34.

6. R. S. Kaplan and D. P. Norton, "Using the Balanced Scorecard as a Strategic Management System," *Harvard Business Review* (January–February 1996), pp. 75–85; R. S. Kaplan and D. P. Norton, "The Balanced Scorecard—Measures That Drive Performance," *Harvard Business Review* (January–February, 1992), pp. 71–79.

7. P. D. Heaney, "Can Performance Be Measured?" *Progressive Grocer*, Vol. 82 (2003), pp. 11–13.

8. S. P. Mader, D. Vuchot, and S. Fukushima of Korn/Ferry International, *33rd Annual Board of Directors Study* (2006), p. 9.

9. *Management Tools and Trends 2009*, Bain & Company, www.bain.com.

10. R. J. Kennedy, "Benchmarking and Its Myths," *Competitive Intelligence Magazine* (April–June 2000), pp. 28–33.

11. L. Mann, D. Samson, and D. Dow, "A Field Experiment on the Effects of Benchmarking & Goal Setting on Company Sales Performance," *Journal of Management*, Vol. 24, No. 1 (1998), pp. 73–96.

12. D. B. Balkin and L. R. Gomez-Mejia, "Matching Compensation and Organizational Strategies," *Strategic Management Journal* (February 1990), pp. 153–169.

13. P. J. Stonich, "The Performance Measurement and Reward System: Critical to Strategic Management," *Organizational Dynamics* (Winter 1984), pp. 45–57.

11

SUGGESTIONS FOR CASE ANALYSIS

An analysis of a corporation's strategic management calls for a comprehensive view of the organization. The case method of analysis provides the opportunity to move from a narrow, specialized view that emphasizes technical skills to a broader, less precise analysis of the overall corporation that emphasizes conceptual skills.

11.1   THE CASE METHOD

The analysis and discussion of case problems has been the most popular method of teaching strategy for many years. Cases present actual business situations and enable you to examine both successful and unsuccessful corporations. In case analysis, you might be asked to critically analyze a situation in which a manager had to make a decision of long-term corporate importance. This approach gives you a feel for what it is like to be faced with making and implementing strategic decisions.

11.2   FRAMEWORKS FOR CASE ANALYSIS

There is no one best way to analyze or present a case report. Each instructor has personal preferences for format and approach. Nevertheless, we suggest an approach for both written and oral reports in **Appendix 11.A**, which provides a systematic method for successfully dealing with a case.

Case discussion focuses on critical analysis and logical development of thought. A solution is satisfactory if it resolves important problems and is likely to be implemented successfully. How the corporation actually dealt with the case problems has no real bearing on the analysis because management might have analyzed its problems incorrectly or implemented a series of flawed solutions.

The presentation of a case analysis can be organized on the basis of several frameworks: One framework is SWOT analysis, followed by a discussion of strategic alternatives and a recommendation; another is the strategic audit as discussed in **Appendix 11.C**. Regardless of the framework chosen, be careful to include a complete analysis of key environmental variables, especially industry trends, the competition, and international developments.

11.3   RESEARCHING THE CASE SITUATION

Depending on your instructor, you should undertake outside research into the environmental setting of the case. Find out the date when the case situation occurred and then screen the business periodicals for that time period. An understanding of the economy during that period will help you avoid making a serious error in your analysis; for example, suggesting a sale of stock when the stock market is at an all-time low or taking on more debt when the prime interest rate is over 15 percent. Information on the industry will provide insights on its competitive activities. This background will give you an appreciation for the situation as the participants in the case experienced it. In the United States, a company's 10-K (annual report), 10-Q (quarterly report), and 14-A (proxy statement) reports from the year of the case can be very helpful. These reports can usually be found at the corporation's Web site or at the U.S. Securities and Exchange Commission (www.sec.gov). Some resources available for research into the economy and a corporation's industry are suggested in **Appendix 11.B**.

Important Note: Before obtaining additional information about the company profiled in a particular case, ask your instructor if this is appropriate for your class assignment. Your strategy instructor may want you to stay within the confines of the case information provided in the book. In this case, it is usually acceptable to at least learn more about the natural and societal environments at the time of the case.

11.4   FINANCIAL ANALYSIS: A PLACE TO BEGIN

Ratio analysis is the calculation of ratios from data in a company's financial statements. It is done to identify possible financial strengths or weaknesses; thus, it is a valuable part of SWOT analysis. A review of key financial ratios can help you assess the company's overall situation and pinpoint some problem areas. Ratios control for firm size and enable you to compare a company's ratios with industry averages. Table 11.1 lists some of the most important financial ratios: (1) *liquidity ratios*, (2) *profitability ratios*, (3) *activity ratios*, and (4) *leverage ratios*.

How are Financial Statements Analyzed?

Calculate all relevant ratios and discuss those ratios that have an impact on the company's problems. Compare these ratios with industry averages to discover whether the company is out of line with others in the industry. If industry averages are not available, use those of a successful competitor. A typical financial analysis of a firm would include a study of the operating statements for five or so years, including a trend analysis of sales, profits, earnings per share, debt to equity ratio, and return on investment, plus a ratio analysis comparing the firm under study with industry standards. As a minimum, undertake the following five steps in basic financial analysis:

1. *Scrutinize historical income statements and balance sheets.* These two basic statements provide most of the data needed for analysis. Statements of cash flow may also be useful.
2. *Compare historical statements over time* if a series of statements is available.
3. *Calculate changes that occur in individual categories from year to year*, as well as the cumulative total change.
4. *Determine the change as a percentage* as well as an absolute amount.
5. *Adjust for inflation* if that was a significant factor.

Table 11.1 Financial Ratio Analysis

	Formula	How Expressed	Meaning
1. Liquidity Ratios			
Current ratio	$\dfrac{\text{Current assets}}{\text{Current liabilities}}$	Decimal	A short-term indicator of the company's ability to pay its short-term liabilities from short-term assets; how much of current assets are available to cover each dollar of current liabilities.
Quick (acid-test) ratio	$\dfrac{\text{Current assets} - \text{Inventory}}{\text{Current liabilities}}$	Decimal	Measures the company's ability to pay off its short-term obligations from current assets, excluding inventories.
Inventory to net working capital	$\dfrac{\text{Inventory}}{\text{Current assets} - \text{Current liabilities}}$	Decimal	A measure of inventory balance; measures the extent to which the cushion of excess current assets over current liabilities may be threatened by unfavorable changes in inventory.
Cash ratio	$\dfrac{\text{Cash} + \text{Cash equivalents}}{\text{Current liabilities}}$	Decimal	Measures the extent to which the company's capital is in cash or cash equivalents; shows how much of the current obligations can be paid from cash or near-cash assets.
2. Profitability Ratios			
Net profit margin	$\dfrac{\text{Net profit after taxes}}{\text{Net sales}}$	Percentage	Shows how much after-tax profits are generated by each dollar of sales.
Gross profit margin	$\dfrac{\text{Sales} - \text{Cost of goods sold}}{\text{Net sales}}$	Percentage	Indicates the total margin available to cover other expenses beyond cost of goods sold, and still yield a profit.
Return on investment (ROI)	$\dfrac{\text{Net profit after taxes}}{\text{Total assets}}$	Percentage	Measures the rate of return on the total assets utilized in the company; a measure of management's efficiency, it shows the return on all the assets under its control regardless of source of financing.
Return on equity (ROE)	$\dfrac{\text{Net profit after taxes}}{\text{Shareholders' equity}}$	Percentage	Measures the rate of return on the book value of shareholders' total investment in the company.

(continued)

Table 11.1 (continued)

	Formula	How Expressed	Meaning
Earnings per share (EPS)	$$\frac{\text{Net profit after taxes} - \text{Preferred stock dividends}}{\text{Average number of common shares}}$$	Dollars per share	Shows the after-tax earnings generated for each share of common stock.

3. Activity Ratios

	Formula	How Expressed	Meaning
Inventory turnover	$$\frac{\text{Net sales}}{\text{Inventory}}$$	Decimal	Measures the number of times that average inventory of finished goods was turned over or sold during a period of time, usually a year.
Days of inventory	$$\frac{\text{Inventory}}{\text{Cost of goods sold} \div 365}$$	Days	Measures the number of one day's worth of inventory that a company has on hand at any given time.
Net working capital turnover	$$\frac{\text{Net sales}}{\text{Net working capital}}$$	Decimal	Measures how effectively the net working capital is used to generate sales.
Asset turnover	$$\frac{\text{Sales}}{\text{Total assets}}$$	Decimal	Measures the utilization of all the company's assets; measures how many sales are generated by each dollar of assets.
Fixed asset turnover	$$\frac{\text{Sales}}{\text{Fixed assets}}$$	Decimal	Measures the utilization of the company's fixed assets (i.e., plant and equipment); measures how many sales are generated by each dollar of fixed assets.
Average collection period	$$\frac{\text{Accounts receivable}}{\text{Sales for year} \div 365}$$	Days	Indicates the average length of time in days that a company must wait to collect a sale after making it; may be compared to the credit terms offered by the company to its customers.
Accounts receivable turnover	$$\frac{\text{Annual credit sales}}{\text{Accounts receivable}}$$	Decimal	Indicates the number of times that accounts receivable are cycled during the period (usually a year).
Accounts payable	$$\frac{\text{Accounts payable}}{\text{Purchase for year} \div 365}$$	Days	Indicates the average length of time in days that the company takes to pay its credit purchases.
Days of cash	$$\frac{\text{Cash}}{\text{Net sales for year} \div 365}$$	Days	Indicates the number of days of cash on hand, at present sales levels.

Table 11.1 (continued)

	Formula	How Expressed	Meaning
4. Leverage Ratios			
Debt to asset ratio	$\dfrac{\text{Total debt}}{\text{Total assets}}$	Percentage	Measures the extent to which borrowed funds have been used to finance the company's assets.
Debt to equity ratio	$\dfrac{\text{Total debt}}{\text{Shareholders' equity}}$	Percentage	Measures the funds provided by creditors versus the funds provided by owners.
Long-term debt to capital structure	$\dfrac{\text{Long-term debt}}{\text{Shareholders' equity}}$	Percentage	Measures the long-term component of capital structure.
Times interest earned	$\dfrac{\text{Profit before taxes + Interest charges}}{\text{Interest charges}}$	Decimal	Indicates the ability of the company to meet its annual interest costs.
Coverage of fixed charges	$\dfrac{\text{Profit before taxes + Interest charges + Lease charges}}{\text{Interest charges + Lease obligations}}$	Decimal	A measure of the company's ability to meet all of its fixed charge obligations.
Current liabilities to equity	$\dfrac{\text{Current liabilities}}{\text{Shareholders' equity}}$	Percentage	Measures the short-term financing portion versus that provided by owners.
5. Other Ratios			
Price/earnings ratio	$\dfrac{\text{Market price per share}}{\text{Earnings per share}}$	Decimal	Shows the current market's evaluation of a stock, based on its earnings; shows how much the investor is willing to pay for each dollar of earnings.
Dividend payout ratio	$\dfrac{\text{Annual dividends per share}}{\text{Annual earnings per share}}$	Percentage	Indicates the percentage of profit that is paid out as dividends.
Dividend yield on common stock	$\dfrac{\text{Annual dividends per share}}{\text{Current market price per share}}$	Percentage	Indicates the dividend rate of return to common shareholders at the current market price.

Note: In using ratios for analysis, calculate ratios for the corporation and compare them to the average and quartile ratios for the particular industry. Refer to Standard and Poor's and Robert Morris Associates for average industry data. Special thanks to Dr. Moustafa H. Abdelsamad, Dean, Business School, Texas A & M University–Corpus Christi, Texas, for his definitions of these ratios.

Examination of this information may reveal developing trends. Compare trends in one category with those in related categories. For example, an increase in sales of 15 percent over three years may appear to be satisfactory until you note an increase of 20 percent in the cost of goods sold during the same period. The outcome of this comparison might suggest that further investigation into the manufacturing process is necessary. If a company is reporting strong net income growth but negative cash flow, this would suggest that the company is relying on something other than operations for earnings growth. Is it selling off assets or cutting R&D? If accounts receivable are growing faster than sales revenues, the company is not getting paid for the products or services it is counting as sold.

What are Common-Size Statements?

Common-size statements are income statements and balance sheets in which the dollar figures have been converted into percentages. For the income statement, net sales represent 100 percent: Calculate the percentage of each category so that the categories sum to the net sales percentage (100%). For the balance sheet, give the total assets a value of 100 percent and calculate other asset and liability categories as percentages of the total assets. (Individual asset and liability items, such as accounts receivable and accounts payable, can also be calculated as a percentage of net sales.)

When you convert statements to this form, it is relatively easy to note the percentage that each category represents of the total. Look for trends in specific items, such as cost of goods sold, when compared to the company's historical figures. To get a proper picture, however, compare these data with industry data. If a firm's trends are generally in line with those of the rest of the industry, the likelihood of problems is less than if they are worse than industry averages. These statements are especially helpful in developing scenarios and pro forma statements because they provide a series of historical relationships (e.g., cost of goods sold to sales, interest to sales, and inventories as a percentage of assets).

What Other Financial Calculations are Useful in Analysis?

If the corporation being studied appears to be in poor financial condition, use *Altman's Bankruptcy Formula* to calculate its Z-value. The **Z-value** indicates how close a company is to bankruptcy. It combines five ratios by weighting them according to their importance to a corporation's financial strength. The formula is:

$$Z = 1.2\,x_1 + 1.4\,x_2 + 3.3\,x_3 + 0.6\,x_4 + 1.0\,x_5$$

where:

x_1 = Working capital/Total assets (%)
x_2 = Retained earnings/Total assets (%)
x_3 = Earnings before interest and taxes/Total assets (%)
x_4 = Market value of equity/Total liabilities (%)
x_5 = Sales/Total assets (number of times)

Scores below 1.81 indicate significant credit problems, whereas scores above 3.0 indicate a healthy firm. Scores between 1.81 and 3.0 indicate question marks.[1]

The **index of sustainable growth** is useful to learn if a company embarking on a growth strategy will need to take on debt to fund this growth. The index indicates how much of the growth rate of sales can be sustained by internally generated funds. The formula is:

$$g^* = \frac{[P(1 - D)(1 + L)]}{[T - P(1 - D)(1 + L)]}$$

where:

P = (Net profit before tax/Net sales) × 100

D = Target dividends/Profit after tax

L = Total liabilities/Net worth

T = (Total assets/Net sales) × 100

If the planned growth rate calls for a growth rate higher than its g^*, external capital will be needed to fund the growth unless management is able to find efficiencies, decrease dividends, increase the debt to equity ratio, or reduce assets by renting or leasing arrangements.[2]

How Should Inflation, Interest Rates, and GDP be Used?

If you are analyzing a company over many years, you may want to adjust sales and net income for inflation to arrive at "true" financial performance in constant dollars. **Constant dollars** are dollars adjusted for inflation to make them comparable over various years. In the United States, the *consumer price index (CPI)* is an easy way to adjust for inflation (see **Table 11.2**). Dividing sales and net income by the CPI factor for that year changes the figures to 1982–1984 constant dollars.

Table 11.2 *U.S. Economic Indicators:* Gross Domestic Product (GDP); Consumer Price Index (CPI) for All Items (1982–1984 = 1.0); Prime Interest Rate (PIR)

Year	GDP (in $ billions) Gross Domestic Product	CPI (for all items) Consumer Price Index	PIR (in %) Prime Interest Rate
1986	4,460.1	1.096	8.33
1990	5,800.5	1.307	10.01
1995	7,414.7	1.524	8.83
1996	7,838.5	1.569	8.27
1997	8,332.4	1.605	8.44
1998	8,793.5	1.630	8.35
1999	9,353.5	1.666	7.99
2000	9,951.5	1.722	9.23
2001	10,286.2	1.771	6.92
2002	10,642.3	1.799	4.68
2003	11,142.1	1.840	4.12
2004	11,867.8	1.889	4.29
2005	12,638.4	1.953	6.10
2006	13,398.9	2.016	7.94

(continued)

	GDP (in $ billions) Gross Domestic Product	CPI (for all items) Consumer Price Index	PIR (in %) Prime Interest Rate
Year			
2007	14,077.6	2.073	8.08
2008	14,441.4	2.153	5.21
2009	14,256.3	2.145	3.25

Table 11.2 (continued)

Notes: Gross domestic product in billions of dollars; consumer price index for all items (1982–1984 = 1.0); prime interest rate in percentages.

Sources: Gross domestic product from U.S. Bureau of Economic Analysis, National Economic Accounts (*www.bea.gov*). Consumer price index from U.S. Bureau of Labor Statistics (*www.bls.gov*). Prime interest rate from *www.moneycafe.com*.

Another helpful analytical aid is *prime interest rate (PIR)*—;the rate of interest banks charge on their lowest risk loans. To better assess strategic decisions, note the level of the PIR at the time of the case (see Table 11.2). A decision to borrow money to build a new plant would have been very costly in 2000, but inexpensive in 2003.

In preparing a scenario for your pro forma financial statements, you may want to use the *gross domestic product (GDP)* from Table 11.2. The GDP is used worldwide and measures the total output of goods and services within a country's borders. It is a good indicator of a country's overall economic health.

11.5 USING THE STRATEGIC AUDIT IN CASE ANALYSIS

Appendix 11.C is an example of a strategic audit proposed for use not only in strategic decision making, but also as a framework for the analysis of complex strategy cases. The questions in the audit parallel the eight steps depicted in Figure 1.3, the strategic decision-making process. The **strategic audit** provides a checklist of questions, by area or issue that enables a person to make a systematic analysis of various corporate activities. It is extremely useful as a diagnostic tool to pinpoint problem areas and to highlight strengths and weaknesses. It is not an all-inclusive list, but it presents many of the critical questions that need to be addressed in the strategic analysis of any business corporation. Some questions or even some areas might be inappropriate for a particular case; in other cases, the questions may be insufficient for a complete analysis. However, each question in a particular area of the strategic audit can be broken down into an additional series of subquestions. Develop these subquestions as they are needed.

Discussion Questions

1. Why should you begin a case analysis with a financial analysis? When are other approaches appropriate?

2. What are common-size financial statements? What is their value to case analysis? How are they calculated?

3. When should you gather information outside a case by going to the library or using the Internet? What should you look for?

4. When is inflation an important issue in conducting case analysis?

5. How can you learn what date a case took place?

Key Terms (listed in order of appearance)

ratio analysis *162*
common-size statements *166*
Z-value *166*

index of sustainable
  growth *166*

constant dollars *167*
strategic audit *168*

Notes

1. M. S. Fridson, *Financial Statement Analysis* (New York: John Wiley & Sons, 1991), pp. 192–194.

2. D. H. Bangs, *Managing by the Numbers* (Dover, N.H.: Upstart Publications, 1992), pp. 106–107.

APPENDIX 11.A

Suggested Techniques for Case Analysis and Presentation

A. CASE ANALYSIS

1. Read the case to get an overview of the nature of the corporation and its environment. Note the date in which the case took place (not the year in which the case was written) so that you can put the case into proper context.

2. Read the case a second time, and give it a detailed examination according to the strategic audit (**see Appendix 11.C**) or some other framework of analysis. Regardless of the framework used, you should end up with a list of the salient issues and problems in the case. Perform a financial analysis.

3. Undertake outside research, when appropriate, to uncover economic and industrial information. **Appendix 11.B** suggests possible sources for outside research. These data should provide the environmental setting for the corporation. Conduct an in-depth analysis of the industry. Analyze the important *competitors*. Consider the bargaining power of both *suppliers* and *buyers* that might affect the firm's situation. Consider also the possible threats of *new entrants* to the industry and the likelihood of new or different products or services that might be *substitutes* for the company's present ones. Consider *other stakeholders* who might affect strategic decision making in the industry.

4. Compile facts and evidence to support selected issues and problems. Develop a framework or outline to organize the analysis. Consider using one of the following methods of organization:
   a. The strategic decision-making process or the strategic audit
   b. The key individual(s) in the case
   c. The corporation's functional areas: production, management, finance, marketing, and R&D
   d. SWOT analysis

5. Clearly identify and state the central problem(s) as supported by the information in the case. Use the SWOT format to sum up the strategic factors facing the corporation: strengths and weaknesses of the company; opportunities and threats in the environment. Develop an EFAS Table (Table 3.3) for external factors and an IFAS Table (Table 4.2) for internal factors. Identify the strategic factors using an SFAS Matrix (Figure 5.1).

6. Develop a logical series of mutually exclusive alternatives that evolve from the analysis to resolve the problem(s) or issue(s) in the case. One of the alternatives should be to continue the company's current strategy. Develop at least two other strategy alternatives. However, don't present three alternatives and then recommend that all three be adopted, which is actually one alternative presented in three parts!

7. Evaluate each of the alternatives in light of the company's environment (both external and internal), mission, objectives, strategies, and policies. Discuss pros

and cons of each. Also, for each alternative, consider both the possible obstacles to its implementation and its financial implications.

8. Make recommendations assuming that action must be taken regardless of whether the needed information is available. The individuals in the case may have had the same or even less information than is given in the case.
   a. Base your recommendations on a total analysis of the case.
   b. Provide the evidence gathered earlier in Step 4 to justify suggested changes.
   c. List the recommendations in order of priority.
   d. Show clearly how your recommendations deal with each of the strategic factors that were mentioned earlier in Step 5. How do they build on corporate *strengths* to take advantage of environmental *opportunities*? How do they deal with environmental *threats* and corporate *weaknesses*?
   e. Explain how each recommendation will be implemented. How will the plan(s) deal with anticipated resistance?
   f. Suggest feedback and control systems to ensure that the recommendations are carried out as planned and to give advance warning of needed adjustments.

B. WRITTEN REPORT

1. Use the outline from Step A.4 to write the first draft of the case analysis. Follow Steps A.5 through A.8.
   a. Don't rehash the case material; rather, supply the salient evidence and data to support your analysis and recommendation.
   b. Develop exhibits on financial ratios and other data, such as strategic factors summary, for inclusion in your report. The exhibits should provide meaningful information. Reference key elements of an exhibit in the text of the written analysis. If you include a ratio analysis as an exhibit, explain the implications of the ratios in the text and cite the critical ones in your analysis.

2. Review your written case analysis for content and grammar. Compare the outline (Step A.4) with the final product. Make sure you've presented sufficient data or evidence to support your problem analysis and recommendations. If the final product requires rewriting, do so. Keep in mind that the written report is going to be judged not only on what is said, but also on the manner in which it is said. *Style, grammar, and spelling are just as important as the content in a written case analysis!*

3. If your written report requires pro forma statements, you may wish to develop a scenario for each year in your forecast. A well-constructed corporate scenario helps improve the accuracy of your forecast. (See Chapter 7 for corporate scenarios.)

C. ORAL PRESENTATION BY TEAMS

1. The team should first decide on a framework or outline for analysis, as suggested in Step A.4. Although teams often divide the analysis work, each team member should follow Steps A.5 through A.8 to develop a preliminary analysis of the entire case and share it with team members.

2. The team should combine member input into one consolidated team analysis, including SWOT analysis, alternatives, and recommendation(s). Obtain agreement on the strategic factors and the best alternative(s) to support.

3. Divide further development and presentation of the case analysis and recommendation(s). Agree on responsibilities for the preparation of visual aids and handouts. As in written reports, scenarios and pro forma financial statements should support any recommendation.

4. Modify the team outline, if necessary, and have one or two rehearsals of the presentation. If exhibits are used, make sure to allow sufficient time to explain them. Check to ensure that any visual aids can be easily seen from the back of the room. Critique one another's presentations and make the necessary modifications to the analysis. Again, style, grammar, and delivery are just as important in an oral presentation as is content. Prepare PowerPoint handouts as backup in case of computer problems.

5. Begin your presentation by handing out a copy of the agenda specifying not only the topics to be covered, but also who will deal with each topic area. Introduce yourselves. Dress appropriately. If a presenter misses a key fact during the class presentation, deal with it in the summary speech.

6. Encourage questions from both the instructor and classmates. You may wish to begin the questioning period by calling on someone you consider a friend who can be expected to ask a question you can easily answer. You may want to have one person act as a moderator who refers questions to the appropriate team member.

APPENDIX 11.B

Resources for Case Research

A. COMPANY INFORMATION

1. Annual Reports (prepared by individual corporations and usually included in 10-K reports)
2. *Moody's Manuals on Investment* (a listing of companies within certain industries that contains a brief history and a five-year financial statement of each company)
3. Securities and Exchange Commission Report Form 10-K (annually), Report Form 10-Q (quarterly), and Report Form 14-A (annual proxy statement including in-depth information on the board of directors)
4. Standard and Poor's *Register of Corporations, Directors, and Executives*
5. Value Line *Investment Survey*
6. COMPUSTAT, *Compact Disclosure, CD/International, Hoover's Online Corporate Directory*, and *SEC's Edgar database* (computerized operating and financial information on thousands of publicly held corporations)

B. ECONOMIC INFORMATION

1. Regional statistics and local forecasts from large banks
2. *Business Cycle Development* (U.S. Department of Commerce)
3. Chase Econometric Associates' publications
4. U.S. Census Bureau publications on population, transportation, and housing
5. *Current Business Reports* (U.S. Department of Commerce)
6. *Economic Indicators* (U.S. Joint Economic Committee)
7. *Economic Report of the (U.S.) President to Congress*
8. *Long-Term Economic Growth* (U.S. Department of Commerce)
9. *Monthly Labor Review* (U.S. Department of Labor)
10. *Monthly Bulletin of Statistics* (United Nations)
11. *Statistical Abstract of the United States* (U.S. Department of Commerce)
12. *Statistical Yearbook* (United Nations)
13. *Survey of Current Business* (U.S. Department of Commerce)
14. *U.S. Industrial Outlook* (U.S. Department of Defense)
15. *World Trade Annual* (United Nations)
16. *Overseas Business Reports* (by country, published by U.S. Department of Commerce)
17. *World Fact Book* (by country, published by U.S. Central Intelligence Agency)

C. INDUSTRY INFORMATION

1. Analyses of companies and industries by investment brokerage firms
2. *Business Week* and *Economist* (provide weekly economic and business information)
3. *Fortune* (each April publishes listings of financial information on corporations within certain industries)

4. *Industry Survey* (published quarterly by Standard and Poor's)
5. *Industry Week* (late March/early April issue provides information on 14 industry groups)
6. *Forbes* (mid-January issue provides performance data on firms in various industries)
7. *Inc.* (May and December issues give information on fast-growing entrepreneurial companies)

D. DIRECTORY AND INDEX INFORMATION ON COMPANIES AND INDUSTRIES

1. *Business Periodical Index* (on computer in many libraries)
2. *Directory of National Trade Associations*
3. *Encyclopedia of Associations*
4. Funk and Scott's *Index of Corporations and Industries*
5. Thomas *Register of American Manufacturers*
6. *Wall Street Journal Index*

E. RATIO ANALYSIS INFORMATION

1. *Almanac of Business and Industrial Financial Ratios* (Prentice Hall)
2. *Annual Statement Studies* (Risk Management Associates; also Robert Morris Associates)
3. *Dun's Review* (Dun and Bradstreet; published annually in September–December issues)
4. *Industry Norms and Key Business Ratios* (Dun and Bradstreet)

F. ONLINE INFORMATION

1. *Hoover's Online*: Financial statements and profiles of public companies (www. hoovers.com)
2. *U.S. Securities and Exchange Commission*: Official filings of public companies in Edgar database (www.sec.gov)
3. *Fortune 500*: Statistics for largest U.S. corporations (www.fortune.com)
4. *Dun & Bradstreet's Online*: Short reports on 10 million public and private U.S. companies (www.smallbusiness.dnb.com)
5. *Ecola's 24-Hour Newsstand*: Links to Web sites of 2,000 newspapers, journals, and magazines (www.ecola.com)
6. *Competitive Intelligence Guide*: Information on company resources (www.fuld.com)
7. *Society of Competitive Intelligence Professionals*: Information on competitive intelligence (www.scip.org)
8. *The Economist*: Provides international information and surveys (www.economist.com)
9. *CIA World Fact Book*: International information by country (www.cia.gov)
10. *Bloomberg*: Information on interest rates, stock prices, currency conversion rates, and other general financial information (www.bloomberg.com)
11. *The Scannery*: Information on international companies (www.thescannery.com)

12. *CEO Express*: Links to many valuable sources of business information (www. ceoexpress.com)
13. *Wall Street Journal*: Business news (www.wsj.com)
14. *Forbes*: Information on America's largest private companies (www.forbes.com/lists/)
15. *CorporateInformation.com*: Subscription service for company profiles (www. corporateinformation.com)
16. *Kompass International*: Industry information (www.kompass.com)
17. *CorpTech*: Database of technology companies (www.corptech.com)
18. ADNet: Data on the information technology industry (www.companyfinder.com)
19. *CNN company research*: Provides company information (http://money.cnn.com/news/crc/)
20. *Paywatch*: Database of executive compensation (www.aflcio.org/corporatewatch/paywatch/)
21. *Global Edge Global Resources*: International resources (http://globaledge.msu.edu/resourceDesk/)
22. *Google Finance*: Data on North American stocks (http://finance.google.com/finance)
23. *World Federation of Exchanges*: International stock exchanges (www.world-exchanges.org/)
24. *SEC International Registry*: Data on international corporations (www.sec.gov/divisions/corpfin/internatl/companies.shtml)
25. *Yahoo Finance*: Data on North American companies (www.yahoo.com)
26. *Guide to Financial Reports*: How to read a financial statement (www.ibm.com/investor/help/guide/introduction.wss)

APPENDIX 11.C

Strategic Audit of a Corporation

I. CURRENT SITUATION

A. Current Performance

How did the corporation perform the past year overall in terms of return on investment, market share, and profitability?

B. Strategic Posture

What are the corporation's current mission, objectives, strategies, and policies?

1. Are they clearly stated or are they merely implied from performance?
2. *Mission*: What business(es) is the corporation in? Why?
3. *Objectives*: What are the corporate, business, and functional objectives? Are they consistent with each other, with the mission, and with the internal and external environments?
4. *Strategies*: What strategy or mix of strategies is the corporation following? Are they consistent with each other, with the mission and objectives, and with the internal and external environments?
5. *Policies*: What are the corporation's policies? Are they consistent with each other, with the mission, objectives, and strategies, and with the internal and external environments?
6. Do the current mission, objectives, strategies, and policies reflect the corporation's international operations, whether global or multidomestic?

II. CORPORATE GOVERNANCE

A. Board of Directors

1. Who is on the board? Are they internal or external members?
2. Do they own significant shares of stock?
3. Is the stock privately held or publicly traded? Are there different classes of stock with different voting rights?
4. What do the board members contribute to the corporation in terms of knowledge, skills, background, and connections? If the corporation has international operations, do board members have international experience? Are board members concerned with environmental sustainability?

Source: T. L. Wheelen and J. D. Hunger, *Strategic Audit of a Corporation*, Copyright ©1982 and 2005 by Wheelen and Hunger Associates. Thomas L. Wheelen, "A Strategic Audit," paper presented to Society for Advancement of Management (SAM). Presented by J. D. Hunger and T. L. Wheelen in "The Strategic Audit: An Integrative Approach to Teaching Business Policy," to Academy of Management, August, 1983. Published in "Using the Strategic Audit," by T. L. Wheelen and J. D. Hunger in *SAM Advanced Management Journal* (Winter 1987), pp. 4–12. Reprinted by permission of the copyright holders. Revised 1988, 1994, 1997, 2000, 2002, 2004, 2005, 2009 and 2010.

5. How long have board members served on the board?
6. What is their level of involvement in strategic management? Do they merely rubber-stamp top management's proposals or do they actively participate and suggest future directions? Do they evaluate management's proposals in terms of environmental sustainability?

B. Top Management

1. What person or group constitutes top management?
2. What are top management's chief characteristics in terms of knowledge, skills, background, and style? If the corporation has international operations, does top management have international experience? Are executives from acquired companies considered part of the top management team?
3. Has top management been responsible for the corporation's performance over the past few years? How many managers have been in their current position for less than three years? Were they internal promotions or external hires?
4. Has it established a systematic approach to strategic management?
5. What is its level of involvement in strategic management?
6. How well does top management interact with lower level managers and with the board of directors?
7. Are strategic decisions made ethically in a socially responsible manner?
8. Are strategic decisions made in an environmentally sustainable manner?
9. Do top executives own significant amounts of stock in the corporation?
10. Is top management sufficiently skilled to cope with likely future challenges?

III. EXTERNAL ENVIRONMENT: OPPORTUNITIES AND THREATS (SW<u>OT</u>)

A. Natural Physical Environment: Sustainability Issues

1. What forces from the natural physical environment are currently affecting the corporation and the industries in which it competes? Which present current or future threats? Opportunities?
   a. Climate, including global temperature, sea level, and freshwater availability
   b. Weather-related events, such as severe storms, floods, and droughts
   c. Solar phenomena, such as sunspots and solar wind
2. Do these forces have different effects in other regions of the world?

B. Societal Environment

1. What general environmental forces are currently affecting both the corporation and the industries in which it competes? Which present current or future threats? Opportunities?
   a. Economic
   b. Technological
   c. Political-legal
   d. Sociocultural
2. Are these forces different in other regions of the world?

C. Task Environment

1. What forces drive industry competition? Are these forces the same globally or do they vary from country to country? Rate each force as high, medium, or low.
   a. Threat of new entrants
   b. Bargaining power of buyers
   c. Threat of substitute products or services
   d. Bargaining power of suppliers
   e. Rivalry among competing firms
   f. Relative power of unions, governments, special-interest groups, and so on
2. What key factors in the immediate environment (i.e., customers, competitors, suppliers, creditors, labor unions, governments, trade associations, interest groups, local communities, and shareholders) are currently affecting the corporation? What are the current or future threats? Opportunities?

D. Summary of External Factors (Include in an EFAS Table)

Which of these forces and factors are the most important to the corporation and to the industries in which it competes at the present time? Which will be important in the future?

IV. INTERNAL ENVIRONMENT: STRENGTHS AND WEAKNESSES (SWOT)

A. Corporate Structure

1. How is the corporation structured at present?
   a. Is the decision-making authority centralized around one group or decentralized to many units?
   b. Is it organized on the basis of functions, projects, geography, or some combination of these?
2. Is the structure clearly understood by everyone in the corporation?
3. Is the present structure consistent with current corporate objectives, strategies, policies, and programs, as well as with the firm's international operations?
4. In what ways does this structure compare with those of similar corporations?

B. Corporate Culture

1. Is there a well-defined or emerging culture composed of shared beliefs, expectations, and values?
2. Is the culture consistent with the current objectives, strategies, policies, and programs?
3. What is the culture's position on important issues facing the corporation (i.e., on productivity, quality of performance, adaptability to changing conditions, environmental sustainability, and internationalization)?
4. Is the culture compatible with the employees' diversity of backgrounds?
5. Does the company take into consideration the values of each nation's culture in which the firm operates?

C. Corporate Resources

1. Marketing

a. What are the corporation's current marketing objectives, strategies, policies, and programs?
   i. Are they clearly stated, or merely implied from performance and/or budgets?
   ii. Are they consistent with the corporation's mission, objectives, strategies, policies, and with internal and external environments?

b. How well is the corporation performing in terms of analysis of market position and marketing mix (i.e., product, price, place, and promotion) in both domestic and international markets? How dependent is the corporation on a few customers? How big is its market? Where is it gaining or losing market share? What percentage of sales comes from developed versus developing regions of the world? Where are current products in the product life cycle?
   i. What trends emerge from this analysis?
   ii. What impact have these trends had on past performance and how might these trends affect future performance?
   iii. Does this analysis support the corporation's past and pending strategic decisions?
   iv. Does marketing provide the company with a competitive advantage?

c. How well does this corporation's marketing performance compare with that of similar corporations?

d. Are marketing managers using accepted marketing concepts and techniques to evaluate and improve product performance? (Consider product life cycle, market segmentation, market research, and product portfolios.)

e. Does marketing adjust to the conditions within each country in which it operates?

f. Does marketing consider environmental sustainability when making decisions?

g. What is the role of the marketing manager in strategic management?

2. Finance

a. What are the corporation's current financial objectives, strategies, policies, and programs?
   i. Are they clearly stated or merely implied from performance and/or budgets?
   ii. Are they consistent with the corporation's mission, objectives, strategies, policies, and with internal and external environments?

b. How well is the corporation performing in terms of financial analysis? (Consider ratios, common-size statements, and capitalization structure.) How balanced in terms of cash flow is the company's portfolio of products and businesses? What are investor expectations in terms of share price?
   i. What trends emerge from this analysis?
   ii. Are there any significant differences when statements are calculated in constant versus reported dollars?

      iii. What impact have these trends had on past performance and how might these trends affect future performance?

      iv. Does this analysis support the corporation's past and pending strategic decisions?

      v. Does finance provide the company with a competitive advantage?

  c. How well does this corporation's financial performance compare with that of similar corporations?

  d. Are financial managers using accepted financial concepts and techniques to evaluate and improve current corporate and divisional performance? (Consider financial leverage, capital budgeting, ratio analysis, and managing foreign currencies.)

  e. Does finance adjust to the conditions in each country in which the company operates?

  f. Does finance cope with global financial issues?

  g. What is the role of the financial manager in strategic management?

3. Research and Development (R&D)

  a. What are the corporation's current R&D objectives, strategies, policies, and programs?

      i. Are they clearly stated, or merely implied from performance or budgets?

      ii. Are they consistent with the corporation's mission, objectives, strategies, policies, and with internal and external environments?

      iii. What is the role of technology in corporate performance?

      iv. Is the mix of basic, applied, and engineering research appropriate, given the corporate mission and strategies?

      v. Does R&D provide the company with a competitive advantage?

  b. What return is the corporation receiving from its investment in R&D?

  c. Is the corporation competent in technology transfer? Does it use concurrent engineering and cross-functional work teams in product and process design?

  d. What role does technological discontinuity play in the company's products?

  e. How well does the corporation's investment in R&D compare with the investments of similar corporations? How much R&D is being outsourced? Is the corporation using value-chain alliances appropriately for innovation and competitive advantage?

  f. Does R&D adjust to the conditions in each country in which the company operates?

  g. Does R&D consider environmental sustainability in product development and packaging?

  h. What is the role of the R&D manager in strategic management?

4. Operations and Logistics

  a. What are the corporation's current manufacturing/service objectives, strategies, policies, and programs?

      i. Are they clearly stated, or merely implied from performance or budgets?

      ii. Are they consistent with the corporation's mission, objectives, strategies, policies, and with internal and external environments?

b. What are the type and extent of operations capabilities of the corporation? How much is done domestically versus internationally? Is the amount of outsourcing appropriate to be competitive? Is purchasing being handled appropriately? Are suppliers and distributors operating in an environmentally sustainable manner? Which products have the highest and lowest profit margins?

   i. If the corporation is product-oriented, consider plant facilities, type of manufacturing system (e.g., continuous mass production, intermittent job shop, or flexible manufacturing), age and type of equipment, degree and role of automation and/or robots, plant capacities and utilization, productivity ratings, and availability and type of transportation.

   ii. If the corporation is service-oriented, consider service facilities (e.g., hospital, theater, or school buildings), type of operations systems (e.g., continuous service over time to same clientele or intermittent service over time to varied clientele), age and type of supporting equipment, degree and role of automation, use of mass communication devices (e.g., diagnostic machinery and video machines), facility capacities and utilization rates, efficiency ratings of professional and service personnel, and availability and type of transportation to bring service staff and clientele together.

c. Are manufacturing or service facilities vulnerable to natural disasters, local or national strikes, reduction or limitation of resources from suppliers, substantial cost increases of materials, or nationalization by governments?

d. Is there an appropriate mix of people and machines, in manufacturing firms, or of support staff to professionals (in service firms)?

e. How well does the corporation perform relative to the competition? Is it balancing inventory costs (warehousing) with logistical costs (just-in-time)? Consider costs per unit of labor, material, and overhead; downtime; inventory control management and scheduling of service staff; production ratings; facility utilization percentages; and number of clients successfully treated by category (if service firm) or percentage of orders shipped on time (if product firm).

   i. What trends emerge from this analysis?

   ii. What impact have these trends had on past performance and how might these trends affect future performance?

   iii. Does this analysis support the corporation's past and pending strategic decisions?

   iv. Does operations provide the company with a competitive advantage?

f. Are operations managers using appropriate concepts and techniques to evaluate and improve current performance? Consider cost systems, quality control and reliability systems, inventory control management, personnel scheduling, TQM, learning curves, safety programs, and engineering programs that can improve the efficiency of manufacturing or service.

g. Do operations adjust to the conditions in each country in which it has facilities?

h. Do operations consider environmental sustainability when making decisions?

i. What is the role of the operations manager in strategic management?

5. **Human Resources Management (HRM)**

   a. What are the corporation's current HRM objectives, strategies, policies, and programs?

      i. Are they clearly stated, or merely implied from performance and/or budgets?

      ii. Are they consistent with the corporation's mission, objectives, strategies, policies, and with internal and external environments?

   b. How well is the corporation's HRM performing in terms of improving the fit between the individual employee and the job? Consider turnover, grievances, strikes, layoffs, employee training, and quality of work life.

      i. What trends emerge from this analysis?

      ii. What impact have these trends had on past performance and how might these trends affect future performance?

      iii. Does this analysis support the corporation's past and pending strategic decisions?

      iv. Does HRM provide the company with a competitive advantage?

   c. How does this corporation's HRM performance compare with that of similar corporations?

   d. Are HRM managers using appropriate concepts and techniques to evaluate and improve corporate performance? Consider the job analysis program, performance appraisal system, up-to-date job descriptions, training and development programs, attitude surveys, job design programs, quality of relationship with unions, and use of autonomous work teams.

   e. How well is the corporation managing the diversity of its workforce? What is the company's record on human rights? Does the corporation monitor the human rights record of key suppliers and distributors?

   f. Does HRM adjust to the conditions in each country in which the company operates? Does the company have a code of conduct for itself and for key suppliers in developing nations? Are employees receiving international assignments to prepare them for managerial positions? Are they being utilized appropriately?

   g. What is the role of outsourcing and temporary employees in HRM planning?

   h. What is the role of the HRM manager in strategic management?

6. **Information Technology (IT)**

   a. What are the corporation's current IT objectives, strategies, policies, and programs?

      i. Are they clearly stated, or merely implied from performance and/or budgets?

      ii. Are they consistent with the corporation's mission, objectives, strategies, policies, and with internal and external environments?

   b. How well is the corporation's IT performing in terms of providing a useful database, automating routine clerical operations, assisting managers in making routine decisions, and providing information necessary for strategic decisions?

      i. What trends emerge from this analysis?

      ii. What impact have these trends had on past performance and how might these trends affect future performance?

      iii. Does this analysis support the corporation's past and pending strategic decisions?

      iv. Does IT provide the company with a competitive advantage?

    c. How does this corporation's IT performance and stage of development compare with that of similar corporations? Is it appropriately using the Internet, intranet, and extranets?

    d. Are IT managers using appropriate concepts and techniques to evaluate and improve corporate performance? Do they know how to build and manage a complex database, establish Web sites with firewalls, conduct system analyses, and implement interactive decision-support systems?

    e. Does the company have a global IT and Internet presence? Does it have difficulty with getting data across national boundaries?

    f. What is the role of the IT manager in strategic management?

D. Summary of Internal Factors (Include in an IFAS Table)

Which of these factors are core competencies? Which, if any, are distinctive competencies? Which of these factors are the most important to the corporation and to the industries in which it competes at the present time? Which might be important in the future? Which activities or functions are candidates for outsourcing?

V. ANALYSIS OF STRATEGIC FACTORS (SWOT)

A. Situational Analysis (Include in a SFAS Matrix)

What are the most important internal and external factors (*Strengths, Weaknesses, Opportunities, Threats*) that strongly affect the corporation's present and future performance?

B. Review of Mission and Objectives

    1. Are the current mission and objectives appropriate in light of the key strategic factors and problems?

    2. Should the mission and objectives be changed? If so, how?

    3. If changed, what will be the effects on the firm?

VI. STRATEGIC ALTERNATIVES AND RECOMMENDED STRATEGY

A. Strategic Alternatives

    1. Can the current or revised objectives be met by the simple, more careful implementation of those strategies presently in use (e.g., fine-tuning the strategies)?

    2. What are the major feasible alternative strategies available to this corporation? What are the pros and cons of each? Can corporate scenarios be developed and agreed upon? (Alternatives must fit the natural physical, societal and industry environments, and the corporation for next three to five years.)

   a. Consider *stability, growth,* and *retrenchment* as corporate strategies.

   b. Consider *competitive strategies,* such as lower cost or differentiation, and *cooperative strategies,* such as joint ventures or licensing, as possible business strategies.

   c. Consider any functional strategic alternatives that might be needed for reinforcement of an important corporate or business strategic alternative.

B. Recommended Strategy

1. Specify which of the strategic alternatives you are recommending for the corporate, business, and functional levels of the corporation. Do you recommend different business or functional strategies for different units of the corporation?
2. Justify your recommendation in terms of its ability to resolve both long- and short-term problems and effectively deal with the strategic factors.
3. What policies should be developed or revised to guide effective implementation?
4. What is the impact of the recommended strategy on the company's core and distinctive competencies?

VII. IMPLEMENTATION

   A. What kinds of programs (e.g., restructuring the corporation or instituting TQM) should be developed to implement the recommended strategy?

     1. Who should develop these programs?

     2. Who should be in charge of these programs?

   B. Are the programs financially feasible? Can pro forma budgets be developed and agreed upon? Are priorities and timetables appropriate to individual programs?

   C. Will new standard operating procedures need to be developed?

VIII. EVALUATION AND CONTROL

   A. Is the current information system capable of providing sufficient feedback on implementation activities and performance? Can it measure strategic factors?

     1. Can performance results be pinpointed by area, unit, project, or function?

     2. Is the information timely?

     3. Is the corporation using benchmarking to evaluate its functions and activities?

   B. Are adequate control measures in place to ensure conformance with the recommended strategic plan?

     1. Are appropriate standards and measures being used?

     2. Are reward systems capable of recognizing and rewarding good performance?

INDEX